CW00736144

DIEPPE

DIEPPE
A NECESSARY FAILURE

HENRY BUCKTON

AMBERLEY

First published 2022

Amberley Publishing
The Hill, Stroud
Gloucestershire, GL5 4EP

www.amberley-books.com

Copyright © Henry Buckton, 2022

The right of Henry Buckton to be identified as
the Author of this work has been asserted in
accordance with the Copyright, Designs and
Patents Act 1988.

ISBN 978 1 3981 0386 3 (hardback)
ISBN 978 1 3981 0387 0 (ebook)

All rights reserved. No part of this book may
be reprinted or reproduced or utilised in any
form or by any electronic, mechanical or other
means, now known or hereafter invented,
including photocopying and recording, or in any
information storage or retrieval system, without
the permission in writing from the Publishers.

British Library Cataloguing in Publication Data.
A catalogue record for this book is available
from the British Library.

1 2 3 4 5 6 7 8 9 10

Typesetting by SJmagic DESIGN SERVICES, India.
Printed in the UK.

CONTENTS

INTRODUCTION

The Allied assault on the German-occupied port of Dieppe in France on 19 August 1942 was codenamed Operation *Jubilee*. It was a battle that lasted for only a few hours but has gone down in history as a military disaster. This book revisits the story to mark the 80th anniversary of that ill-fated event and does of course reaffirm the negatives and failures surrounding the operation and the fact that few of its objectives were actually met.

Operation *Jubilee* was not an isolated incident and was one in a series of raids carried out on Hitler's Atlantic Wall. As such we will also look at the bigger picture and its place in those wider operations.

After the evacuation of the British Expeditionary Force from Dunkirk in May and June 1940, Prime Minister Winston Churchill set about creating a programme by which raiding parties of varied sizes and with a wide range of objectives could return to occupied territories to inflict casualties on the Germans, gain intelligence about their disposition, bolster British morale, and ultimately pave the way for the time when Britain and its Allies could open a second front in Europe.

The men who perpetrated these raids were mainly British Commandos, but the two largest, Operation *Gauntlet* and Operation *Jubilee,* would draw heavily on Canadian troops that had been training in England since the outbreak of war but hadn't seen any action.

In each of these raids, the size of the force deployed depended on the objective. The smallest, Operation *JV*, involved only two men. The attack on Dieppe was the largest and involved over 10,500 troops. Most of the raids would only occur overnight, but some, like Operation *Gauntlet,* were conducted over a number of days.

These Commando raids collectively caused such a nuisance to the enemy that in October 1942, Hitler issued the Commando Order, which required the execution of all those captured while carrying them out. Most would be shot against a wall shortly after apprehension. The men captured at Dieppe didn't fall victim to this directorate but the raid did result in changes to the way prisoners were treated on both sides and led to some occasionally terrible consequences.

In total, there were fifty-seven raids directed against Germany's Atlantic defences between Dunkirk and D-Day, mainly against targets in France, which experienced thirty-six raids. There were twelve raids in Norway, seven in the Channel Islands and one each in Belgium and the Netherlands. Operation *Jubilee* was number twenty-one in this list, so roughly halfway through the programme. There were also Commando raids in other theatres, including North Africa, Italy and Greece.

Theses raids met with widely different fortunes. Operation *Jubilee* was considered to be a failure, whereas Operation *Chariot*, the raid against dock installations at Saint-Nazaire, is regarded as the greatest Commando raid in history. Others, like Operation *Aquatint* and Operation *Musketoon*, resulted in the capture or death of all of those involved.

This programme of raiding targets in Europe, for whatever purpose, ended in early 1944 on the orders of Major General Robert Laycock, the chief of Combined Operations headquarters. He suggested that they were no longer as effective and simply resulted in the Germans strengthening their beach defences, which would only be detrimental to Allied plans for the forthcoming invasion. However, each of these raids and perhaps Dieppe more so than any other, were critical rehearsals and provided crucial lessons for what was to come.

During Operation *Jubilee* itself, the three armed services worked together in a true combined operation which we will review in detail. The Royal Navy would do the donkey work of ferrying the ground troops from several ports in southern England across the English Channel to alight at their various objectives. They would also provide off-shore fire power and the means of evacuation at the conclusion. RAF Fighter Command would attempt to gain air supremacy over the landing beaches by doing battle with their counterparts in the Luftwaffe. They would also attack ground targets thought to be occupied by German defences.

The ground forces would be made up of men from combined nations. Canadian troops had arrived in Britain shortly after the war began in 1939, but they hadn't participated greatly with the British Expeditionary Force in France and Belgium, so they were keen to take part in an operation and show what they could do. With that in mind, they were given the main responsibility. Around 5,000 Canadian infantry soldiers would come ashore during the raid, supported by a regiment of Churchill tanks from the 1st Canadian Tank Brigade. Tanks brought yet another untried dimension to the operation as they had not been used in an amphibious assault prior to this.

As well as the Canadians, the force would include around 1,000 British troops, mainly Commandos and smaller numbers of French and US troops. By now the United States had begun to send men to Britain and they were also keen to experience combat against Germany. Consequently, fifty United States Army Rangers were included in the force. These were the first US troops to go into action in Western Europe. They were skilled in things like scaling cliffs in order to destroy gun batteries. All of this would have echoes on D-Day.

What were the objectives of Operation *Jubilee*? They were both political and physical. On the political front, Winston Churchill had repeatedly promised Stalin that the Western Allies would open a second front in Europe. But time was running out for the Russians after Germany had invaded in Operation *Barbarossa*. If the Allies launched an attack in the west, this would draw much of the German army away from the eastern front and alleviate some of the pressure on the Soviets. But as time went on, Churchill became fearful that Stalin might be forced into making an agreement with Hitler, which would have the reverse effect and once again, all of the Wehrmacht's resources could be deployed in the west to prevent a future Allied invasion.

Although the Allies didn't yet possess the capability to launch a real attack in the west, they thought the operation at Dieppe might confuse the enemy and convince the Soviets that they were committed to victory. A secondary consideration was the boost to morale this would have, not only to the people of Russia, but to the people of Britain and its Allies.

As for the physical objectives, the main one was for the Allied force to seize and hold Dieppe for a given period of time, to show that a major seaport could be captured and quickly utilised by the invaders. The idea was that if a real invasion was to succeed, it would be critical first to capture ports from where the western front could be reinforced and supplied.

On conclusion of the operation, the force was to destroy coastal defences, port structures and all strategic buildings.

They were also to gain intelligence and capture German prisoners, from whom more information could be extracted regarding the enemy's disposition.

As well as these main objectives there were sub plots to the story. For instance, amidst the confusion a specialist team was tasked with entering a radar station on the cliffs to analyse its equipment and learn its secrets. Another party was tasked with capturing a new German 4-rotor Enigma code machine, plus its associated code books and rotor setting sheets.

Although there were one or two minor successes during the operation, only one of its main objectives was realised. For a start, the German defences had been underestimated because of poor reconnaissance and were not sufficiently neutralised before the attack. The terrain also seems completely wrong for this type of operation with the landing beaches surrounded by high cliffs, which meant that the German defenders had the best possible topographical advantage as the troops and tanks came ashore beneath them. Much of the force that did get ashore was trapped on the beach and unable to carry out any of their tasks.

Roughly ten hours after the first troops came ashore, the last soldiers to be evacuated were on their way home. Of the men who did disembark, a vast number were dead, wounded, or had been captured. RAF Fighter Command lost 106 aircraft on the day, many falling victim to anti-aircraft fire, or accidents. In contrast, the Luftwaffe lost forty-eight aircraft. As for the Royal Navy, they suffered the loss of thirty-three landing craft and one destroyer.

The raid on Dieppe was a military disaster and afterwards questions were asked about who was to blame and why it had gone so horrendously wrong. But in times of war things move quickly and soon the whole fiasco had been forgotten. The events at Dieppe as well as other raids mounted by Combined Operations against the Nazi war machine nevertheless influenced all aspects of planning for Operation *Torch*, the invasion of

North Africa, and finally, Operation *Overlord,* the successful Normandy landings in June 1944.

In writing this book to mark the 80th anniversary of these events I was worried that I would find nothing new to add to what has already been said. I then discovered an initiative called *The Memory Project* organised by Historica Canada. This project has interviewed Canadians about many aspects of their country's past. Trawling through this vast database I discovered numerous transcripts of interviews with Dieppe veterans. I have been given permission to use these interviews and have not altered them, other than to edit them for clarity. Collectively, they give a timely and very poignant account of one of the darkest days in Canada's history.

I

COMBINED OPERATIONS

Following the evacuation of the British Expeditionary Force from Dunkirk and other places in western Europe in May and June 1940, it was obvious to the politicians and military leaders of Great Britain and her few surviving Allies that in order to win the war they would have to return one day to the continent, probably through France. With this in mind, the Prime Minister Winston Churchill gave the order to develop a substantial raiding force called Combined Operations.

The ground forces deployed by this new headquarters would largely consist of British Commandos. These would learn to work in co-operation with both the Royal Navy and ultimately the Royal Air Force to carry out tri-service raids in occupied Europe. For larger raids they would also work alongside more substantial military formations including those from Allied armies based in Britain, notably Canada.

Most of these raids would be on coastal targets and would have a range of objectives, from the reconnaissance of beaches and coastal defences to the gaining of intelligence, capture of enemy personnel for interrogation, and the destruction of shipping, harbour installations and factories contributing to Germany's war effort. The raids would add to the Allied understanding of Germany's defences and hopefully pinpoint their weaknesses.

This would undeniably be extremely dangerous and daring work and required the services of a certain type of individual, one who in Churchill's words must be 'of the hunter class who can develop a reign of terror down the enemy coast'. Once an operation was set in motion, these men, operating effectively behind enemy lines, would only have their own ingenuity and resourcefulness, together with that of their comrades, to rely upon to survive and hopefully return to base.

The raids that Combined Operations would plan and carry out in the years and months before D-Day would give the Allies a more detailed understanding of how to plan and prepare for an amphibious assault against a heavily defended coast. Dieppe would be the largest and costliest of these, in terms of the loss of men and equipment. It was also, without doubt, the most informative in terms of lessons learned that were invaluable to the eventual launching of the second front.

About a week after Dunkirk, Churchill ordered Sir John Dill, the chief of the imperial general staff, to prepare a scheme for what he had in mind, basically for the Royal Navy to convey bands of trained raiders up and down the length of the occupied coasts of Europe, from Narvik in Norway to Bordeaux in France, to demonstrate the point that Britain still nurtured an offensive spirit in spite of her recent defeat.

Much of the target area would later become known as the Atlantic Wall, and from 1942 onwards the Germans defended it by building an extensive system of coastal defences and fortifications. But for now, their newly acquired territories remained vulnerable to daring raiders as they had not had sufficient time to secure them. However, as each month passed, the situation became more difficult as the Nazis continually strived to improve their front line against attacks. In order to compensate for this, the operations mounted would have to be more thoroughly researched and prepared for. By the time of Dieppe, the Atlantic Wall was quite formidable, and Allied intelligence would underestimate its effectiveness.

Sir John Dill passed the job of looking into Churchill's requirements to one of his trusted staff, Lieutenant Colonel Dudley Clarke, who already possessed a great knowledge of guerrilla warfare gained from service in Palestine at the time of the Arab Rebellion, where he witnessed small bands of Arabs hinder entire units of regular troops. He set to work and, in a few days, produced the outline of a scheme which had been long in his own mind. The men for this type of irregular warfare should, he suggested, be formed into units to be known as Commandos, a word first used to describe Boer guerrillas during the South African War.

His ideas were studied and considered at length by the general staff and without much hesitation accepted. The first of the Commando units was formed in June 1940. They were drawn from what were originally known as independent companies and later special service battalions. These men had been raised at the time of the campaign in Norway and their purpose was to raid and hinder the enemy in small numbers with maximum effect. They were all volunteers taken from regiments in the regular British Army and Territorial Army and placed under specially selected officers. However, due to the fast-moving nature of the campaign in Norway they were never used for the purposes for which they were formed and instead fought conventionally alongside regular units of the British Army. On returning to the British Isles they were established at camps in Scotland and Northern Ireland in order to continue their training.

On 12 June 1940, Winston Churchill appointed Lieutenant General Sir Alan Bourne, who at that time was the Adjutant

General of the Royal Marines, as Director of Combined Operations. He was a hugely experienced officer, who at the time of his retirement in 1943 was the last officer in the Royal Marines to hold a commission from the time of Queen Victoria, having been commissioned on 1 September 1899. He had served throughout the First World War in France and Belgium, where he was mentioned in dispatches twice and awarded the Distinguished Service Order (DSO).

His second in command and chief of staff would be Lieutenant Colonel A. H. Hornby of the Royal Artillery. Other senior officers drafted to this new organisation included Lieutenant Colonel Dudley Clarke himself and Captain Gerald Garnons-Williams of the Royal Navy.

For this clandestine and very secretive work a set of vacant offices were made available at the Admiralty in Whitehall, where Lieutenant General Bourne established his headquarters. Here, with his various members of staff, he would plan each raid and then submit proposals to the joint planning committee of the three services. Once approved by the chiefs of staff, the necessary men and equipment required for the task at hand would also be organised from these premises.

The men who would carry out the raids would largely come from Lieutenant Colonel Clarke's Commandos. However, in order to reach their objectives they needed to work together with the Royal Navy, which is where Captain Garnons-Williams stepped up to the plate. During the initial setting up of Combined Operations, it seems the raids were very much designed around using the Army and Royal Navy together, with very little thought of including air support, which ultimately would become a crucial part in the success of any operation.

Captain Garnons-Williams was tasked with acquiring the necessary small craft that would be used during raids as well as the officers and men who would sail them. The obvious solution to this would be what we now think of as the landing craft used at Dieppe and in Normandy on D-Day and other later operations, but at this early stage of the war such dedicated vessels were not available. Assault landing craft had been developed as early as 1936, but these were precious commodities, so none were provided to Combined Operations in the first instance. Instead, he was forced to trawl the rivers and harbours of south east England in an attempt to recruit an assorted collection of what were mainly privately owned motor-boats. This inevitably draws comparisons with the little boats of Dunkirk, also mostly civilian craft, which answered the call in Britain's hour of need.

Few of the officers he managed to recruit were from the Royal Navy and mostly belonged to the Royal Naval Reserve, or the Royal Naval Volunteer Reserve. Similar to the Territorial Army, before the war these men had trained at weekends or in the evenings alongside their full-time counterparts. But most were very experienced and capable yachtsmen. In their professional capacities they might have been the skipper of a trawler, tanker, cruise ship, or even a fishing boat. The ordinary seamen on the other hand, had mainly worked the fishing boats before the war and continued to do so as this was mainly, although not entirely, a reserved occupation. Nevertheless, they were enthusiastic and willing to participate in this heroic scheme, even though unaccustomed to the naval discipline that accompanied it.

By 15 June 1940, Garnons-Williams had largely gathered his armada of small craft and established a training depot, first in a converted yacht until suitable on-shore quarters were established on the south coast of England. Training in amphibious warfare began.

Lieutenant General Bourne was now in a position to report to the Prime Minister that his organisation was ready to begin planning raids on the shores of western Europe, wherever required. He gave his opinion that he now possessed both the men and equipment necessary to carry out such raids.

As the weeks following Dunkirk ticked away, Churchill was eager to begin raiding operations as soon and as regularly as possible, to illustrate to the enemy that Britain still possessed teeth. He wanted to show Hitler that although Germany had prevailed in France and Belgium, his forces were still able to go on the offensive and one day would return to retake the territories he had gained.

Aware of Churchill's desire, Lieutenant General Bourne and his staff began to work frantically in their new headquarters in Whitehall and within days had put together the plan for their first proposed operation. They subsequently presented it to the chiefs of staff who without hesitation approved it for action. This opening raid was to be named Operation *Collar* and would be executed on the night of 24/25 June 1940.

The plan was for the Royal Navy to carry 200 men and land them on the coast of France around the Pas-de-Calais. The raid would be perpetrated by six separate parties who would make a reconnaissance of the German defences in the area and bring back any prisoners they could capture for interrogation. It was a small beginning but would test the feasibility of operating in this clandestine way.

The men chosen to carry out this inaugural raid belonged to No. 11 Independent Company, which at the time was based in Scotland. Once given their orders they were moved to the port of Southampton in the south of England to make the necessary preparations for the mission. In order to be ready for the task in hand a series of training exercises were designed and carried out in the River Hamble, a local infantry battalion acting as the enemy.

During these exercises it became quite evident that the boats with which they had been issued were totally inadequate for the job of taking them safely across the English Channel and back again. So at very short notice they managed to enlist the services of four air-sea rescue motor launches belonging to the Royal Air Force, which were stationed at Newhaven, Ramsgate and Dover.

The final plan, which had to be amended due to the number of boats available, was for a force of 115 officers and other ranks to be landed on four target beaches at Neufchâtel Hardelot, Stella Plage, Berck and Le Touquet. To confuse the enemy if they were detected, they would land simultaneously. Each party had its own objective and would spend no more than eighty minutes ashore before returning to the boats.

The senior naval officer was Lieutenant Commander J. W. F. Milner-Gibson and the troops were under the command of Major Ronnie Tod of the Argyll and Sutherland Highlanders. Lieutenant Colonel Clarke also accompanied the raid but was under strict orders not to go ashore with the men. He was there merely to observe the proceedings and report back to Whitehall after the raid with his conclusions.

Although the air-sea rescue launches were infinitely preferable to the boats they were originally issued with, they were still far from ideal and were certainly not equipped for a mission of this nature. For a start, their navigational systems were not good enough to locate exact locations, little more than a rudimentary and unreliable compass. The fact that their skippers managed to reach the various targets in the dark was nothing short of a miracle, especially having narrowly escaped being attacked by a patrol of British aircraft which was unaware of their presence and having spotted them, closed in to investigate. But get them to the beaches they did and at roughly 02:00 on 24 June, the launches reached the coast of France.

The objective of the group that landed at Le Touquet was a hotel named the Merlimont Plage, which according to intelligence sources had been taken over by the Germans for use as a barracks. However, on reaching the hotel undetected, they found it boarded up and empty of any occupants, military or otherwise. It was possible that their sources had identified the wrong target, so the group spent a little time searching for others that might have been employed by the enemy but to no avail. With time running out, they returned to the beach.

On arrival they discovered that their launch had put back out to sea, so they had to wait for its return. While waiting they were happened upon by two German soldiers on patrol. The Commandos quickly and silently killed both with bayonets. Unfortunately, a second larger German patrol appeared on the scene and the group decided not to engage with them. Instead, they discarded any heavy equipment and non-essential weapons they were carrying and leaving them on the sand, swam out to the launch and made their escape.

The job of the group that landed at Neufchâtel Hardelot was to hunt out any German military personnel they could find at that location. Any discovered would be taken prisoner and brought back to their launch for removal to England for interrogation, although if this proved impossible, they were to kill them instead. However, having spent their allotted time ashore searching far and wide and having not encountered any German soldiers, they returned to their boat empty-handed and withdrew.

The group approaching Berck discovered a number of enemy seaplanes anchored in the small harbour and gave a lot of thought to the possibility of sabotaging one or more of them. Unfortunately, the whole place was too heavily defended to carry out such a task, so the Commandos had to give up any such notion as such an attack would have been futile. Also, as they were still in the process of discussing the possibility of implementing an attack on one of the seaplanes, it took off and flew directly over them.

The final group, under the command of Major Tod, came ashore at Stella Plage and, having penetrated a little way inshore, stumbled upon a German patrol. There was a short exchange of fire before the Commandos tactically withdrew to their boat. The only casualty was Lieutenant Colonel Clarke himself, who was very slightly wounded when a bullet grazed him just behind the ear as he waited in the bow of the launch for the men to escape.

This first mission enjoyed what can only be described as mixed success and was certainly not a triumph, yet at its conclusion the Ministry of Information issued a glowing communiqué designed to boost the morale of a country which was ostensibly teetering on the brink of an invasion and needed reassurances that its armed forces was still in a position to be able to fight the aggressors. Any news of a positive nature was a valuable tool to Churchill and his government in helping to bolster the spirits of the nation at one of the country's most precarious moments in its modern history. It also left Churchill wanting more of the same, as any successful attack on German held territory was a huge tonic to him and other Allied commanders. They didn't have long to wait for the next instalment.

The second raid, codenamed Operation *Ambassador*, took place on the night of 14/15 July 1940. The target was the island of Guernsey in the Channel Islands, which had been occupied by the Germans. Prior to the mission, a secret reconnaissance of the island by Lieutenant Hubert Nicolle revealed that there were an estimated 469 Germans on the island, mostly stationed in St Peter Port. Elements of No. 3 Commando and No. 11 Independent Company were to attack an airfield on the island and destroy whatever facilities they could, then kill as many of the enemy as possible and capture others for interrogation.

In charge of the Commandos was Major John Durnford-Slater of the Royal Artillery. The independent company was once again led by Major Tod with Captain Goodwin as his second in command. Durnford-Slater would go on to lead No. 3 Commando during the Dieppe Raid and was evidently already building the experiences he would need to tackle progressively bigger tasks for him and his men.

The plan was for No. 3 Commando in this instance to make a diversionary landing on the north coast of the island, while the men of No. 11 Independent Company attacked the airfield. Durnford-Slater would therefore draw the occupying forces away from the target while Tod and his men destroyed as much of the airfield, its aircraft and infrastructure as was possible in the time. The Royal Navy provided the destroyers HMS *Scimitar* and HMS *Saladin* to ferry the force to a point close enough to the island from where they could climb into a series of motor launches that had been following in their wake across the Channel, which would ultimately put them ashore.

At the very last moment the plans were changed after new information was forthcoming that indicated the German garrison had been reinforced. It was decided that the party under Major Durnford-Slater would now land to the west of the Jerbourg peninsula (or Jerbourg Point) where they would establish a roadblock in order to isolate the peninsula, while Major Tod attacked the airfield.

Once again, the operation was completed with mixed success, bordering on failure, with one of the launches completely missing Guernsey altogether because of an unreliable compass. This group eventually found themselves skirting around an island of high cliffs with no apparent beaches, making it impossible for them to come ashore. After returning home and analysing the mission it was deduced that they had been circumnavigating the island of Sark.

Another group also experienced difficulties with their motor launch and attempted to use HMS *Saladin's* whaler to support their endeavours instead. However, this was leaking and going nowhere. Consequently, they also failed to make land and were left with no other option but to return to England, making the last part of their perilous journey under the watchful eye of the Royal Air Force.

The third and final landing party commanded by Durnford-Slater met with slightly more success. Having said that, although the crews of the launches managed to locate and reach the correct beach on the Jerbourg peninsula, there was a problem that their reconnaissance and planning had not picked up. All along the front of the beach there was a series of treacherous rocks into which the surf was crashing, which made any landing from the boats impossible as these could not get close enough to the beach for the men to alight on dry land. Because of this, the troops had to leave their boats some way out to sea and wade ashore in waist-deep water with their guns and equipment raised over their heads. This they succeeded in doing and once ashore had to negotiate a steep, narrow path, which they managed to climb in almost complete silence. Luckily, the pre-arranged movement of Anson aircraft belonging to Coastal Command drowned out the few sounds they did make.

With the attack on the airfield itself having now been cancelled because of the failure of any of the other troops in the group to land, Durnford-Slater decided he would make a thorough search of the peninsula for a supposed army barracks where the enemy on the island were thought to be accommodated. If he could locate the buildings in question, it might still be plausible to carry out the secondary objectives of the raid, which was to kill enemy personnel and capture others for interrogation. However, on eventually pinpointing and arriving at the suspect buildings, they were found to be completely unoccupied, so Durnford-Slater and his Commandos retraced their tracks back to the beach for re-embarkation on the waiting launches.

Even this part of the operation went badly as the motor boats waiting to extract the party were unable to get closer than fifty yards from the beach because of the jagged rocks and surging waves. Using a small dinghy, most of the men managed to make it out to the waiting boats a few at a time. However, on its fifth trip the dinghy capsized and was lost, and one man was drowned. Those left on the beach decided to swim to the boats, except for three who were not strong enough swimmers and had to be left behind, who later surrendered. The boats eventually reached HMS *Scimitar* and the exhausted Commandos climbed aboard for the trip back to England.

These first two raids planned and executed by Lieutenant General Bourne and his new Combined Operations headquarters were small and largely unsuccessful. They would not have worried the Nazi occupation forces in the west, or indicated that Britain was capable of mounting any sort of second front in Europe in the foreseeable future – or any operations on a large scale for that matter. What was gained from these operations is of course debatable, other than to gather information about the build-up of enemy forces along the Atlantic Wall and to boost morale at home. By 1941 it was decided that these were not enough, and although small reconnaissance missions should continue, something larger was also needed.

In the meantime, new combined operational training centres were being established in secret locations where the troops could be prepared for their varied missions. This all took time and while training steamed ahead, more suitable craft were being sourced for future raids.

To mark the move from small to larger-scale missions it was decided that a change of command was required at the top. To this end, on 17 July 1940, Admiral of the Fleet Sir Roger Keyes was appointed Director of Combined Operations, replacing Lieutenant General Sir Alan Bourne, who gracefully accepted the role of his second in command.

This was very much the culmination of a glittering career in the Royal Navy for Keyes, which began in 1885 as a naval cadet. During the Boxer Rebellion he had led a mission to capture a flotilla of four Chinese destroyers and was one of the first men to climb the walls of Peking in order to break through and free the besieged diplomatic legations. During the First World War he was involved in the organisation of the Dardanelles campaign, was director of plans at the Admiralty, and commanded the Dover Patrol. He also planned and led the famous raids on the German submarine pens in the Belgian ports of Zeebrugge and Ostend. Between the wars he commanded the Battlecruiser Squadron, the Atlantic Fleet and then the Mediterranean Fleet before eventually becoming commander in chief, Portsmouth. And during the Second World War, prior to his appointment as Director of Combined Operations, he had acted as liaison officer to King Leopold III of Belgium. So, he was a hugely experienced officer possessing the qualities required for the job in hand.

Admiral Keyes, according to Churchill's expressed wishes, was keen to keep up the impetus and not allow the Nazis to rest easy in their captured Atlantic nests. He immediately and wholeheartedly got to grips with his new responsibilities. The first of these larger-scale raids was codenamed Operation *Claymore*.

Thinking that the Germans might now be expecting incursions along the coast of France and the Channel Islands, he turned his attention to the north. The raid would take place in the Lofoten Islands, which was situated 100 miles north of the Arctic Circle. Along with the rest of Norway, the islands had been occupied by the Germans in the early summer of 1940. Here there were a number of factories producing fish oil, which the Germans used in the production of glycerine for munitions. It was an important resource contributing to Hitler's war machine. These factories were located in the four ports of Stamsund, Henningsvaer, Svolvaer and Brettesnes. The Germans had taken the factories over and had already begun to supply themselves with this vital commodity using the local population to work in them.

The plan was to locate and destroy the factories and capture as many Germans as possible, as well as quislings, the term used from about 1940 for Nazi collaborators. They would also offer safe passage back to Britain to any Norwegian citizens willing to enlist in the Norwegian forces established there. Finally, any ships supporting the enemy's war effort found in the ports would be captured or sunk.

For this daring sortie a naval force of five destroyers under the command of Captain Clifford Caslon went from Scapa Flow in the Orkney Islands to the Faroe Islands for final preparations: HMS *Somali*, HMS *Bedouin*, HMS *Tartar*, HMS *Eskimo* and HMS *Legion*. From here they would escort two infantry landing ships to Norway, HMS *Queen Emma* and HMS *Princess Beatrix*. These were carrying 500 men of Nos 3 and 4 Commandos, a few sappers from the Royal Engineers, and fifty Norwegian soldiers and sailors. In charge of this military force was Brigadier Joseph Haydon, although the Norwegian soldiers and ratings sailed under their own officers, who had taken an active role in planning the raid.

In the early hours of Monday 3 March 1941, the force entered Vestfjorden, which lies between the Lofoten archipelago and the Salten district of mainland Norway. Each of the ships had a Norwegian pilot on board to help them navigate to their targets. All the navigational lights in the vicinity were clearly on, indicating that the British raiders had arrived with complete surprise.

Four separate landings took place, No. 3 Commando coming ashore at Stamsund and Henningsvaer, and No. 4 Commando at Svolvaer and Brettesnes. No enemy forces were initially encountered at any of the landing sites and in fact the surprise was so complete that local people who were heading off early to work thought that the soldiers were Germans taking part in a training exercise. On realisation of the truth the locals were far from resentful about the fact that the British had come to destroy their factories and effectively, their livelihoods. On the contrary, many were eager to help, especially in the identification and rounding up of officials and collaborators.

315 individuals volunteered to return to Britain to join the Norwegian forces, including eight women who expressed their interest in joining the Norwegian Red Cross. No one had been expecting to take women back with them, but a quick radio message was sent to operational headquarters asking for advice on the matter and they were given the all clear to be taken off.

Although the raid met with no military opposition, some 225 German personnel and ten quislings were rounded up, including the head of the local police force. In fact, the Commandos were so disappointed at not facing the enemy that Lieutenant Richard Lloyd Wills sent a telegram from the telegraph office at Stamsund addressed to Mr A. Hitler in Berlin, which read: 'You said in your last speech, German troops would meet the British wherever they landed. Where are your troops?'

On shore the demolition parties from the Royal Engineers set to work planting their explosive charges with which they destroyed eleven fish oil or fish-meal factories, an electric-light plant, and oil tanks containing an estimated 800,000 gallons. Naval demolition parties boarded and destroyed four enemy ships, while a fifth, the SS *Hamburg* which was a large factory and refrigerator ship, was sunk by gunfire from HMS *Tartar*.

The only opposition the raiders faced came at sea from an armed trawler, the *Krebs*, which came out of Stamsund at around 06:00. Although her captain could see the overwhelming forces ahead of him he bravely engaged HMS *Somali*, which unknown to him was the force headquarters ship. The German ship took fire and ran aground on a small island, from which she drifted off and surrendered a few hours later. Her captain had by now been killed. The surviving crew members were taken prisoner and the ship was finally sunk by gunfire.

By 13:00 all of the troops had re-embarked along with their prisoners, and the force set sail for Scapa Flow as the burning fish oil factories clouded the fjord with smoke. Operation *Claymore* had been a complete success and to add to it was the capture of a set of spare rotors for a German Enigma coding machine from the *Krebs*, which was sent directly to Bletchley Park near Milton Keynes, the top secret code-breaking establishment. The only British casualty suffered during the raid was an officer who wounded himself accidentally by firing his own revolver into his thigh.

Following the success of *Claymore*, the next raid was on a much smaller scale again. This was Operation *Chess* directed against a beach near the village of Ambleteuse, in the Pas-de-Calais. It was treated very much as an operational training exercise and its objective was to test a new prototype landing craft recently arrived from the USA. The craft was newly designed for landing on beaches and had a ramp which could be lowered for the men to run straight onto the sand. Secondary to this, they were to make a reconnaissance of the area and if possible, take prisoners. It was executed by seventeen soldiers belonging to No. 12 Commando under the orders of Second Lieutenant Philip Pinckney during the night of 27/28 July 1941.

The raiding party were towed across the English Channel in two of these landing craft by a motor launch. When they reached a point about two miles from the small target beach, the launch cast them off. It was supposed to have been undefended but as the boats drew close inshore a flare shot up to illuminate them and heavy machine gun fire was directed towards them. The gun appeared to be situated on a small cliff top and had to be silenced. The soldiers went ashore and a party under Lieutenant Pinckney took the machine gun nest out with hand grenades. Among the party was Commander Sir Geoffrey Congreve, a veteran of the Lofoten Islands raid. He had joined the mission as an observer and was killed by the machine gun fire.

The Commandos remained in the area for one hour before being extracted by the landing craft. It was not a great success and no Germans were taken prisoner, but at least it succeeded in its primary purpose of evaluating new equipment being phased in for future operations.

During most of the period in which the early raids took place, Britain was under serious threat of invasion as the Nazis built up troops and barges in continental ports. They planned to invade at any moment, if and when thee Luftwaffe won air supremacy, which would enable their troops to assault the southern coast of England without interference from the RAF or Royal Navy. Britain would be in this precarious predicament throughout the summer of 1940. However, thanks to the relentless bravery of the pilots of RAF Fighter Command during the Battle of Britain, by the end of October Hitler had cancelled any plans to launch an invasion that year. Instead, he turned his attentions to the east and in doing so, provided Britain with a new military and economic partner.

On 22 June 1941 the Nazis launched Operation *Barbarossa*, the codename for the Axis invasion of the Soviet Union. Their ambition was to occupy the western part of the country and to repopulate it with German citizens. The local inhabitants would be enslaved and used as forced labour for German war industries. The Nazis also wished to acquire the oil reserves of the Caucasus and the agricultural resources of the area, and eventually to annihilate the Slavic peoples and create *Lebensraum* for Germany.

What this meant for Britain was that many of Germany's troops, as well as a large part of its air force, which had been deployed against them in the west, were now redirected to the eastern front. For the first time since June 1940, Britain could sigh with relief and more seriously consider a possible second front at some time in the future.

From the onset of the invasion Churchill made it clear that he would offer to support the Soviet Union in any way possible, particularly if it also proved beneficial to the British. With this in mind, a plan was hatched to establish British naval and air forces in Spitsbergen, which is the largest island of the Svalbard archipelago in northern Norway and borders the Arctic Ocean, the Norwegian Sea and the Greenland Sea, some 650 miles south of the North Pole. This could be the ideal base from which to supply the Soviets and bring the fight to the Germans in Norway. A reconnaissance was made of the area, which found that the enemy was heavily reinforcing the whole of northern Norway. This fact made establishing a base there impractical.

Spitsbergen had a number of highly productive coal mines at Longyearbyen that were owned and operated by Norway, while others at Barentsburg were owned and run by Soviet companies. If these fell into German hands the coal would be very useful in their war effort and as neither the Norwegians nor the Soviets were in a position to benefit from this supply, a suggestion was made that a British task force could be sent to destroy the mines. This was agreed by the governments of both Russia and Norway and the task was handed to Admiral Keyes and Combined Operations headquarters.

Admiral Keyes set about planning Operation *Gauntlet,* a raid that was much more ambitious than anything so far attempted. It would occur over a longer period of time and involve substantially more troops, many of whom would be Canadian. These untried troops would get their first taste of battle almost exactly a year before Dieppe. The naval part of the operation would be planned and undertaken by Rear Admiral Philip Vian in command of Force K, consisting of the troopship RMS *Empress of Canada*, the cruisers HMS *Nigeria* and HMS *Aurora,* and the destroyers HMS *Icarus*, HMS *Anthony*, HMS *Eclipse*, HMS *Tartar* and HMS *Antelope*.

The objectives of the raid were to destroy the coal mines, coal supplies, mining and shipping infrastructure and stores on

Spitsbergen. They were also to evacuate miners from the island and suppress the wireless stations on the archipelago, from which the Germans received their weather reports.

The original plan was for the deployment of two complete battalions, but after it was discovered that the enemy had not actually invaded the island yet, this was reduced to one. The task was handed to the 2nd Canadian Infantry Brigade under the command of Brigadier Arthur Potts. His force numbered forty-six officers and 599 other ranks, of which twenty-nine officers and 498 other ranks were Canadian. These were provided by the Edmonton Regiment, the 3rd Field Company Royal Canadian Engineers, and the Saskatoon Light Infantry. There were also three Norwegian officers and twenty-two other ranks under Captain Aubert, and ninety-three British from Nos. 2, 5, 9 and 12 Commandos. Here for the first time we begin to see the development of a raid somewhere on the scale of Dieppe and using troops from combined nations together with British Commandos.

To prepare for the raid the Canadians made their way to No. 1 Combined Training Centre at the shore establishment HMS *Quebec* at Inveraray on Loch Fyne, where they began rehearsing the landings and other aspects of the mission. Then from the Clyde the naval force, with the troops aboard the converted liner *Empress of Canada*, first sailed to the south-west of Iceland for refuelling before setting course for Spitsbergen on 21 August 1941. On 24 August they rendezvoused with the oiler *Oligarch* and its escorting trawlers *Elm* and *Hazel,* and together the whole force approached Spitsbergen on the morning of 25 August.

Before their arrival an air reconnaissance was made of the area, which indicated that the Germans had still not arrived on the island. At 04:30 a group of signallers was put ashore near the wireless station at Kap Linne and were welcomed by the Norwegian operators with open arms. In order that the Germans did not suspect that anything was wrong it was imperative that the station maintained its weather reports throughout the duration of the raid. They also sent out false fog reports to try and stall any German activity in the area. Once this had been arranged, at around 08:00 the ships entered Green Bay and anchored off the Soviet mining village at Barentsburg.

As pre-arranged with the Soviet government, 1,800 of its citizens, most of whom were miners, were evacuated from the island aboard the *Empress of Canada* along with vital mining equipment and ferried to a rendezvous point with a small fleet of Russian vessels for onward transportation to the Soviet Union. While this was being done the engineer demolition parties set about destroying all of their targets on Spitsbergen, including coal mines, mining equipment not transported with the Soviets, an estimated 450,000 tons of stocked coal and an estimated 275,000 gallons of fuel, oil, petrol and grease.

On 2 September the *Empress of Canada* and her escorts returned from their rendezvous bringing with them around 200 free French soldiers who had escaped from German prison camps and had made their way to the Soviet Union. At this point the Germans had still not arrived on the island and with all their tasks complete the ground forces re-embarked for the journey back to Britain. They also evacuated 800 Norwegian civilians, mainly miners who would be able to either work in British mines for the rest of the war or join the Norwegian free forces. Finally, just before leaving, the wireless stations that had been sending out false reports throughout the raid were destroyed.

Operation *Gauntlet* was a complete success. It had been achieved without the Germans even being aware of it. The raiders had suffered no casualties, all of its objectives were met and the Canadians were now ready for bigger and better things, full of confidence about whatever was required of them in the future.

Following the success of Operation *Gauntlet* the next raids were small and largely designed to make a reconnaissance of potential beaches in north-west France where landing craft could be beached. The first of these was Operation *Acid Drop*, which saw twenty-five men of No. 5 Commando target beaches at Neufchâtel-Hardelot and Merlimont on the night of 30/31 August 1941. If possible, they were to take prisoners for interrogation. The Commandos came ashore for around half an hour, but no German opposition was encountered, although a thorough evaluation of the beaches was made.

Next came Operations *Chopper* and *Deep Cut*, mounted simultaneously by No. 1 Commando on the night of 27/28 September. In the first, twenty-five men led by Captain Tom Hemming raided the coast at St Aubin. The raid met a German patrol and suffered a number of casualties including two killed. The second raid against St Vaast led by Lieutenant Scaramanga ambushed a German bicycle patrol. In the exchange two Commandos were wounded. Again, no prisoners were taken but reconnaissance was achieved.

Collectively, all of these early raids were adding to the experience of the men who would both plan and carry out the future invasion. No matter how big or small the raids appear, or how diverse their objectives were, each was an important lesson. Each was a small piece in a bigger puzzle that would one day lead to the beaches of Dieppe and beyond.

2

A NEW DIRECTION

On 27 October 1941, Admiral of the Fleet Sir Roger Keyes was succeeded as Director of Combined Operations by Captain the Lord Louis Mountbatten, who was promoted to Commodore First Class. On 18 March 1942, he was further promoted to the rank of Acting Vice Admiral, when his title was changed from Director to Chief of Combined Operations. He would also be given honorary commissions in both the Army and the Royal Air Force as a Lieutenant General and Air Marshal respectively.

Mountbatten belonged to royal lineage and was born Prince Louis of Battenberg on 25 June 1900 at Frogmore House in Windsor. His father, of whom he was the youngest child and second son, was also called Prince Louis of Battenberg. His mother was Princess Victoria of Hesse and by Rhine. His maternal grandparents were Louis IV, Grand Duke of Hesse and Princess Alice of the United Kingdom, who was a daughter of Queen Victoria and Prince Albert of Saxe-Coburg and Gotha. During the First World War, in a bid to appease British nationalist sentiment, King George V issued a royal proclamation changing the name of the British royal house from the German House of

Saxe-Coburg and Gotha to the House of Windsor. The King's British relatives followed suit with Louis's side dropping their German titles and name and adopting the surname Mountbatten. He remained a favourite with the Royal Family, Churchill and the British public, so was destined for great things.

His military career began at the Royal Naval College, Osborne, in May 1913. He was thereafter posted as midshipman to the battlecruiser HMS *Lion* in July 1916 and, after seeing action, transferred to the battleship HMS *Queen Elizabeth* during the closing phases of the First World War.

At the end of the hostilities, he was posted to the battlecruiser HMS *Renown* in March 1920 and accompanied Edward, Prince of Wales, on a royal tour of Australia in her. Promoted to lieutenant, he transferred to the battlecruiser HMS *Repulse* in March 1921 and accompanied the Prince of Wales on a Royal tour of India and Japan. Edward and Mountbatten formed a close friendship during this trip. Pursuing his interests in technological development and gadgetry, Mountbatten joined the Portsmouth Signals School in August 1924 and then went on briefly to study electronics at the Royal Naval College, Greenwich.

He was posted to the battleship HMS *Centurion* in the Reserve Fleet in 1926 and became Assistant Fleet Wireless and Signals Officer of the Mediterranean Fleet under the command of Admiral Sir Roger Keyes. Promoted lieutenant commander on 15 April 1928, he returned to the Signals School in July 1929 as senior wireless instructor. He was appointed fleet wireless officer to the Mediterranean in August 1931, and having been promoted commander on 31 December 1932, was posted to the battleship HMS *Resolution*.

In 1934, Mountbatten was given his first command, HMS *Daring*. His ship was a new destroyer, which he was to sail to Singapore and exchange for an older ship, HMS *Wishart*. He successfully brought *Wishart* back to port in Malta and then attended the funeral of King George V in January 1936. Mountbatten was appointed a personal naval aide-de-camp to King Edward VIII on 23 June 1936. Having joined the Naval Air Division of the Admiralty in July 1936, he attended the coronation of King George VI and Queen Elizabeth in May 1937. He was promoted captain on 30 June 1937 and was then given command of the destroyer HMS *Kelly* in June 1939.

When war broke out in September 1939, Mountbatten became Captain (D) (commander) of the 5th Destroyer Flotilla aboard HMS *Kelly*, which became famous for its exploits. In late 1939 he brought the Duke of Windsor back from exile in France and in early May 1940 he led a British convoy in through the fog to evacuate the Allied forces participating in the Namsos Campaign in Norway.

In August 1941, Mountbatten was appointed captain of the aircraft carrier HMS *Illustrious* before finally replacing his old boss Sir Roger Keyes as Director of Combined Operations. It would be under Mountbatten's watch that the Dieppe Raid would be planned and executed.

In the meantime, other raids continued, the next being Operation *Astrakan* carried out by No. 6 Commando on the night of 12/13 November 1941. The target was the area around Houlgate and Les Hemmes. Again, the mission of a four-man patrol was to test the suitability of the local beaches for use by landing craft. No Germans were encountered but vital information was ascertained.

The next event of any real size was Operation *Sunstar* on the night of 22/23 November. This was carried out by ninety men of No. 9 Commando in the area to the east of Houlgate and was led by Lieutenant Colonel J. M. Sagaert. Their objective was to attack and destroy the four-gun coastal emplacement, the Batterie de Tournebride, and to capture prisoners for interrogation.

The raiding party was ferried to the objective from Portsmouth aboard the infantry landing ship HMS *Prince Leopold*, escorted by four motor gun boats. From the landing ship they climbed into smaller assault landing craft for the final approach to the beach. However, some of the men came ashore at the wrong location, Vaches Noires, which was a little way from their intended landing beach. Here they were confronted by a cliff and because of this they were unable to press home their attack. Things got worse when the Germans became aware of their presence and illuminated the beach with flares and searchlights. The raiders on the beach were forced to hastily extract themselves by swimming back out to their landing craft after exchanging signals with the boats. The gunners on the craft did not fire at the enemy in order not to give away their positions.

Elsewhere, another group of raiders had made it as far as a French farmhouse where they were informed that a two-man German bicycle patrol would be passing there imminently. They decided to lay an ambush for the cyclists by setting a rope across the road. However, while they were doing this the landing craft came under attack from a Junkers Ju 87 dive bomber and the Commandos decided to make it back to their boats.

Again, it was hardly an auspicious success. The raiders failed to complete any of their tasks. As before, there were problems with navigation and communication between the raiding parties and the landing craft. It was becoming increasingly clear that there was a requirement for better planning and execution. At Dieppe both of these problems would nevertheless recur, with dire consequences.

Mountbatten was immediately concerned about the lack of success of the raids carried out so far by Combined Operations and the inadequate planning with which they had often been undertaken. He was also aware of Churchill's desire to provide the public and Britain's Allies with some sort of morale boost by these incursions. With these concerns in mind, for his first raid in overall charge he decided to return to the Lofoten Islands of

Norway, which had been the scene of Operation *Claymore,* one of the group's previous successes. This was the least defended part of the Atlantic coast, so logically where the Germans would least expect an attack to take place.

Operation *Anklet* would be the last substantial raid undertaken without the support of the Royal Air Force. A force of 300 men, consisting of 223 men of No. 12 Commando accompanied by seventy-seven soldiers of a Norwegian independent company, would attack and destroy radio transmitters, sink enemy shipping and take prisoners. A considerable task force of twenty-two ships was assembled for the mission at three separate locations, Scapa Flow, Greenock and Lerwick. This was codenamed Force J and set sail for the Lofoten Islands between Monday 22 December and Tuesday 23 December 1941. During the journey, the infantry landing ship HMS *Princess Josephine Charlotte* developed engine trouble and returned to Scapa Flow accompanied by her escort destroyer HMS *Wheatland,* which, after delivering her charge safely, returned to the task force. As Force J made its final approach to the Lofotens, a British submarine HMS *Sealion* was already in position to act as a navigational beacon for the attack, scheduled for 26 December.

The approaching naval force included ships from several navies with the Royal Navy naturally providing the lion's share: the light cruiser HMS *Arethusa*; six destroyers HMS *Somali,* HMS *Ashanti,* HMS *Bedouin,* HMS *Eskimo,* HMS *Lamerton* and HMS *Wheatland*; three minesweepers HMS *Speedwell,* HMS *Harrier* and HMS *Halcyon*; the corvette HMS *Acanthus*; two infantry landing ships HMS *Prins Albert* and (the aborted) HMS *Princess Josephine Charlotte*; two submarines HMS *Tigris* and HMS *Sealion*; and the survey ship HMS *Scott.* The Royal Fleet Auxiliary sent two fleet tankers RFA *Grey Ranger* and RFA *Black Ranger,* the freighter *Gudrun Maersk,* and the tugboat *Jaunty.*

The Royal Norwegian Navy which was operating out of British naval bases sent two corvettes, HNoMS *Andenes* and HNoMS *Eglantine*. And the Polish Navy, also exiled to Great Britain, provided the destroyers ORP *Krakowiak* and ORP *Kujawiak*.

On arrival in the area, the infantry landing ship HMS *Prins Albert* headed for the island of Moskenesøya escorted by the destroyer HMS *Lamerton* and the corvettes HNoMS *Eglantine* and HMS *Acanthus*. Here they would land the Commandos. Meanwhile, other ships took part in separate operations around the islands. The destroyer HMS *Bedouin* destroyed a radio transmitter at Flakstadøya and the cruiser HMS *Arethusa* entered the Vestfjorden, along with the destroyers HMS *Somali*, HMS *Ashanti* and HMS *Eskimo*. Here they discovered and captured the Norwegian coastal steamers *Kong Harald* and *Nordland*. The *Ashanti* also managed to sink a German patrol boat.

The landing had been planned to take place at 06:00 on Boxing Day. The planners had hoped that the German garrison would be enjoying Christmas celebrations and consequently off their guard and unprepared. The Commandos, wearing white camouflage overalls, landed on the western side of the island and came ashore unopposed and quickly occupied the villages of Reine and Moskenes. They captured the small German garrison and a handful of Norwegian quislings as well as the radio station.

On 27 December, the Luftwaffe made an appearance when a German seaplane bombed HMS *Arethusa*. Although not directly hit, she sustained partial damage. This prompted Rear Admiral Louis Keppel Hamilton, the commander of Force J, to bring the operation to a close and return to Scapa Flow before they faced any further counterattacks. After occupying the Norwegian villages for two days, the force withdrew unopposed and arrived back at Scapa Flow on 1 January 1941 after registering a resounding success for Lord Mountbatten.

Two radio transmitters had been destroyed, several small German boats had been captured or sunk, and a number of Germans and quislings had been taken prisoner. Also during the raid, an Enigma coding machine had been captured from a German patrol ship that had been sunk and the force had returned to Britain with 200 volunteers for the Free Norwegian Forces. Mountbatten had leant several lessons from the raid, most crucially that any raid of this size should enjoy a degree of air support.

At the same time as *Anklet* another larger and more daring raid also took place in Norway, Operation *Archery*, which targeted the islands of Vaagso and Maaloy. Its objective was the destruction of German fish oil and glycerine production facilities, particularly in the small port of South Vaagso. The target was some 350 miles north of Norway's southern coast and about halfway between Bergen and Trondheim.

Because of its timing it has been suggested that *Anklet* was a diversion for this greater adventure, which is unlikely as *Anklet* had clear objectives of its own. It was more probable that Mountbatten was keen to up the game and make his impact felt. There was also a desire to tie up more German troops in Norway and therefore away from both the Russian front and the defence of France. *Archery* was groundbreaking as it was the first operation to be undertaken by all three services, with the Royal Air Force using bombers and fighter-bombers to give close air support.

The ground forces for the operation would number 570 and were under the command of Major John Durnford-Slater and his second in command Major Jack Churchill, although in overall charge of the mission was Brigadier Joseph Charles Haydon. Durnford-Slater's troops would come from Nos. 2, 3, 4, and 6 Commandos, with a small contingent from a Norwegian independent company.

The seagoing element provided by the Royal Navy consisted of the light cruiser HMS *Kenya,* and the destroyers HMS *Onslow,* HMS *Oribi,* HMS *Offa,* and HMS *Chiddingfold.* HMS *Tuna,* the sole submarine, was employed as a navigational aid. The troops would be ferried in and out of the area by HMS *Prince Charles* and HMS *Prince Leopold.*

In order to assist with the raid, intelligence officers in Whitehall had constructed a detailed model of the entire town of South Vaagso, along with its factories. This was taken to Scapa Flow by Major Durnford-Slater and used for the training of his troops, although the exact location of the attack would not be revealed to the men until the very last moment.

Ahead of the raid Durnford-Slater rehearsed his troops thoroughly and each morning they would undertake between twenty-five and thirty beach landings from landing craft. The men would then learn to sprint approximately eighty feet from craft to cover with full equipment and could do this in under ten seconds.

The force set sail from Scapa Flow on Christmas Eve. The main raiding-force arrived exactly to schedule on 27 December but was spotted by the Germans as it sailed into the fjord. The German response was confused, however, as although the German Navy was alerted, its Army units around the town were not. They first became aware of the situation when the combined guns of HMS *Kenya,* HMS *Offa* and HMS *Onslow* began to shell their batteries on Maaloy Island. They were subjected to a severe barrage with around 400-450 shells dropping on their positions in less than ten minutes. In the meantime, the main force of Commandos raced ashore in US-made Higgins assault boats as RAF Hampden bombers flew over the landing sites and laid down a smoke screen to obscure the assault troops.

On Maaloy Island, Jack Churchill came ashore with 105 Commandos with the objective of destroying a large herring oil factory, as well as German shore batteries and an anti-aircraft gun. At the same time Durnford-Slater would lead 200 men into South Vaagso itself, while thirty troops set up road blocks on the route into the port from the direction of Rodberg. Another group were to clear the village of Hollevik, then reform and become the onshore reserve.

Disaster struck when one of the Hampden bombers was hit by German flak guns onboard the armed trawler the *Foehn*. One of its phosphorous bombs inadvertently hit a landing craft, killing almost half of those aboard and badly burning others.

The remaining troops under Durnford-Slater rushed ashore and entered the town, where they faced fierce opposition from an estimated fifty German soldiers belonging to an Alpine regiment who were based in the area while on leave from the eastern front. These troops established a redoubt in a large building which the Commandos had to clear with hand grenades, room by room. Other Germans had barricaded themselves in the Ulvesund Hotel where they repulsed two attacks from British and Norwegian forces before finally succumbing after a mortar shell dropped down the chimney of the building, setting it ablaze and inflicting large casualties on those inside.

The German garrison continued to fight, and Durnford-Slater's men went from house to house clearing them in turn. They were soon joined by Major Churchill's men, who had already captured the guns on Maaloy Island and taken several prisoners. By noon the town had been secured and by 15:00 with the mission complete, all of the Commandos were back aboard their boats.

The German trawler the *Foehn*, which had shot down the Hampden, was one of several enemy ships attacked and disabled. It was targeted by several RAF aircraft and eventually ran aground with its crew deserting it. A British party boarded the deserted vessel where they were to discover an invaluable set of codebooks, which contained the radio call-signs of every German ship in northern Europe, as well as other important code words and signs. It was a massive boost for Allied intelligence.

Although perhaps the fiercest battle fought by Combined Operations thus far, Operation *Archery* was an overwhelming success for Mountbatten and his team. Ten enemy ships were destroyed and four oil factories were blown up, as well as numerous warehouses, fuel tanks and other facilities. Among other targets successfully put out of action were telephone exchanges, wharfs, a lighthouse and the German barracks. On Maaloy Island the coastal guns had also been destroyed along with a tank.

During the raid around 130 Germans were killed and this figure does not include those aboard the ships that were destroyed. Another ninety-eight were captured and returned to Britain as prisoners, including two ladies described as 'comfort' women.

The Commandos suffered the loss of twenty dead and fifty-three wounded. Three of the dead were from the Norwegian contingent. The local population also sustained one death and five wounded, while seventy returned to England as volunteers for the free Norwegian forces. The RAF in its first full operational raid with Combined Operations lost eight aircraft along with their crews.

Just as important, the combined raids at Vaagso and the Lofoten Islands convinced German high command that the British were attempting to open a major theatre of operations in Norway and potentially launch the second front from there. Because of this they moved considerably more men into the area and away from the Russian front and France. By the time of D-Day, some 40,000 German troops were tied up in the north, along with much of their navy.

1942 began with an altogether smaller affair, Operation *Curlew*, on the night of 11/12 January. The target area was near Saint-Laurent-sur-Mer in France and the objective was to return to the basics of beach reconnaissance and to ascertain the strength of the German defences. However, it did have one notable difference to its predecessors.

So far, all of these raids had been mounted by British Commando units with the occasional participation of other bodies of men, such as the Canadians or Norwegians. It was time to let others have a go, as it was realised that the invasion, when it happened, would mainly involve soldiers of regular army units. So in some ways this very much had the feel of a training exercise: in other words, an opportunity to train regular troops in irregular methods. Although sanctioned by Combined Operations, a separate school was established for this and future raids of a similar nature.

The V Corps School of Raiding was the brainchild of Brigadier Gerald Templer, who was a staff officer in V Corps, a major formation of the British Army then based at Tidworth under the command of Lieutenant General Sir Edmund Schreiber. The school consisted of two officers, with four non-commissioned officers acting as the instructors. The purpose of the establishment was to train one infantry company from V Corps per month in raiding tactics and techniques. Part of this training would be the opportunity to carry out a small-scale raid somewhere on the coast of France. But it was a short-lived exercise, and the school was disbanded in September 1942.

Operation *Curlew* itself would see four officers and eleven soldiers of the 15th Battalion of the Welsh Regiment landing on the coast from two Eureka boats and staying ashore for about an hour to gather whatever intelligence they could, before being extracted by the Royal Navy. It was not considered a success from the military point of view as no enemy forces were encountered and little useful information gleaned.

The next raid was another milestone in preparations for the second front. For the first time on the Atlantic Wall paratroopers would lead the raid and they would of course be a crucial element in the success of D-Day. This was Operation *Biting*, also sometimes referred to as the Bruneval Raid, which took place on the night of 27/28 February 1942. Its objective was to capture German radar technology and return it to England for examination by Allied scientists.

During the Battle of Britain in the summer of 1940, radar had played an important role in tracking Luftwaffe aircraft as they crossed the coast of England and because of it RAF Fighter Command was able to scramble its aircraft and intercept the enemy wherever they appeared. In 1942 the tables had turned, as British aircraft of RAF Bomber Command were the targets of German radar installations along the coast of France. Because of mounting losses, it was obvious that the Nazis had developed a highly sophisticated system. Allied aircraft always seemed to be met by German fighter aircraft or anti-aircraft batteries when they flew over occupied territory.

Germany had developed a radar system codenamed *Würzburg*. During a photo-reconnaissance mission the crew of a British aircraft returned with a picture that showed a saucer-shaped structure on the French coast near Saint-Jouin-Bruneval. Experts in Britain were confident that this was a radar site and they were also convinced that if they could get access to German technology, they would be able to find a way to block or fool the Nazi detecting system. So Lord Mountbatten and his team were given the task of capturing some of the German radar equipment and they set to work at once to come up with a plan.

Studying maps and pictures of the area, it soon became clear that their usual tactic of a seaborne assault would be futile. The site was near the top of some sheer cliffs and the area was defended by some formidable coastal fortifications. The obvious way to assault the radar installation was from inland and that could only be achieved by using parachute troops of the newly formed British 1st Parachute Brigade. These men had already seen some action as jump-trained Commandos of the Special Air Service in small raids in Italy and Libya. They formed the nucleus of the new brigade.

The task required by Operation *Biting* was delegated to C Company of the 2nd Parachute Battalion, commanded by Major Johnny Frost. Their aircraft for the mission would be converted twin-engine Armstrong-Whitworth Whitley bombers flown by No. 51 Squadron of the RAF.

Frost divided the 120 men of his command into five sections, each of which was named after a famous naval hero. Sections Drake, Hardy and Jellico would make the main assault on the radar station as well as a nearby chateau being used as the German barracks. Nelson section would attack and neutralise the coastal defences which was critical for the evacuation of all the Paras after the job had been completed, as they would be taken off the beach by landing craft and torpedo boats belonging to No. 12 Commando. Finally, Rodney section would be in place to protect the rear of the troops from any counterattack.

Three days of bad weather delayed the operation from taking place when the moon was at its brightest, but nevertheless it went ahead on 27 February. True to form, the Whitley bombers encountered intense flak as they crossed the coast of France, which meant that the radar was undoubtedly doing its job and had detected them. The group experienced a few uncomfortable minutes before safely navigating through the gun fire and over the drop zone, where Major Frost gave the order to 'hit the silk'.

Once on the ground a few problems began to arise. First, none of the radios the group had been issued with appeared to be working, so Frost was unable to contact any of his men, other than to appoint runners to carry communications between sections. The other problem was that some of Rodney section, which was supposed to be the action's rear guard, had overshot their drop zone by about two miles.

Taking all of this in his stride, Frost carried on with the task in hand and ordered the three designated sections to assault the chateau and radar station. Luckily, the barracks were almost empty as the occupants had recently moved to another site. A solitary German sentry made a fight of it and was killed in an exchange of gunfire. The radar site was also easily overrun and a German radar technician captured.

Accompanying the operation was an RAF radar technician called Flight Sergeant Charlie Cox. It was his job to dismantle certain components of the *Würzburg* and return the pieces to England for examination. In the time available to him this proved difficult and in the end he had to use a crow bar and brute force to extract the necessary bits. Then having achieved all their objectives Frost led his men towards the evacuation beach.

On their arrival Nelson section had gone ahead to neutralise the shore defences, but when Frost arrived this had not been completely achieved and he and his men found themselves pinned down by a heavy machine gun nest. It also became evident that the Germans had now recaptured the chateau and they were being fired upon from the rear as well. Frost had two choices, he could either face the machine gun or retake the chateau. He chose the latter and the Paras returned to rout the Germans in the rear. Having done this they returned to the beach, only to find that the missing troops of Rodney section under the command of Lieutenant Euen Charteris had fought their way through the German lines and had knocked out the enemy machine gun post, allowing Frost and his men onto the beach.

On arrival at their point of extraction there was no sign of their boats and they were unable to raise their relief force on their radios. With the Germans closing in on them, Frost formed his men into a defensive position with their backs to the sea: not an ideal situation to be in. But then, out of the darkness, the landing craft of No. 12 Commando appeared with Bren guns blasting cover fire against the German positions on the cliffs. The Paras boarded the boats along with two prisoners, the bodies of two of their dead comrades, and the all-important radar components. Frost waited until the last possible moment to board himself, as six of his men were unaccounted for. These men never made it to the beach and were later captured.

The raid had been a tremendous success and once the radar components were in the hands of British scientists, a way actually was soon discovered to fool the technology. Basically, dropping long thin strips of reflective material known as chaff from bombers on their way to their targets created thousands of false radar echoes, which rendered *Würzburg* ineffective. This simple tool would work brilliantly during the rest of the war and the technique is still employed today. Operation *Biting* illustrated the effectiveness of British airborne troops and the success at Bruneval paved the way for the establishment of the British 1st Airborne Division.

The next raid, Operation *Chariot,* was another ambitious landmark. Its objective was the destruction of dock facilities in the French port of Saint-Nazaire in Brittany, which is roughly six miles upstream from the mouth of the River Loire. This was the only port on the Atlantic seaboard with the capability to dock the formidable German battleship The *Tirpitz,* which had become the scourge of the British Merchant Navy during the Battle of the Atlantic. If the British could destroy the docks, the ship would be unable to use it for servicing and repairs and would be forced to return to Germany for necessary work. This would keep her out of the battle for longer periods of time and also make her more vulnerable to Allied attacks.

Mountbatten and his team were asked to draw up a plan, as an aerial bombardment of the port by the Royal Air Force had already been ruled out due to the high number of French civilian casualties that would be expected. The town had a population of roughly 50,000 in 1942. The only practical solution would be a Commando raid on a large scale mounted from the sea, but this would not be easy and losses would be expected to be high; the town had a large military garrison positioned there to give protection to ships and submarines moored in the harbour. The town was protected by numerous searchlights, anti-aircraft guns and coastal batteries.

Mountbatten submitted the plans for Operation *Chariot* to the chiefs of staff on 6 February 1942 and it was approved on 3 March. Most of the details had been worked out by the commanding officer of No. 2 Commando, Lieutenant Colonel Augustus Charles Newman, who would also lead the ground forces during the mission. The outlined set of objectives was to destroy the dry dock, its pumping stations and nearby U-boat pens. The main force under Newman would consist of 100 soldiers belonging to No. 2 Commando. Their task was to destroy enemy gun positions and then provide cover for the demolition parties who were drawn from Nos. 1, 3, 4, 5, 9 and 12 Commando.

An important part of the plan was for a ship of some description, which would be brimming with explosives, to ram into the gates of the dock and afterwards explode. The ship would also carry part of the assault force, while others would disembark from motor launches. Following the successful conclusion of the raid the men would gather at a mole in the harbour, from where they would be taken off by the motor launches and ferried back to Britain. The naval force during the operation would be under the direction of Commander Robert Edward Dudley (Red) Ryder.

The ship which would be used to destroy the dock gates was the HMS *Campbeltown*, an old destroyer that had previously belonged to the United States Navy when it was known as the USS *Buchanan*. Britain had acquired it as part of an exchange programme between the two countries with the US receiving land in Bermuda under the agreement. Before the operation the ship was stripped of all unnecessary equipment and had her bow packed with an enormous amount of explosives. In an attempt to fool the enemy defences, she had two of her four funnels removed to make her resemble a German frigate.

Reconnaissance photographs provided by the RAF established that the dock gates in Saint-Nazaire were not dissimilar to those of the King George V Dock in Southampton, so these became an extremely useful training aid. The Commandos who would carry out the raid also underwent training in street fighting techniques, while the demolition parties practised preparing charges and running at night with rucksacks filled with 90lbs of high explosives.

By 13 March 1942, the force numbering some 630 men in total was ready and assembled at Falmouth and aboard HMS *Campbeltown* waiting for the order to go. It would include sixteen Fairmile B Class motor launches to carry some of the assault troops in the latter stages and extract them from the mole afterwards. But these were made of wood and with 500-gallon petrol tanks strapped to their decks, extremely vulnerable to enemy fire. For protection they were fitted with machine guns and Oerlikon cannon. Two of these launches also carried delayed action torpedoes to fire at the dock gates if HMS *Campbeltown* was sunk before it could ram the gates. The force would be escorted by two hunt class destroyers.

Lieutenant Colonel Newman had reservations about some aspects of the mission. The RAF had been instructed to bomb areas away from the intended target, both as a distraction and to avoid civilian casualties in the town. Newman was concerned that this might have an adverse effect and in fact alert the enemy to the fact that something was about to take place. Also, further reconnaissance by the RAF had shown that four German frigates had berthed close to the landing site and didn't seem in a hurry to move on. However, the operation would progress regardless and the force set sail, first heading out into the Atlantic Ocean in three columns to make the Germans believe that they were an anti-submarine force going on a sweep. Luckily, to add to the illusion, on the second day out they spotted a German submarine, which was consequently attacked by one of the escorts, HMS *Tynedale*.

The British submarine HMS *Sturgeon* had gone ahead of the convoy and positioned itself at the mouth of the river estuary to act as a beacon by revealing a light. This was sighted at 22:00 on Saturday 28 March and the convoy immediately headed towards it and consequently towards the dock. As they proceeded, a group of RAF Whitley bombers flew overhead having been tasked with carrying out a diversionary bombing raid. This proved difficult because of low level cloud and as Lieutenant Colonel Newman had suspected, it alerted the enemy to the possibility of an attack. They had soon observed the convoy heading towards Saint-Nazaire.

The Germans were immediately suspicious, especially after the harbour master confirmed that he was not aware of any of their own convoys being active in the area. The various elements of the town's defences, particularly gun emplacements, were put on alert. But Ryder had a card up his sleeve and the *Campbeltown* was able to send signals to the enemy using codes that had been captured during the Commando raid on Vaagso. This temporarily fooled the enemy and Ryder pushed the *Campbeltown* to full speed. They were now only two nautical miles from the dock gates. But the Germans were not tricked for long and realising that it was an enemy ship, opened fire. At 01:27 the British had the dock gates in their sights. They took down the German ensign they had been flying and hoisted the British battle ensign. At 01:34, while under fire, the *Campbeltown* crashed into the gates.

The Commandos on *Campbeltown* now rushed ashore. They were made up of two assault teams and five demolition teams.

Three of the demolition teams were given the job of destroying the dock pumping machinery and other installations associated with the dry dock. Another team under Captain Donald William Roy, complete with kilt, had to knock out two pump-house roof-top gun emplacements high above the quayside and then secure a bridge to provide a route for the raiding parties to exit back to the dock area, both of which objectives they achieved.

The other two Commando groups were not as successful as the motor launches transporting them had almost all been destroyed on their approach by enemy fire. One boat did land its Commandos at the mole and another managed to reach the gates at the old entrance to the basin. That team succeeded in planting charges on two tugboats moored in the basin.

Lieutenant Colonel Newman directed much of the onshore action himself, first directing mortar fire onto a gun position on top of the submarine pens that was causing heavy casualties among the Commandos. He next directed machine gun fire onto an armed trawler, which was forced to withdraw upriver. He then organised a defence that succeeded in keeping the increasing numbers of German reinforcements at bay until the demolition parties had completed all their tasks.

The enemy position was getting stronger all the time however, and with 100 of his men still fighting ashore, Newman realised that evacuation by sea was no longer possible. He gathered the survivors and issued three orders: 'to do their best to get back to England; not to surrender until all ammunition was exhausted; not to surrender at all if it can be helped'. Following this he led a charge from the old town across a bridge which was being raked by machine gun fire and advanced into the new town of Saint-Nazaire. They then attempted to fight their way through the narrow streets of the town and into the surrounding countryside but were eventually surrounded. With all their ammunition expended, they finally surrendered. Not all of the Commandos were taken and five men managed to evade capture, reached neutral Spain and eventually returned to England.

At 10:35 the *Campbeltown* finally exploded, to the relief of the prisoners. The force of the charges destroyed the caisson and seawater gushed into the empty dock. The remains of some 150 Germans aboard her at the time of the blast were found up to a mile away. The dock was put out of action and would not be used again by the Germans for the remainder of the war.

This raid was undoubtedly a success for the British, despite the heavy casualties and Operation *Chariot* has often been called 'the greatest raid of all'. For their actions on the day five Victoria Crosses were awarded, including one for Newman himself.

The next operation, which was codenamed *Myrmidon,* was another ambitious affair although it resulted in complete failure. Its objective was to land some 3,000 troops made up of one and a half battalions of Royal Marines, an armoured regiment and one motor battalion, supplemented by Nos. 1 and 6 Commando, in the area of Bayonne, at the confluence of the rivers Nive and Adour. The area in question was relatively close to the border between France and Spain where the men were to disrupt road and rail transport between the two countries.

After the force was gathered together, they set sail on the transport ships HMS *Queen Emma* and HMS *Princess Beatrix,* spending a month sailing off the coast of France disguised as Spanish merchant ships. On 5 April 1942, despite bad weather, they finally approached the mouth of the estuary in order to carry out the landing. However, they discovered an uncharted sandbar and finding no obvious way to cross it, reluctantly returned to England having called the operation off.

Operation *JV* was by far the smallest of all the raids carried out on Hitler's Atlantic Wall. It involved two men, Captain Gerald Montanaro and Sergeant Preece of 101 (Folbot) Troop No. 6 Commando, paddling a two-man canoe into the harbour at Boulogne-sur-Mer on the night of 11/12 April 1942, after being transported across the Channel in a Royal Navy patrol boat. There they planted a limpet mine on a German ore tanker before withdrawing unseen. The mission was a success, although the extent of the damage caused to the tanker appears to be unknown.

Canadians would again feature in Operation *Abercrombie,* which was an Anglo-Canadian reconnaissance raid on the area around the French coastal village of Hardelot. Its objectives were to make observations of the beaches, capture prisoners and destroy military installations and equipment, including a searchlight battery. It was scheduled to take place on the night of 19/20 April 1942 but delayed until 21/22 April. Even though the raid was generally unopposed, its benefits were later considered to have not been worth the effort. And because of a navigation error the Canadian detachment lost their way and had to abort.

The force comprised B and C troops of No. 4 Commando, which was about 100 men, fifty men from the Canadian Carleton and York Regiment (2nd Canadian Infantry Brigade), and some Royal Engineers, under the overall command of Major The Lord Lovat of No. 4 Commando. Training for the operation took place in the New Forest and at Lepe near Southampton, based aboard the landing ship HMS *Prins Albert,* on which the Commandos were transported to Dover on 18 April. From Dover the force would be ferried to France on motor gun boats before being transferred on to assault landing craft the MGBs had towed across the Channel behind them.

C Troop would land first, and their task was to clear obstacles and establish a beachhead. B Troop would then come ashore and pass through C Troop, head inland and execute their tasks. The return journey would be in the landing craft. This raid was notable as the first time the new landing craft support (LCS) was employed, equipped with two machine guns and a mortar.

The convoy set sail on the evening of April 19, but after two hours one of the landing craft took on water and sank. The two crewmen were recovered but two Commandos who had manned a Bren gun were lost and after the search was abandoned the force returned to Dover.

A second attempt was made on 21 April, with a replacement landing craft. However, something went wrong with the Canadian contingent, who experienced navigational problems and became separated from the rest of the force. Worse, they were observed by the enemy and attracted tracer fire from the shore. In disarray they decided to return to England employing their accompanying motor gun boats. Consequently, none of the Canadian troops actually took part in the raid.

The Commandos landed a little further north than planned but were unopposed and escaped detection until among the deep sand dunes and wire entanglements. Support fire from the landing craft partially suppressed moderate German tracer fire from the flanks and the Commandos were able to progress.

The German defences in the area were assessed as being very light, some emplacements even found to be abandoned. Only three German soldiers were encountered at close quarters, who withdrew immediately. The official report recorded, 'no determined opposition'. Lovat sent a fighting patrol of twelve men to destroy the search lights but because of the time constraints they were forced to retire before being able to achieve this.

The British suffered one casualty during the raid, which was a Commando who was shot through the ankles after failing to respond to a beachhead sentry's challenge quickly enough. Supporting craft of the Royal Navy encountered and engaged several enemy vessels, including E Boats, one of which is believed to have been sunk and several more damaged. The Royal Navy suffered three casualties.

Next up was Operation *Bristle* on the night of 3/4 June 1942. The target of the raid was a German radar site at Plage-Ste-Cecile between Boulogne-sur-Mer and Le Touquet. The raiding force which was provided by No. 6 Commando was defeated by strong German defences. During the return voyage, at around dawn the naval force was attacked by German fighter aircraft which damaged two motor launches and one motor gun boat. One Commando and two naval personnel were killed with another nineteen wounded. It could have been far worse but for the appearance of the RAF, who fought off the attackers and prevented further losses.

This brings us to Operation *Barricade,* the last of the raids on the Atlantic Wall prior to Operation *Jubilee.* This was to be carried out approximately one mile to the east of Reville on the coast of the Cherbourg Peninsula in Normandy.

The objectives of the raid originally included targeting a German radar station situated some 600 metres from the coast. They were to capture any papers and documents found inside and then destroy some anti-aircraft gun sites located in the fields immediately bordering the shore. They were also to kill as many Germans as possible while bringing back others for interrogation. The original plan would have been carried out by 120 men of the East Yorkshire Regiment and a naval force of HMS *Prins Albert* carrying eight landing craft with motor gun boats in close support. Air cover would be provided by No. 11 Group of RAF Fighter Command.

On reflection, Mountbatten and his staff at Combined Operations headquarters decided against a large-scale assault and instead opted to use only eleven officers and men of the Small Scale Raiding Force under the command of Major Gustavus Henry March-Phillipps. The revised operation was reduced to only attacking the anti-aircraft gun sites to the north-west of Pointe de Saire and to capture and kill the enemy, with the radar site part of the operation completely dropped.

The raid took place on the night of 14/15 August 1942. A motor torpedo boat (MTB) named 'Little Pisser' under the command of Lieutenant Freddie Borne would be used to transport the raiding party across the Channel to within a mile of the French coast. It sailed from Gosport at 20:45 heading for Pointe de Barfleur. Not long after leaving, the port engine of the MTB began to give trouble and eventually cut out, which meant that their approach was made using only the starboard engine. At 23:00 the lighthouse at Cape Barfleur was sighted, which was a great aid in the final approach.

When they were approximately three miles off the French coast, the skipper cut the starboard engine and switched to silent running at a reduced speed of some seven knots. They dropped anchor three-quarters of a mile due east of Pointe de Fouli, but because of the failure of the port engine and trouble navigating, it was now 01:30, which made them an hour and a half behind schedule.

A Goatley collapsible boat was lowered from the motor torpedo boat which the raiders used to paddle to the shore in silence, but a strong current running northward took them three-quarters of a mile north of their intended landing site where they climbed out of the craft. Leaving one man behind to guard the boat, the rest of the team moved off in single file through fields towards their objective. Along the way they encountered fences which they had to cut their way through.

They finally reached the perimeter of a German encampment where they observed a sentry and here split to attack the site from different sides. It soon became clear that the encampment was much larger than anticipated and as they attempted to cut through a perimeter fence their actions attracted the attention of the sentry who retired to his hut and re-emerged accompanied by more guards.

Because of the delay in arriving at the target the raid was now well beyond schedule, so in order to keep to their rendezvous with the MTB, Major March-Phillipps decided to engage the guards but then give up any attempt of destroying the installations within the encampment and instead beat a retreat back to the coast. Three plastic bombs were thrown that landed amongst the approaching enemy and as they exploded the raiders opened fire with their Tommy guns. It is estimated that three of the Germans were killed and another three killed or very seriously wounded.

The raiders made their way back to the waiting Goatley boat and cast off without difficulty but at least half an hour was spent searching for the MTB, which was not found until 03:45. The party finally arrived back in England at 07:00.

So the final raid before Operation *Jubilee* was only a partial success but provided useful information about the German disposition along the Atlantic Wall and helped in the bigger picture being built up to plan for the invasion, as did all the other raids that had taken place since June 1940. During this series of raids nearly every aspect of what would become Operation *Overlord*, the Normandy invasion, seems to have been covered to some degree; but Operation *Jubilee* would take the whole thing one step further.

Although there were a number of successful raids during this outlined programme, there were also numerous failures. Many of the raids were hampered by poor planning, lack of reconnaissance and the breakdown in communications systems. Operation *Jubilee* would be a larger raid than all of its predecessors, but it would be approached in the same way and therefore we should not be surprised to find that its deficiencies largely fell into these familiar brackets.

3

WHY DIEPPE?

On 7 December (8 December in Asian time zones) 1941, the armed forces of Japan attacked both British and American holdings in the Far East with near-simultaneous offensives, which included an attack on the American fleet at Pearl Harbor, and landings in Thailand and Malaya. These attacks led the United States, Britain, and several other Allied states to formally declare war on Japan. The Soviet Union, being heavily involved in large-scale hostilities with Germany, preferred to maintain a neutrality agreement with Japan. However, because the Third Reich had a military pact with Japan, Hitler subsequently declared war on the United States on 11 December 1941, which was reciprocated by the US the same day.

In August 1941, Winston Churchill had met with President Franklin D. Roosevelt and even though America was not in the war at that time they began to discuss what would happen in the post-war period. Much of their discussions would form the basis of the Atlantic Charter. In the 'Declaration by United Nations' of 1 January 1942, the Allies, including China, the Soviet Union and twenty-two other countries, many of which had exiled governments operating from Britain, affirmed the charter and made an obligation not to broker separate peace deals with the Axis powers.

During 1942, Allied officials debated the appropriate grand strategy to pursue. All agreed that defeating Germany was the primary objective, even though enough troops should be committed to the Far East in order to keep the Japanese checked. With this in mind, America began to send troops to Britain in order to prepare for the invasion. These would include many squadrons of aircraft that would enter operations immediately from bases in East Anglia, where they would begin their strategic bombing of Nazi targets on the continent. At the same time US ground forces would build up and begin the process of training for the amphibious assault against Hitler's Atlantic Wall.

The Americans favoured a straightforward, large-scale attack on Germany through France. The Soviets were demanding an attack from the east. But the British persuaded its Allies that a landing in France was not feasible in 1942 and they should instead focus on driving the Axis out of North Africa before any action in Europe was started.

The truth of the matter was that by the summer of 1942 the Allied armies still did not have a large enough force in Britain, trained and equipped for an attack on Europe. To be in a position to launch a full-scale invasion would take time and planning. An attack on the French coast was one thing, but in order for the invasion to succeed, the established front would have to be reinforced and constantly supplied with arms and equipment. There was also the question of transportation, as at that particular time the United Nations forces in Britain did not have enough ships to execute the initial thrust and thereafter maintain it. In the summer of 1942, the invasion of western Europe was still considered to be some way off.

Although an actual invasion was unrealistic at that time, what could be done was to scale up the attacks on the coast of France and raid Europe in force. This would keep the Soviet Union happy and convince them that America and Britain were dedicated to opening a second front. What was required was a raid on a much bigger scale than anything which had been carried out so far, even greater than the attack on Saint-Nazaire.

With America now in the war, it was also time to begin planning for the actual invasion, as up until now the raids carried out by Combined Operations were not realistically contributing to that final goal. Now an invasion, although still some way off, was most certainly the end result. Raiding on a large scale would be a means of providing the Allied general staffs with essential information about the enemy's disposition. They needed to learn about his strengths and weaknesses, where he could be most successfully attacked, which beaches could accommodate an amphibious assault, which ports could be most easily captured and used to supply the front. All of this and much more would have to be ascertained through the raiding before any multinational invasion force could set sail across the English Channel.

Encouraged by events at Saint-Nazaire, the possibility of carrying out an even more substantial raid on another French port was discussed by the chiefs of staff in early April 1942. The job of planning this was given to Lord Mountbatten and his staff at Combined Operations headquarters. The Royal Air Force sent aircraft on reconnaissance missions over each potential target to bring back aerial photographs to be studied by the planners.

The general area in question was the Pas-de-Calais and the coast between Le Havre in the west and Dunkirk to the east. For obvious reasons, this was regarded as the most likely launching pad for the invasion and where the Germans would expect it to come. From this area Dieppe was finally chosen as being suitable for their objectives, which were many.

First and foremost, the plan was to test the feasibility that an enemy port could be assaulted and captured on the first day of the invasion and thereafter held and fortified in order to supply the invasion front. There were several ports along the coast of northern France that were possibilities including Le Havre, Calais, Boulogne-sur-Mer and Dunkirk. All of these and a few more were considered, studied and subsequently rejected as targets.

As this was only a raid as opposed to being the actual invasion, whichever port was chosen would only be held for the duration of at least two tides and have its facilities and infrastructure destroyed at the conclusion of the mission in the same way that those at Saint-Nazaire had been. This would render the port in question useless to the Nazis, who would no longer be able to use it for berthing and repairing warships for the Atlantic theatre, or for supplying their garrisons in other parts of the world.

Most of the ports studied were equally well defended, having been subjected to a building plan of pillboxes, gun emplacements and other concrete fortifications which had been ordered by German high command throughout 1942. In fact, attacking any part of this coast was a daunting prospect. So from the photographic appraisals it was decided that Dieppe was a suitable example of what could be expected at any point along the potential invasion coast.

Another factor to be considered was the importance of the chosen target in terms of its ability to help maintain Germany's war machine. Dieppe was blessed with many facilities that contributed to this and it would be very beneficial to the Allies if they were destroyed. As well as the harbour itself, there were railway marshalling yards in the vicinity. There was also a large gas works, an electric power station, quite considerable petrol dumps and supplies, and a pharmaceutical factory which could potentially be contributing to the Nazi weapons industry. All of these were attractive propositions for an Allied strike that would cause a hindrance to the enemy with their elimination.

A major and important part of the battle and perhaps just as significant as the raid on the ground, was the role intended for RAF Fighter Command. Since the Battle of Britain the men and aircraft of Fighter Command had not been tested in a major battle, a situation they were desperate to rectify. They knew that in order for the invasion to succeed, they would have to win air supremacy over the English Channel. In 1940 the Luftwaffe had failed to do this, which was one of the main reasons why the Wehrmacht was unsuccessful in launching its own invasion of Britain. The raid on Dieppe would therefore be the ideal opportunity to test the Luftwaffe's capabilities in the west.

Another important consideration for the planners was that Dieppe was within range of the Royal Air Force's fighter aircraft, similar to anywhere else in the Pas-de-Calais. They would be able to operate from their airfields in the south of England without the need to secure advanced landing strips nearer the target. This would enable them to provide the raiding force with a complete fighter umbrella of protection, meaning that aircraft would be immediately available and in situ to tackle any enemy aircraft that attempted to interdict the boats as they crossed the English Channel and attacked the target beaches. They would have limited time and fuel for this, but at least it was feasible that they could.

Most of the raids planned by Combined Operations headquarters so far had taken place at night, but Mountbatten and his team considered that if this one was carried out at daybreak and continued in broad daylight, against a coastline which the enemy regarded as a stronghold, this would provoke the Luftwaffe into giving battle on a much larger scale. This would also draw the Luftwaffe away from the eastern front where most of its resources were concentrated against the Russians.

If they suffered heavy losses of both aircraft and men over France, *Reichsmarschall* Hermann Göring, the commander in chief of the Luftwaffe, might be compelled to switch bombers and fighters from the east to the west and alleviate some of the pressure on Moscow.

The attack on Dieppe was given the codename Operation *Rutter* and the English ports of Newhaven, Shoreham, Southampton and Portsmouth, were chosen as its principal embarkation points, roughly seventy miles from the French town and close enough to allow for a surprise attack. The ships would be able to use the cover of darkness for their approach and similarly, the soldiers going ashore would benefit from the daylight at dawn as they hit their beaches, if the operation went according to its exact timing.

On 4 April 1942, Lord Mountbatten was given the order to instruct his staff at Combined Operations headquarters to draw up the plans. They subsequently produced two variants, which he thereafter presented to the chiefs of staff.

The first plan would see Dieppe captured by a pincer movement with tanks and infantry landing on either side of the town and then moving across two headlands on each flank of the port. The second plan was for a frontal assault in which the tanks and infantry would be landed directly on to the main beach in front of the town. They would be supported by more troops landing to both the east and west of the town.

For either plan to succeed it was imperative to first capture or destroy the heavy coastal gun batteries that commanded the approaches to Dieppe, which were located at Varengeville-sur-Mer to the west and Berneval-le-Grand to the east. These, it was decided would be captured by airborne troops parachuting in slightly ahead of the main assault. There were also a number of other batteries that would need taking out before the main event. Basically, Dieppe sat in a dip in the cliffs with headlands towering over it to both the east and west, which the Germans had defended with heavy guns. In order for the Allied forces to come ashore in front of the town, both of these headlands would need to be captured and their weaponry put out of action.

On 18 April 1942 the committee of the chiefs of staff decided that further planning should commence on the second variation, with the main frontal assault being preceded by a heavy aerial bombardment provided by the Royal Air Force. Mountbatten was asked to draw up more detailed plans for *Rutter* with a suggested D-Day of early July, when meteorologists advised that the tides would be suitable.

Before any raid the planners were faced with two main considerations, the first being the geography of the target area and whether or not there were any natural obstacles that could hamper its success. The other consideration was the strength and type of the enemy's defences.

In terms of its geography, Dieppe would appear to have been a difficult prospect under any circumstances. The town sat on a coastline that was mainly comprised of high cliffs, many being sheer and not easily climbed. It was known as 'The Iron Coast', which gives some indication of the task. In places, the cliffs were broken by river mouths, where the high ground came down to sea level and where towns and harbours were positioned. These would have been seen as the best possible access areas for troops trying to break inland.

The town of Dieppe was located at the mouth of the River Arques where the gap in the cliffs was roughly a mile wide, and where it flowed into a medium-sized harbour. So if you were going to consider an amphibious assault anywhere along this stretch of coast, Dieppe would have been one of the most likely spots to attempt it.

Another problem was the beach itself, which was quite steep in places and had large rocks on the seabed as you approached it. Therefore, trying to get a landing craft on or off it at low tide would have been a difficult and dangerous task. However, the planners considered that at high tide this was perfectly feasible. So for the raid to succeed, timing would be of the essence. The problem was that Allied air reconnaissance photographs could not physically show the suitability of the beaches in terms of gradient, surface and sub-surface for heavy tanks, so these things were assessed by examining holiday snapshots and postcards. The outline plan for Operation *Rutter* stated that 'Intelligence reports indicate that Dieppe is not heavily defended and that the beaches in the vicinity are suitable for landing infantry, and armoured fighting vehicles at some.' In fact, both of these statements were completely wrong.

As for the German defences, these were certainly considerable. The defenders on the high cliffs around the beach had an array of fire power with every inch of the ground below covered. Therefore, to succeed, surprise would have been essential, followed by a swift plan of attack to knock out the German defences as quickly as possible. If this part of the operation failed it surely must have been obvious to the planners and those approving the plans that the troops on the beach would have been at the mercy of the defenders.

It was also clear that the Germans had placed their two heavy coast batteries at Varengeville-sur-Mer and Berneval-le-Grand in such a way as to prevent unwanted ships from coming too close to the shore and harbour and remaining there for long. Their presence, unless eliminated, would have made a daylight attack almost impossible as the approaching armada would have been easy targets for their guns. This was the reason why it was imperative for airborne troops to seize the batteries ahead of the main assault.

As for the seafront of the town itself, this was a typical seaside resort of the day, although the beaches were predominately made up of shingle. Along the seafront was an esplanade where there were typical hotels and other seafront buildings, some of which the Germans had demolished to aid in coastal defence. The ones that remained were integrated into the town's defence capabilities by housing troops and weapons. These included the casino, which would feature heavily in the fighting.

Dieppe and the flanking cliffs were well defended; the 1,500-strong garrison from the 302nd Static Infantry Division under the command of *Generalleutnant* Konrad Haase comprised the 570th, 571st and 572nd Infantry Regiments, each consisting of two battalions. The division was also supplemented by the 302nd Artillery Regiment, the 302nd Reconnaissance Battalion, the 302nd Anti-tank Battalion, the 302nd Engineer Battalion and the 302nd Signal Battalion. These were deployed along the beaches and cliffs and in the neighbouring towns, covering all the likely landing places. They also had reserve troops stationed at the rear, which collectively provided the defenders with and impressive all-round fighting ability, ready and trained to repel an incursion in their sector. The town and port were protected by a concentration of heavy weapons on the main approach and in caves situated in the cliffs themselves, which were unseen by aerial reconnaissance, and a complete fighting force with all necessary supporting units.

The size and scale of Operation *Rutter* made the task much too big to be carried out by British Commandos alone, so the plan was to use regular troops deployed in the UK. The obvious choice were the men of South Eastern Army, which were already based in the general area under the command of Lieutenant General Bernard Montgomery.

In April 1941 Montgomery became commander of XII Corps, who were responsible for the defence of Kent. He famously instituted a regime of continuous training and insisted on high levels of physical fitness for both officers and other ranks.

He was ruthless in sacking officers he considered would be unfit for command in action. Following this success, in December 1941 Montgomery was put in charge of South Eastern Command, which oversaw the defence of Kent, Sussex and Surrey. Here he again insisted on every soldier being battle fit and ready for action and in order to promote an offensive spirit, regardless of his command's defensive responsibilities, he renamed his command the South Eastern Army. During this time, he further developed and rehearsed his ideas and trained his soldiers hard, culminating in Exercise Tiger in May 1942, a combined forces exercise involving 100,000 troops. With all of this in the minds of the chiefs of staff, Montgomery and his army seemed the ideal soldiers for the task.

At this time, some of his command consisted of Canadian troops and although select Canadians had been involved during previous missions under the umbrella of Combined Operations, most had not. To a large degree, these troops, already located in the south of England, had been there since the beginning of the war, training but not seeing any action. Montgomery later claimed that the final decision to use the untested Canadians was not his, but was taken by his superior, General Sir Bernard Paget and even then under pressure from Canadian senior officers and politicians to get their boys involved.

In the spring of 1942, there were over 200,000 Canadian soldiers in Britain who served in one of three infantry divisions, two armoured divisions, or in one of several armoured brigades or artillery formations. They were all volunteers and as such were eager to see action and prove their worth. Since arriving in Britain three years previously they had spent their time training or performing garrison duties and they now wanted to fight the enemy for real.

In command of the Canadian forces in Britain was Lieutenant General Andrew George Latta McNaughton. He was asked to recommend and select units for the operation and chose the 2nd Canadian Infantry Division, which was commanded by Major General John Hamilton Roberts, a man who had already seen action. Roberts had graduated from the Royal Military College of Canada in Kingston, Ontario, in 1914. He came to England in 1939 where he was among the Canadian troops that were deployed to Northern France at that time, commanding the 1st Regiment, Royal Canadian Horse Artillery. It was while he was serving in that position that the Germans launched the Battle of France in May 1940. Roberts managed to save his regiment's guns while evacuating from Brest in Brittany during the unsuccessful attempt to establish a second British Expeditionary Force in France after the evacuation at Dunkirk. He was later promoted to Major General and appointed General Officer Commanding the 2nd Canadian Infantry Division in 1941.

The principal elements of the 2nd Canadian Infantry Division consisted of the 4th Canadian Infantry Brigade under Brigadier Sherwood Lett, which included The Essex Scottish Regiment under Lieutenant Colonel Frederick K. Jasperson; The Royal Hamilton Light Infantry under Lieutenant Colonel Robert Ridley Labatt; and The Royal Regiment of Canada under Lieutenant Colonel Douglas Cato. Then there was the 6th Canadian Infantry Brigade commanded by Brigadier William Southam, which included Les Fusiliers Mont-Royal under Lieutenant Colonel Dollard Menard; The Queen's Own Cameron Highlanders of Canada under Lieutenant Colonel Alfred Gosling; and The South Saskatchewan Regiment under Lieutenant Colonel Charles Merritt. There were also elements of the 5th Canadian Infantry Brigade that included three platoons of The Black Watch (Royal Highland Regiment) of Canada; and a mortar platoon of The Calgary Highlanders. Also included in Robert's formation was the 14th Canadian Tank Regiment (Calgary Regiment) commanded by Lieutenant

Colonel John Andrews, with various supporting arms. All of these troops would be destined for Dieppe.

Being on a larger scale than anything previously attempted, Operation *Rutter* would require the participation of all three services. As usual, the Royal Navy would ferry the ground troops to their objectives and provide their means of extraction afterwards. They would also provide supporting gunfire to neutralise enemy positions. The aircraft of RAF Fighter Command would be used to protect the operation, while at the same time they would attempt to provoke the Luftwaffe into fighting a major air battle as already outlined. In order to achieve this, they would send the largest fighter screen that had been used since the Battle of Britain. They would also send aircraft ahead of the landings to attack known enemy positions.

For the planning, Mountbatten largely permitted the three force commanders to iron out the details. These were Captain John Hughes-Hallett for the Royal Navy, who was the chief naval planner at Combined Operations headquarters; Major General John Roberts who was of course commander of the ground element; and for the Royal Air Force, Air Vice Marshal Trafford Leigh-Mallory, the commanding officer of No. 11 Group Fighter Command.

By 9 May 1942, the updated plan was ready and had been submitted to the committee of the chiefs of staff who read it and finally gave it the all-clear. It seems that the intelligence that had been gathered from different sources, including the aerial photographs taken by the RAF, indicated that Dieppe was no more heavily defended than any other part of the coast. It also stated that the beaches around the town were deemed to be suitable for the landing of infantry and tanks when the right conditions prevailed.

Some had their reservations about the plan, including Mountbatten himself, who was not particularly in favour of a direct frontal assault on the most heavily defended part of the Dieppe seafront. But others were buoyant and optimistic about its chances of success, thinking that once the enemy's heavy guns were silenced ahead of the landings and the headlands to the east and west were in Allied hands, the outcome would be a formality.

But what exactly was the plan? Using mainly elements of the 2nd Canadian Infantry Division, the essence of the plan was to assault the coast around Dieppe by landing on six different beaches, four in front of the town itself, and two to the eastern and western flanks. From east to west, the beaches were codenamed Yellow, Blue, Red, White, Green and Orange. Yellow and Orange, which were on the extreme flanks, were not landing beaches as such, but the points from which paratroopers would be extracted at the end of the raid.

For the first stage of the battle and slightly ahead of the main attack, elements of the 1st Parachute Battalion of the 1st Parachute Brigade would be dropped into the flanks to attack and capture the heavy coastal batteries around Varengeville-sur-Mer and Berneval-le-Grand. Next, which was roughly half an hour before the main assault, battalions from the South Saskatchewan Regiment and the Royal Regiment of Canada would attack and neutralise two further German batteries that overlooked the main beach in front of Dieppe. The South Saskatchewan Regiment was to land on Green Beach, capture Pourville-sur-Mer and the headland overlooking Dieppe to the west, on their way destroying a radio-location station and a battery of light anti-aircraft guns. The Royal Regiment of Canada was to land on Blue Beach at Puys, seize another heavy battery, situated some distance inland, and capture the headland overlooking Dieppe to the east.

A battalion of the Queen's Own Cameron Highlanders of Canada would follow the South Saskatchewans and after they had captured Pourville-sur-Mer, they would pass through them and with armoured support move down the valley of the Scie

River to attack and capture an airfield located just behind the town near Saint-Aubin-sur-Scie.

The men of the Essex Scottish Regiment and the Royal Hamilton Light Infantry would assault the main two beaches in front of the town, Red and White, which stood behind the long esplanade. The former were detailed to land to the east and the latter to the west. They would then proceed into and capture the town and harbour.

Just before coming ashore the Royal Navy would lay down a short and intense bombardment on the main defences covering the beach, which would be provided by the guns of four destroyers. Also, while the landing craft were touching down, a curtain of smoke was to be laid across the eastern headland from which it was expected that the heaviest fire would come.

Once the two regiments were ashore and had cleared the beach they would be followed and supported by the tanks of the 14th Canadian Tank Regiment (Calgary Tanks) along with Royal Canadian Engineers, there to destroy tank obstacles. The tanks would enter the town and support the infantry in seizing and holding it while various objectives were destroyed.

The 14th Canadian Tank Regiment could deploy up to fifty-eight of the newly designed and British-built Churchill tanks, consisting of variants of the models I, II and III, which would be delivered to the beaches by the very latest landing craft tanks (LCT). In fact, it would be the Churchill's first outing to a combat zone, and it was therefore untested in battle but was considered suitable for beach landings and street warfare.

The hull of the Churchill was made up of simple flat plates, which were bolted together in earlier models and later welded. The hull was split into four compartments: the driver's position at the front, then the fighting compartment including the turret, the engine compartment, and the gearbox compartment. The suspension was fitted under the two large panniers on either side of the hull, the track running over the top. There were eleven bogies either side, each carrying two ten-inch wheels. Only nine of the bogies normally took the vehicle weight, the front coming into play when the vehicle nosed into the ground or against an obstacle, the rear acting in part as a track tensioner. Due to the number of wheels, the tank could survive losing several without much in the way of adverse effects as well as traversing steeper terrain obstacles.

The first Churchill turrets were rounded in shape and provided sufficient space to accommodate a relatively small two pounder gun. For its role as an infantry support vehicle, the first models were also equipped with a three-inch howitzer. This gave the tank a useful high-explosive capability while retaining the anti-tank capabilities of the two-pounder gun. However, like other multi-gun tanks, it was limited by a poor fire arc – the entire tank had to be turned to change the aim of the hull gun. The Mk II dispensed with the howitzer and replaced it with a bow machine gun and on the Mk III, the two pounder was replaced with the six pounder, significantly increasing the tank's anti-tank capabilities. In addition, three of the models at Dieppe were equipped with flame-thrower equipment and all had adaptations enabling them to operate in the shallow water near the beach.

A battalion from Les Fusiliers Mont-Royal would be used as a floating reserve unit and would wait aboard the ships until committed as and when Major General Roberts saw fit. Towards the end of the operation, they would form a defensive perimeter through which the other units would withdraw. Behind them were Royal Marines Commandos in small fast motor boats, which were manned by the Fighting French. Their task was to destroy the dock and all its facilities and recover documents thought to be held in the port office. A small group attached to the Royal Marines was given the separate job of trying to acquire some of the enemy's latest Enigma technology, thought to be located in a hotel situated in the harbour area.

The plans were much more thorough and elaborate than anything Combined Operations had committed to paper before, and they needed to be. They considered all of the information and intelligence that was either already available or had been gathered specially for the mission. For instance, the plan contained information regarding the nature and size of the possible landing sites, with particular attention given to the tides and tidal streams flowing around the beaches.

Maps were prepared of the town and surrounding area which showed all of the known enemy defences, particularly the various gun batteries. And the plans were certainly not hurried, as more information was gathered daily from various sources, sifted and passed on. A lot of the final information was gathered from aerial photographs taken by aircraft flying at very low and dangerous altitudes, some as late as only thirty-six hours before the raid was finally scheduled. Models of the coastline were built, studied and used as training aids.

Having said all of that, it seems that the intelligence that was gathered was patchy to say the least, in terms of both the disposition of enemy forces and the local topography. What the aerial reconnaissance photographs had failed to pick up was the series of caves and tunnels built into the cliffs around Dieppe, which housed guns. As they had not been observed, there were no plans put forward for their elimination.

The force commanders issued detailed orders that covered each phase of the operation from start to finish. These were studied by the officers and NCOs of the various force contingents, although the troops remained in complete ignorance of their real objective until the very last minute. Everyone would have to know their task fully and most importantly would have to stick rigidly to the timing of each successive phase. The success of the operation would rely on synchronisation, so this was stressed over and over again. The timings were methodically worked out and would have to be followed to the letter.

Even before the date of *Rutter* was set, the Canadians and other units involved began to exercise for the mission. On 20 May all infantry units were stationed on the Isle of Wight, which was sealed off, and a programme of rigorous training was initiated. They practised climbing cliffs and other steep places, street fighting, negotiating wire, attacking pillboxes, advancing with tanks, and handling weapons of all kinds. They also carried out two full dress rehearsals. And while the plans were being perfected, large quantities of stores, ranging from ammunition for the tanks to the food which would be carried in the landing craft were being collected in secret.

Operation *Rutter* was eventually scheduled for some time between 4 and 8 July. After weeks of training and preparation the troops made their way to Newhaven and other embarkation points, where they boarded their ships, which thereafter assembled in The Solent. This coincided with a period of inclement weather, so the order to sail was not given and the force commander was instructed to wait for further orders. The problem was that the entire mission was weather dependent because of the airborne element. It would be impossible for parachute troops to make the drop unless the conditions were suitable. Because of this the whole convoy had to wait until the time was right.

In the meantime, the ships were spotted by German aircraft and were bombed and strafed. This attack caused minor damage and injury to the convoy, but it made the chiefs of staff think twice about giving the order to go, as surely the enemy would have been suspicious as to the purpose of the ships they had spotted and attacked. Potentially, they would suspect that some sort of operation was about to be mounted. Taking this into consideration along with a worsening weather situation it was finally decided to cancel the whole plan on 7 July, and the ships returned to their docks and the soldiers disembarked, some even going on leave. For now at least, the raid on Dieppe had been shelved.

On board one of the ships at Newhaven prior to the cancellation of Operation *Rutter* was Roland Gravel, who was serving with Les Fusiliers Mont-Royal. He remembered the occasion during an interview, along with his training on the Isle of Wight. The interviews with Dieppe veterans quoted below are by kind permission of *The Memory Project*, Historica Canada:

Our regiment, Les Fusiliers Mont-Royal, was in England for a year and a half to train. We were there with two or three other regiments for special training on an island called the Isle of Wight. It was commando training on how to carry out raids. There's a difference between a raid and an invasion. A raid could be carried out on land, or on sea to land, and so on, and it was an attack with a battle for an objective followed by a quick withdrawal. We trained on the Isle of Wight for four months and then we moved to the English coast. One day, the colonel got the battalion together and said, "Men, we've been here for almost two years. Tomorrow morning, we are going to attack Dieppe." We were in Newhaven. For all the soldiers, it was like they were going on vacation because they had spent a year and a half training all day and all night, all the time. Everyone was happy. It was the beginning of July. Unfortunately, there were only three days per month that we could arrive and attack via the sea because of the tides. We loaded onto the boats but unfortunately it rained and it rained for the three days and everything was cancelled. We went back to our camps and the following month, in August, they decided to carry out the attack again. We were still just as happy to go.

David Mann, who was serving with The Royal Regiment of Canada was also on the ships in The Solent waiting for Operation *Rutter* to kick off and recalls, among other things, the moment when the aircraft of the Luftwaffe spotted them and attacked:

Training for and cancellation of Operation *Rutter* (initial plan to attack Dieppe in July 1942, cancelled chiefly because of poor weather). When they hit the two ships, well the one we were on started to sink so they took us off. And the other one, it didn't roll to the bottom but, anyway, it killed two sailors on its way through. Then they boarded us on another ship, but before we got to our destination, the raid had been cancelled. So, for all intents and purposes, that was the end of that.

The work done in planning Operation *Rutter* would not be wasted and would be quickly resurrected a few weeks later, when the decision was made to target Dieppe again and the wheels were set in motion for Operation *Jubilee*.

There were two main differences to the original plan. First, instead of using paratroopers to capture the large German coastal batteries, they would be seized by Commandos through a seaborne landing. The reason for this was the paratroopers' dependence on favourable weather conditions. By using Commandos there would be no repeat of the situation during *Rutter* when the convoy had to wait in The Solent and ultimately give their position away. Now they could go immediately to Dieppe from their ports of departure and hopefully carry out a surprise attack. These attacks were to be delivered by No. 3 and No. 4 Commandos with the object of destroying the two coast defence batteries, whose fire, as has already been explained, would make it impossible for ships to remain offshore during daylight hours.

The Commandos were to land in pre-dawn darkness. No. 3 Commando to the east of Dieppe was to silence the battery near Berneval-le-Grand. No. 4 Commando and fifty US Rangers were to neutralise the battery near Varengeville-sur-Mer to the west of Dieppe. In both cases they would make two landings to effect a pincer movement on the batteries, which each had a cadre of over 100.

This change meant that the operation would now take place using eight landing zones instead of six. The various beaches kept their original codenames but Yellow and Orange would now both be divided into two areas, so there would now be Yellow I and II, and Orange I and II.

The other main difference between *Rutter* and *Jubilee* was that the air bombardment preceding the operation would be abandoned, as politicians feared for the lives of French civilians in the town. Instead, the assault would be preceded by dawn strikes made by cannon-firing fighter aircraft on military positions only. However, to compensate for this, eight destroyers would now bombard the German shore defences instead of four, and the RAF would make a diversionary bombing raid around Boulogne-sur-Mer.

It has been said that the abandonment of the aerial bombardment was one of the major factors contributing to the failure of the operation and various reasons have been offered to explain why this was the case. The bottom line was that British and Canadian politicians limited the use of both air and naval bombardments in an attempt to limit civilian casualties in the town. This was a very sensitive issue for the Canadians in particular, who had a far greater association with France than the British, with many of their own citizens and soldiers being French-speaking and of recent French descent. Churchill and his transatlantic counterpart feared that unjustifiable civilian losses would anger and alienate the Vichy government further.

Apparently, Major General Roberts, the military force commander, was also said to be uneasy about the bombardment but for very different reasons. He argued that a bombardment and the resulting debris and devastation would make the streets of the town almost impassable for his troops and tanks and might even give the enemy another source of cover. This could only be a hindrance to the smooth running of the operation and could hold up their progress once they had fought their way off the beaches and into the town.

Taking all of this into consideration, it was ultimately decided that in any event a severe bombardment of the town and even the defences was not really necessary as the planners believed that if the operation went according to plan, the combination of speed, surprise and the sheer shock to the defenders of seeing tanks come ashore with the infantry, would almost certainly result in a quick victory. It was thought the enemy would be stunned into submission.

Reusing the plans for *Rutter* so soon after their cancellation for another, almost identical operation, was not a situation that everybody concerned with the initiative was happy about. In particular, Lieutenant General Montgomery, from whose command the troops had been selected, voiced his opinion that he felt the whole thing could now have been compromised. The fact was that all of the troops who were taking part had been briefed while on the ships waiting to go to Dieppe and now knew the name of the town they were due to attack. That was a month prior to the rescheduled operation, a month in which a slip of the tongue in a local pub from a Canadian soldier a little worse for wear, or to a local girlfriend, could drop this intelligence right into the lap of German spies undoubtedly working in the vicinity.

Montgomery was also sure that the Germans would now be aware of Allied interest in Dieppe because of increased radio chatter and the number of aircraft appearing in the sky over the town, which they could no doubt guess were taking reconnaissance photographs of their defences. Had Montgomery not been ordered to Egypt to take command of the Eighth Army, his continued doubts may have prevailed. He arrived in Cairo on 13 August 1942, five days before *Jubilee*.

One interesting and perhaps disturbing fact is the lack of documentation relating to Operation *Jubilee*. It would appear that no records were kept of any of the planning meetings beforehand, which is quite remarkable considering the scale of the task. Previously, Combined Operations had kept detailed plans of even the smallest raid. Winston Churchill explained the lack of plans in his memoirs:

> In discussion with Admiral Mountbatten it became clear that time did not permit a new large-scale operation to be mounted during the summer (after *Rutter* had been cancelled), but that Dieppe could be remounted (with the new codename *Jubilee*) within a month, provided extraordinary steps were taken to ensure secrecy. For this reason no records were kept but, after the Canadian authorities and the chiefs of staff had given their approval, I personally went through the plans with the C.I.G.S., Admiral Mountbatten, and the Naval Force Commander, Captain J. Hughes-Hallett.

The original plan with the outlined amendments was finally adopted and on the night of 18-19 August 1942, the first moment at which the weather was satisfactory and the tides were suitable, the raid began.

David Mann, serving with The Royal Regiment of Canada, gives us some further insight into how things went from *Rutter* to *Jubilee* and his own regiment's final embarkation at very short notice:

> We continued training in a place called Littlehampton bearing our full loads of ammunition and battle gear every day. They marched us one morning after breakfast from the mess hall to the

headquarters building and stopped us there and left us standing while the officers went and had a meeting. Anyway, my brother happened to be in the same unit but he didn't have the invasion training and he was on the steps of the building and I yelled at him, "Hey". He said, "Hey what?" I said, "If I don't come back, look after my gear." "What the hell do you mean, you're not going anywhere." Well, I said, "Maybe yes and maybe no but we smell a rat, so just in case, look after my gear." He did because we just boarded in trucks from there, drove to the harbour and climbed on a mother ship and they told us that we were going to the same place (Dieppe) we had all the training for. We had sat on the ships for a week in the first place and just went over the battle plan and whatnot. And they said, "We're going to the same place, all your objectives are the same, you've seen all the aerial photographs," and they said, "there is one small change." "And what's that?" "Instead of a five percent casualty, we expect fifty percent," which was a nice piece of news. But anyway, the next thing, we were crossing the Channel.

4

THE CROSSING

Tuesday 18 August 1942 was a warm, sunny day in the south of England with perfect conditions in the English Channel for the intended crossing. The force that was about to launch its raid against the French town of Dieppe had been gathering at various ports along the English coast during the preceding few days: Newhaven in East Sussex, Southampton and Portsmouth in Hampshire, and Shoreham in West Sussex.

After their period of training on the Isle of Wight, where many of the troops had been billeted in tents in the grounds of Norris Castle just outside East Cowes, with the officers provided quarters in the castle itself, most of the Canadian troops moved to Witley Camp, a temporary military training establishment on Witley Common in Surrey. This was one of three facilities in the Aldershot Command area established for the Canadian army, the others being Bordon and Bramshott. Where possible, the movement of the troops had been restricted, in an attempt to ensure secrecy concerning the date and target of the raid.

From Witley and the other camps at which troops were stationed, the men would move to their embarkation zones and board the landing ships tethered to the jetties. There was a mass movement of men, tanks and other supporting vehicles, as well as equipment and stores, all heading for the ports. Few people were aware of this situation, especially around Newhaven, as many civilians had been evacuated from Sussex with the county effectively being turned into an international barracks with hotels, large houses and other buildings all commandeered for the war effort.

After everyone and everything was eventually loaded on the ships, the force that put to sea that evening numbered an estimated 237 craft, and contained ships and boats of various types, all under the overall command of the naval force commander Captain John Hughes-Hallett RN. It must have been an awesome sight, the largest amphibious assault force since Gallipoli in the First World War, but still only a fraction of the armada that would set out for the beaches of Normandy nearly two years later.

John Hughes-Hallett had already enjoyed a distinguished career in the Royal Navy and was destined for even greater things in the future. His career began as a midshipman on HMS *Lion* in May 1918. He was later promoted to staff rank and during the Second World War served in a variety of roles. During the Norwegian campaign of 1940 he had seen active service aboard HMS *Devonshire* and was mentioned in despatches. During the rest of 1940 and 1941 he had already played a key role in earlier cross-Channel raids organised by Combined Operations and had been part of Mountbatten's planning staff for a number of these.

Perhaps the most important part of the armada were the infantry landing ships that would ferry the 2nd Canadian Infantry Division and other soldiers across the seventy miles of the English Channel. Swinging from davits at their sides were the landing craft, into which the soldiers would be loaded to make their final assault on the beaches in front of Dieppe.

There were nine of these vessels: HMS *Duke of Wellington*; HMS *Glengyle*; HMS *Invicta*; HMS *Prince Charles*; HMS *Prince Leopold*; HMS *Princess Beatrix*; HMS *Princess Astrid*; HMS *Prins Albert*; and HMS *Queen Emma*.

All of these vessels had originally been built for non-military purposes, normally as ferries, and had subsequently been requisitioned for war service. HMS *Duke of Wellington*, which was originally called the *Duke of York*, was built for the London Midland and Scottish Railways and used as a ferry between Heysham and Belfast from the time she was brought into service in 1935. She was requisitioned in 1939 for use as a troopship and in 1942 was converted into a landing ship infantry (hoisting), when her name was changed to HMS *Duke of Wellington*. This was because there was already an HMS *Duke of York* in service with the Royal Navy at that time. The 'hoisting' refers to the fact that she was designed to lower and hoist the landing craft on hand-operated davits.

Her conversion allowed her to carry 250 troops and ten landing craft assault (LCA). For the Dieppe Raid she was assigned to the landing at Blue Beach to the east of Dieppe. She had the soldiers of C Company of The Black Watch (Royal Highland Regiment) of Canada on board who had embarked at Southampton, which consisted of three infantry platoons and the mortar platoon.

HMS *Glengyle* was built by the Caledon Shipbuilding & Engineering Company for the Glen Line, but in 1938, whilst still under construction, the Inter-Service Training and Development Centre determined that she would be ideal as a landing ship infantry (large). She was therefore acquired by the Admiralty and during April and June 1940 converted into an infantry landing ship capable of carrying a force of up to 700 men. She could also accommodate twelve LCAs on davits and one landing craft mechanised (LCM), which could be launched by derricks. In the build-up to the raid, she was disguised as an oil tanker in order not to draw suspicion on herself whilst in port at Southampton. She was tasked with transporting men of The Royal Hamilton Light Infantry to White Beach.

The Royal Hamilton Light Infantry had originally been formed on 11 December 1862, under the name of the 13th Battalion Volunteer Militia (Infantry) Canada. The Regiment went through various name changes before the 1920s, when it finally became known as the RHLI. The regiment was mobilised on 1 September 1939 but didn't set sail for England until 22 July 1940, after the evacuation from Dunkirk was complete, so this was to be their first action of the war.

The *Invicta* was a passenger ferry built in 1939 for the Southern Railway and was requisitioned on completion by the Admiralty for use as a troopship (small) when she was named HMS *Invicta*. Following conversion, she could carry 250 troops and six LCAs and during the raid sailed from Southampton to land soldiers of the South Saskatchewan Regiment on Green Beach to the west of Dieppe at Pourville-sur-Mer, together with HMS *Princess Beatrix*.

HMS *Princess Beatrix* was built as a passenger liner in 1939 by De Schelde at Vlissingen in the Netherlands, when she was named the MS *Prinses Beatrix*, after Princess Beatrix of the Netherlands, and operated by The Zeeland Steamship Company. After fleeing to Britain after the German invasion in 1940, she was requisitioned by the British Ministry of War Transport, renamed HMS *Princess Beatrix* and converted to a troopship (medium) at Harland and Wolff's yard in Belfast. The upper deck was largely cleared and gravity davits installed enabling six LCAs and two LCMs to be carried, along with 450 troops.

The origins of the South Saskatchewan Regiment date back to 3 July 1905. They were originally called the 95th Regiment and recruited in the districts of Assiniboia and Saskatchewan.

More than thirty years later, on 15 December 1936, the South Saskatchewan Regiment came about with the amalgamation of two existing units, the Weyburn Regiment and the Saskatchewan Border Regiment. They were mobilised on 1 September 1939 and set out for the United Kingdom on 16 December 1939.

Also sailing from Southampton was HMS *Prince Leopold* with part of the Essex Scottish Regiment. She had been completed in July 1930 as the Belgian ferry *Prince Leopold* for the Ostende to Dover route and was one of four ships in the convoy originally ordered by the Belgian government. She was requisitioned by the Admiralty in September 1940 and converted to a landing ship infantry (small), as HMS *Prince Leopold* at Devonport. During the raid she ferried her troops to Red Beach.

The rest of the Essex Scottish left from Portsmouth on board HMS *Prince Charles*, another ship originally ordered by the Belgian government in 1929 as a fast cross-Channel ferry. She was completed in 1930 and named after Prince Charles of Belgium. She was a landing ship infantry (small) and had the capacity to carry 270 troops along with eight LCAs or landing craft personnel (LCP).

The Essex Scottish Regiment traces its history back to the 1860s at a point when Irish Fenians were causing trouble in Canada. This became so acute in the Windsor area of Ontario that it was decided to raise an army for the protection of local citizens. It wasn't until 12 June 1885, however, that the regiment, known as the 21st Essex Battalion of Infantry, was authorised. It was formed by the amalgamation of five infantry companies in the Windsor area. The Regiment went through a number of name changes before settling on the Essex Scottish Regiment on 15 July 1927. Also mobilised on 1 September 1939, the regiment was soon at full strength and included a number of Americans wishing to join the war against the Nazis. They eventually set out for England on 16 August 1940.

The third of the Belgian ferry ships in the convoy was HMS *Princess Astrid*, originally the SS *Prinses Astrid*, which was built in Hoboken, Antwerp, at the Cockerill shipyard in 1929. She was converted into a landing ship infantry (small) at Devonport in May 1941 and sailed from Portsmouth with men of The Royal Regiment of Canada on board, together with her sister ship HMS *Queen Emma*, both heading for Blue Beach.

The *Queen Emma* had also been built as a passenger ferry by De Schelde at Vlissingen in 1939, and was named the MS *Koningin Emma*, after Queen Emma of the Netherlands and operated by The Zeeland Steamship Company along with the already mentioned MS *Prinses Beatrix*. After fleeing to Britain together in 1940, she was also requisitioned by the British Ministry of War Transport and renamed HMS *Queen Emma*. She was thereafter converted to a troopship at Harland and Wolff and designated as a landing ship infantry (medium).

The Royal Regiment of Canada can trace its history to 14 March 1862 when it was first known as the 10th Battalion Volunteer (Infantry) Canada. It was formed because of concerns about a possible American invasion, following the outbreak of the Civil War in the United States. The Regiment, which was based out of the Fort York Armoury in Toronto, Ontario, was first sent into combat during the North West Rebellion in 1885. It went on to serve at the turn of the century in the South African War as well as in the First World War. It became known as the Royal Regiment of Canada in 1936 and was mobilised on 1 September 1939. It moved to Iceland in June 1940 and to the United Kingdom in October of the same year.

The last of the nine landing ships infantry was HMS *Prins Albert*, which sailed from Southampton carrying men of No. 4 Commando and the 1st US Ranger Battalion to Orange Beach in order to knock out the coastal battery at Varengeville-sur-Mer. She was also built as a passenger ship at the Cockerill shipyard in 1937 and requisitioned for service in the Royal Navy in July 1940 when she was converted into a landing ship infantry (small) with the capacity to carry 250 troops and eight LCAs.

Landing craft of various types and sizes formed a large part of the Allied armada and were hoisted aboard the LCIs, from where they could be lowered into the sea ready to assault their respective beaches. The soldiers would get into them after they were in the water, by climbing down rope ladders or nets hung over the sides of the ships. Albert Kirby, who served with the Royal Canadian Navy, was part of the crew of an LCA. He spoke about how these craft operated and his own role at Dieppe:

I was on landing craft. We were practicing with the soldiers in England. Everybody knew that we were eventually going to have to land back in France in order to take France back from Germany. So landings were a big problem and we had to learn how to do it. These are barge-like boats they carry on a ship up to an enemy coast. They lower the boats in the water, fill us up with soldiers and then we drive into the beach and these are specially designed boats, meant for landing on a beach. So we land on the beach, they drop the front door down and out run the soldiers. Then we pull our door up and back off and go back to the ship for another load. And we keep running back and forth because in wartime, you're not going to get a chance to land in a harbour because they are all very highly defended. So we had to find beaches where there would be very little defence. These landing craft were meant for that purpose, for taking soldiers into beaches because there would be no docks for landing and tying up the ships.

Each ship had a fellow up front driving, turning the wheel, steering the thing into the beach. There was also another fellow down in the engine room at the back, operating the engines that drove it. So there were two of us operating the boat. Then there was another additional hand to help with other things that came up. So there were three of us in a crew, on a small landing craft. When I say landing craft, I mean small ones. They were only thirty-five feet long. These days we think of landing ships as huge ships with doors in the front that come up on the beach and they were just starting to experiment on that sort of thing when I was on landing craft. But most of the landings were done from very small boats that were specially built of steel with a door in the front that opened and fell down so the soldiers could run out, down the door, onto the beach.

At that time, I think I was eighteen years old and for me, I was with a special group that they recruited here in Canada. They asked for volunteers to go over to England and drive landing craft in operations against the enemy coastline. And for a kid my age, at eighteen years old, that really sounded exciting. We didn't think much about the danger. To us, it was exciting. And we looked forward to being heroes and all that. I jumped at the chance and away I went over there and we trained with other Royal Navy people who had been conducting raids against the enemy coast all along. The Dieppe Raid was our very first chance to actually do it. And we were very excited about it. We wouldn't have missed it for the world. But we quickly got over that cavalier idea once we were at the receiving end of the enemy fire because it's one thing to talk about it, but it's something else to experience it.

Behind the infantry landing ships en route to Dieppe were twenty-four blunt-nosed landing craft tanks (LCTs) carrying the Churchill tanks of the 14th Canadian Tank Regiment (Calgary Tanks) which would be employed during the operation. These would ferry the vehicles directly to Red and White beaches with half departing from Portsmouth and the others from Newhaven.

The 14th Canadian Tank Regiment had been mobilised on 11 February 1941. Within only a couple of weeks, 400 members from the reserve unit, along with more than 100 men from the

Seaforth Highlanders of Canada and the Edmonton Regiment were formed into one complete unit under the command of Lieutenant Colonel G. R. Bradbook. These men were then sent to the Mewata Armouries in Calgary to begin their training. Only a short time passed before they were sent, on 7 March 1941, to Camp Borden in Ontario, where they immediately started training with tanks and gunnery. On 20 June 1941, the unit left Canada and embarked on a ship bound for the UK. Over the next few months, the Regiment moved to various locations and trained intensely.

As well as the Calgary Tanks the LCTs also ferried supporting troops such as Royal Canadian Engineers. Onboard LCT 163, for instance, which was actually painted with a large white six on the side and skippered by Thomas Andrew Cook RNR, was the mortar platoon of The Calgary Highlanders, which consisted of twenty-one men under the command of Lieutenant Jack Reynolds. They were the only part of the battalion to serve at Dieppe, the remainder had been ordered to Portsmouth to help the wounded disembark after the raid and guard any German prisoners returning with the force. Also on this crowded craft were three Churchill tanks, a bulldozer and other Canadian servicemen including the tank crews of No. 6 Troop of the Calgary Tank Regiment under Lieutenant Jack Dunlap.

Reynolds and his men occupied a space between a tank and one side of the LCT. When the craft pulled away from the dock everyone had the feeling of being inside an overcrowded tin can because the steel sides of the craft only allowed a view of the sky, so throughout the journey across the Channel the men on board could see nothing of the surroundings.

Royal Marines (A) Commando, which largely consisted of No. 40 Commando Royal Marines and No. 30 Commando (Intelligence gathering), sailed from Portsmouth on board HMS *Locust* and seven chasseurs of the Free French Navy. The *Locust* was a dragonfly-class river gun boat which was launched in September 1939 and commissioned in May 1940. The chasseurs were smallish patrol boats which the French had used as anti-submarine vessels before relocating to Britain after the fall of their homeland.

This ensemble was termed the 'cutting-out force' and their specific task was to enter Dieppe harbour to search out and seize any barges or trawlers that in their opinion were being moored there for possible use as boats in which to invade Great Britain. Any such craft they discovered would be boarded and either destroyed or towed back to England behind the chasseurs. This force also included a Royal Navy dockmaster's party, who were there to force lock gates to inner basins in order to ease entry to certain areas; the assistant dockmaster's party; No. 2 Royal Marines demolition party; No. 3 Royal Navy demolition party; and a Royal Navy engine room party tasked with starting up the engines of any captured boats. This group would also destroy dock facilities and search for official German documents in port offices and other buildings.

The cutting-out force was escorted by the sloop HMS *Alresford*, which was launched in 1919 and originally intended to be a minesweeper, but as the war ended while she was still under construction, modifications were made to her super-structure and she entered service as a tender to the Navigation School at Portsmouth. In the early summer of 1942 with a refit and the installation of additional armament, she was detailed to take part at Dieppe. She carried a small number of Free French troops.

No. 3 Commando also left Newhaven, as did the Queen's Own Cameron Highlanders of Canada, while Les Fusiliers Mont-Royal travelled from Shoreham. These latter groups were transported in LCPs (Landing Craft Personnel) directly from their ports of departure to the beaches. In total, using all the various carrying craft, a total of 6,086 officers and men set out from the various ports bound for the beaches of Dieppe.

We know about the history of the British Commandos. As for the Queen's Own Cameron Highlanders of Canada, they were first formed in 1910 as the 79th Highlanders of Canada and were recruited from around Winnipeg, Manitoba. Ten years later, they were renamed and became known as the Cameron Highlanders of Canada and in 1923 the Royal prefix was added. The regiment was mobilised on 1 September 1939 and sailed to England in 1940, seeing their first action at Dieppe, along with all the other units in the 2nd Canadian Infantry Division, including Les Fusiliers Mont-Royal who were based in Montréal and originated in 1869. The Regiment first saw action when the North West Rebellion broke out in 1885, and then again during the First World War. As with all of the other units at Dieppe they were mobilised in 1939, but in their case they set out for Iceland in July 1940, where they spent three months before finally departing for the UK in October.

Sailing with these ships to act as escorts and provide fire power, were eight hunt-class destroyers. Seven of these belonged to the Royal Navy: HMS *Calpe*; HMS *Fernie*; HMS *Albrighton*; HMS *Berkeley*; HMS *Bleasdale*; HMS *Brocklesby*; and HMS *Garth*. The eighth vessel, ORP *Slazak,* belonged to the Polish Navy, which was exiled in Great Britain.

HMS *Calpe* was used as the headquarters ship for the naval force commander, Captain John Hughes-Hallett and the command ship for the officer commanding the 2nd Canadian Infantry Division, Major General John Roberts and their staffs, who would remain aboard throughout the raid. Afterwards it would be used as a hospital ship to evacuate casualties back to Newhaven, as were most of the destroyers. Hughes-Hallett's job of controlling so many vessels in the dark, while negotiating a minefield, was not made any easier by the fact that radio silence had to be maintained throughout. Later, there would be difficulties experienced by all radio systems which would cause a severe headache.

The *Calpe* was ordered in December 1939 from Swan Hunter as part of a 1939 emergency programme and was completed in 1941 at Wallsend-on-Tyne. She was a type II hunt-class destroyer and her main armament was six QF 4-inch (100 mm) Mark XVI guns on twin mounts. She also had an array of anti-aircraft weaponry. The hunt class was meant to fill the Royal Navy's need for a large number of small destroyer-type vessels capable of both convoy escort and operations with the fleet.

HMS *Fernie* acted as the force reserve headquarters ship. She was a type I hunt-class destroyer completed in mid-1940, with a main armament of four QF 4-inch (102 mm) guns. She was built by John Brown & Company on Clydebank. Apparently, as she steamed out of the harbour before the raid, she played her battle cry on the loud hailer, and the sound of the fanfare echoed across the water to inspire the troops embarking at the jetties.

HMS *Albrighton* was also built by John Brown & Company in July 1940 and was one of seven type III hunt-class destroyers ordered as part of the 1940 war emergency programme. The type IIIs differed from the previous type II ships in replacing a twin 4-inch gun mount by two torpedo tubes to improve their ability to operate as destroyers. Her main gun armament again was four QF 4-inch (102 mm) Mk XVI dual purpose (anti-ship and anti-aircraft) guns in two twin mounts.

HMS *Berkeley* was a type I hunt-class destroyer ordered from Cammell Laird in a 1939 build programme and built at their Birkenhead shipyard. She was launched on 29 January 1940 and commissioned on 6 June 1940, with her main armament being four QF 4-inch (102 mm) Mk XIX guns on twin mounts.

HMS *Bleasdale* was a type III hunt-class destroyer built by Vickers Armstrong at Newcastle under the 1940 war emergency programme. The ship was laid down on 31 October 1940 and was the first RN warship to bear the name. She was completed on 16 April 1942 and following a successful warship week national savings campaign in March 1942 she had been adopted by the civil community of Garstang in Lancashire. Her principal armament was four QF 4-inch (102 mm) mark XVI guns on twin mounts.

HMS *Brocklesby* was a type I hunt-class destroyer ordered from Cammell Laird in September 1939 and built at Birkenhead and completed in April 1941. The ship's main gun armament was four QF 4-inch (102 mm) Mk XVI dual purpose (anti-ship and anti-aircraft) guns in two twin mounts, with one mount forward and one aft.

HMS *Garth* was a type I hunt-class destroyer built by John Brown & Company on the River Clyde and launched in December 1939. She was adopted by the community of Wokingham, Berkshire, as part of the warship week campaign in 1942. Her main armament was four QF 4-inch (102 mm) Mk XVI guns on twin mounts.

Finally, ORP *Slazak* (the Polish word for Silesian) was a type II hunt-class destroyer, originally built for the Royal Navy in 1940, when she was named HMS *Bedale*. However, in 1942 she was commissioned by the exiled Polish government for use in their navy. Her principal armament was six QF 4-inch (102 mm) Mk XVI guns deployed in three turrets.

As well as the destroyers, the force was further escorted by an array of twelve motor gun boats (MGBs), four steam gun boats (SGBs), and twenty fast motor launches (MLs).

Ahead of everything in the initial stages of the crossing were two minesweeping flotillas, the 9th (MSF) and the 13th (MSF), with seven ships in each. The 9th Minesweeping Flotilla consisted of HMS *Bangor*; HMS *Bridlington*; HMS *Sidmouth*; HMS *Tenby*; HMS *Bridport*; HMS *Blackpool*; and HMS *Rhyl*.

13th Minesweeping Flotilla comprised HMS *Eastbourne;* HMS *Ilfracombe;* HMS *Blyth;* HMS *Stornoway;* HMS *Clacton;* HMS *Felixstowe;* and HMS *Polruan.*

As a large area of the English Channel off Dieppe was believed to have been mined by the enemy, the minesweepers opened proceedings for the raid by clearing a path for the rest of the force to pass safely through. During the afternoon of 18 August, the 9th and 13th MSFs sailed separately from Portsmouth for the vicinity of Beachy Head. This was to give enemy aircraft that might be operating in the area the impression that one of the groups was carrying out a routine clearance sweep in the area. At the same time, the second group would proceed on passage through the Channel.

The 13th Flotilla began sweeping the Channel which the following force would negotiate at approximately 23:50, finishing their task at 00:51. The 9th Flotilla commenced sweeping at 00:03 and at 01:05 turned to port to get in further sweeps. Everything proceeded smoothly and the two groups were able to mark out a channel which was about four cables wide and clearly marked on both sides and at the ends. During their night's work only one mine was discovered, so the passage was never as heavily mined as intelligence had suggested.

After their work was complete both flotillas turned away to keep clear of the approaching expedition and soon after 05:00 they turned for home. On their way back to port the flotillas left Dan Buoys with flags to mark the channels in daylight for the armada to follow on their return journey at the conclusion of the operation. They returned in company to Portsmouth, having carried out their work with efficiency and precision.

The one thing that was notably missing from the whole Allied armada was the support of a battleship, which could have provided the fire power to confront enemy attackers at sea. This was because of the reluctance of the First Sea Lord, Sir Dudley

Pound, to risk capital ships in an area he believed vulnerable to attacks by German aircraft. Mountbatten had asked Pound to send a battleship to provide fire support for the Dieppe raid, but Pound was mindful that Japanese aircraft had sunk the battlecruiser HMS *Repulse* and the battleship HMS *Prince of Wales* off Malaya in December 1941, and he would not risk sending capital ships into waters where the Allies did not have absolute air superiority.

Once safely through the minefield, the main force formed up in a pre-arranged order, with the two Commandos who were to make the outer flank landings first, being positioned to port and starboard of the van. The hours went by and as the night drew towards morning no enemy ships or aircraft had been spotted and it seemed to the force commanders that complete surprise may well have been achieved.

The following despatch was submitted to the commander-in-chief, Portsmouth, on 30 August, 1942, by Captain Hughes-Hallett, the naval force commander at Dieppe. It was published in a supplement to *The London Gazette* on 12 August 1947 and gives some idea of the Channel crossing made by the convoy that night under his command.

Generally speaking the assembly of the force and the passage were carried out in accordance with the plan and without any major incident. After clearing the gate HMS *Queen Emma* (Captain G. L. D. Gibbs, DSO, RN (Ret.)) leading Groups 1, 2 and 3, appeared to me to be proceeding at an excessive speed, and HMS *Calpe* (Lieut. Commander J. H. Wallace, RN) and the destroyers had some difficulty in taking station ahead. At 00:16 when HMS *Calpe* was abeam of HMS *Queen Emma* a signal was made informing her that she was ahead of station and instructing her to reduce to 18 knots. After this the destroyers formed ahead, and shortly afterwards altered course for the Western passage through the minefield. The Dan Buoys and the ML marking the entrance to this channel were only sighted about two minutes before HMS *Calpe* entered the channel, no signals from the type 78 Beacon being received on account of a breakdown of HMS *Calpe's* RDF. However, HMS *Calpe* and the destroyers of the 2nd Division successfully passed through the Western channel, but HMS *Queen Emma* with Groups 1, 2 and 3 in company, lost touch with the destroyers and passed through the Eastern channel, overtaking HMS *Fernie* (Lieut. W. B. Willett, RN) and certain groups of LCTs and LCPs but fortunately without any collisions.

A word of praise is due to the 9th and 13th Minesweeping Flotillas (Commander H. T. Rust, RN and Commander L. S. J. Ede, DSO, RN) who carried out the task allotted to them with efficiency and precision.

After passing through the minefield HMS *Calpe* stopped in accordance with the plan, and subsequently signalled her position to HMS *Queen Emma*, HMS *Prince Albert* (Lieut. Commander H. B. Peate, RNR) and HMS *Glengyle* (Captain D. S. McGrath, RN), as these vessels respectively came in sight. HMS *Calpe* then proceeded and stopped about one mile to seaward of the position in which HMS *Glengyle* with Group 4 had stopped to lower their boats.

At this point the force had reached its position roughly seven miles off the coast of France and had negotiated the English Channel and the minefields without incident. However, as they began to implement the next stage of the operation, things were about to take an unexpected turn for the worse.

5

YELLOW BEACH

The main landings in front of the town of Dieppe were due to begin at 05:20 on 19 August. Just before the main body of troops and the tanks stormed onto White and Red beaches, their assault would be preceded by attacks on the two coastal batteries that protected the flanks of the main landing area at Varengeville-sur-Mer to the west and Berneval-le-Grand to the east, and further attacks on other batteries that dominated headlands to the east and west of the port. If this part of the operation went according to plan, all of the heavy guns that could fire on the Allied ships as they approached the beaches would be disabled, allowing the landings to go relatively unhindered. However, if it didn't go according to plan and the guns were not knocked out before the assault, the consequences could be catastrophic.

The mission for Lieutenant Colonel John Durnford-Slater and No. 3 Commando was to carry out two landings on separate sections of Yellow Beach to the east of Dieppe to silence the (2/770) Goebbels battery near Berneval-le-Grand about four miles from Dieppe and half a mile inland. This battery, which consisted of three 170 mm (6.7 inch) guns, four 105 mm (4.1 inch) guns, and a 20 mm flak gun, could shell the troops and ships at the main assault beaches. The Commandos were to capture it by using an enveloping manoeuvre to outflank their target and assault it from both sides simultaneously.

As the boats of No. 3 Commando made their final approach towards Yellow Beach at around 03:48, their landing craft and escorts ran into and exchanged fire with a small convoy of German ships made up of several fast trawlers or *Schnellboote* (S Boats), armed with torpedoes, who were escorting an oil carrier which was sailing between Boulogne-sur-Mer and Dieppe. On becoming aware of the presence of the Allied force the Germans sent up a star shell which illuminated all of the boats, leaving no doubt as to their identity and purpose.

For their attack to succeed, No. 3 Commando, who had sailed directly to France from Newhaven aboard their LCPs, needed to operate with complete surprise. With this in mind they planned to arrive just as dawn was breaking, so that their approach was shielded by the darkness while the troops coming ashore would enjoy the first glimmers of dawn light. Unfortunately, in the short engagement that followed, many of the LCPs were scattered, damaged or lost, and the element of surprise had completely disappeared, not just for No. 3 Commando, but for the entire operation.

For operational and communication purposes the Allied ships were divided into groups and the landing craft and escorts heading for Yellow Beach were Naval Group 5. In command of the vessels was Commander Derek Bathurst Wyburd, RN, who was aboard the steam gun boat SGB5. This group had started out with twenty-three LCPs and even before this unlucky brush with the enemy, they had already lost five due to breakdown. During the ensuing encounter with the German convoy, four more of the LCPs would be damaged and another seven widely dispersed. This would leave only seven out of the original twenty-three craft to press on with the mission, together with a motor launch (ML346) and a landing craft flak (LCF1).

As an example of what happened to one of the seven boats that were dispersed, one carried an officer, a sergeant and twenty other ranks of No. 3 Commando, as well as their naval crew. A shell killed all the crew of the boat except the naval officer in command, who was severely wounded. Also killed was the army officer in charge, so the sergeant, Clive Collins who had previously served with the Hampshire Regiment, took charge of the situation. The boat's compass had been put out of action, so Sergeant Collins used his army prismatic compass to set a course back to Newhaven, arriving back some six hours later but obviously unable to take any part in the battle.

Lieutenant Colonel Durnford-Slater was also aboard SGB5 with Commander Wyburd but had become isolated and out of touch with his men when the steam gun boat had been hit and incapacitated during the fighting. Its radio had also been knocked out, so Durnford-Slater was unable to make contact with any of his Commandos to find out what was happening with their part of the operation, or indeed, whether or not any had even manged to make it ashore. It wasn't until 06:30 that he finally managed to find a working radio set on one of the other dispersed LCPs they happened to link up with. He was then able to contact Major General Roberts and his headquarters on board HMS *Calpe* and inform them that No. 5 Group had been dispersed by the enemy.

Not that far away from the fighting at sea, the Allied destroyers HMS *Brocklesby* and ORP *Slazak* had heard the noise of the engagement, but both of their commanders had no notion that enemy ships had been encountered and had incorrectly assumed that the landing craft of No. 3 Commando had come under fire from the shore batteries. Because of this they had decided not to intervene or give assistance to their comrades. It also later transpired that the German convoy had actually been located by British Chain Home radar stations as early as 21:30 the previous evening and had been tracked by them all the time. However, for whatever reason, the Allied force had not been warned of their approach or acquainted with this intelligence. Captain Hughes-Hallett described the encounter in his supplement in the *London Gazette*:

At about 03:50 gun fire was observed to the E.S.E. which it was realised must be in the immediate vicinity of Group 5. At the time I considered this might be caused by an E-boat attack, but with the knowledge that Polish Ship *Slazak* (R. Tyminski, Kmdr.- Ppov.) and HMS *Brocklesby* (Lieutenant Commander E. N. Pumphrey, DSO, DSC, RN) were within about four miles of Group 5 and that HMS *Calpe* was the only ship in the immediate vicinity of HMS *Glengyle* and Group 4, it was decided to keep Group 4 in sight.

Actually Group 5 had made a chance encounter with some armed trawlers, and although Commander D. B. Wyburd, RN, in SGB5 (Lieutenant G. H. Hummel, RNR) maintained a steady course and speed in order that his LCPs should remain in company, SGB5 was soon disabled, and the LCPs disorganised. Commander Wyburd's persistence in remaining the guide of the slow LCPs while himself under heavy fire, showed great gallantry and determination. Nevertheless, I am of opinion that he would have done better to use the speed and smoke-laying capabilities of SGBs in order to protect the LCPs. LCF1 (Lieutenant T. M. Foggitt, RANVR) also in company with Group 5, successfully engaged the German vessels, setting one on fire and claiming to have sunk a second. In the course of this engagement her fire control was unfortunately put out of action.

During the action ORP *Slazak* with HMS *Brocklesby* in company was approximately four miles to the N.N.E. but did not intervene. The Commanding Officer of ORP *Slazak* has since informed me that he considered the firing came from the shore and therefore thought it best to continue with his patrol.

So with the escorting SGB5 disabled, ML346 and LCF1 had combined to drive off the German boats but nevertheless the element of surprise had now gone and because of the time involved with this unfortunate disruption, so had the cover of darkness. The LCPs were now exposed to daylight. In fact, only seven of the LCPS had finally made it to the shore anyway, with six of them landing on Yellow Beach I but only one on Yellow Beach II. The disembarkation of the troops aboard these landing craft would be covered by the fire provided by the motor launch and flak boat, which remained close to the shore for this purpose.

The first five of these landing craft reached Yellow Beach I and began to land their troops sometime between 05:10 and 05:30, which was by now at least twenty minutes behind schedule. The German defenders were now fully aware of their presence and to make things worse, dawn had broken and the craft were beaching in full daylight. Survivors recall seeing German soldiers standing on the cliffs with their weapons poised, almost as though they had been expected. The defenders also waited until the Commandos were tight to the shore before beginning to fire down on them. Some of the soldiers were looking through binoculars and waiting for the best possible moment to cause as much death and destruction as possible among the invaders.

Manning the defences above were men belonging to the 571st Infantry Regiment, who were equipped with rifles and machine guns. These troops were definitely on high alert as the Germans had every reason to suspect an attack was imminent due to the increased radio activity and Allied aerial reconnaissance interest in the town. They also had a network of double agents working within British Intelligence who would have suspected something as well. So in fact, the thought of catching the enemy napping and completely by surprise was probably never a realistic proposition and something the Allied troops were told to bolster their morale.

The whole of the 302nd Static Infantry Division had been trained for just such an eventuality, their very purpose for being there was to defend this small piece of coastline against incursions. They would have been drilled to perfection in their expected duties at such a moment and it would only have taken a matter of minutes to put their resistance in place once the alarm had been raised, with reinforcements arriving where required.

From the shoreline to the foot of the cliffs, Yellow Beach I was roughly 400 yards wide and the enemy soldiers had the whole area completely covered by the arc of their fire, making it almost impossible to operate below without being hit. Commandos were shot and killed in the boats as they approached the beach, as they attempted to alight from their flimsy wooden craft, and as they attempted to traverse the beach. There seemed to be no escaping from the deadly hail of bullets.

On one of the LCPs (No. 42) Lieutenant Commander Charles Corke, its captain, had been hit and mortally wounded and its coxswain killed. The Commandos on board debated turning back but unanimously decided to continue with the mission, with one of the troopers taking the helm of the craft and coxing it to shore. The craft was sinking and before it went down Lieutenant Corke oversaw the transfer of the wounded to another craft before choosing to go down with his vessel. The remaining troopers managed to make it from the stricken vessel to the beach carrying their equipment through the water and through the onslaught of enemy bullets.

As all of this was going on and the men attempted to come ashore, the various weapons on board ML346 and LCF1 continued to fire at the enemy positions on the cliff tops. These included three pounder guns, Oerlikon cannons and Lewis guns, all of which definitely helped to suppress the enemy and keep their heads down while the Commandos rushed across the beach to take shelter beneath the cliffs. Some of the German machine gunners were using the cover of a large white house and what was thought to be a small chapel close to it. These received a torrent of fire from the two boats until they were both seen to be on fire and ferociously blazing and the cover they afforded the soldiers within them was eliminated.

Most of the men who had made it ashore belonged to No. 6 (F) Troop, No. 3 Commando, and in the absence of Lieutenant Colonel Durnford-Slater, the senior officer on the ground, Captain Richard Lloyd Wills, originally from the Duke of Cornwall's Light Infantry, took command of the situation: the same Captain Wills who you will recall sent a message to Mr A. Hitler from the telegraph office in Stamsund, although at that time he was still a lieutenant. The plan was to make towards a point at which the cliffs were at their lowest height. This was in front of the small settlement of Le Petit Berneval, which nestled a short distance to the east of the battery. He led his men across the beach and to the foot of the cliffs where two gullies appeared to lead off the beach and up to higher ground. At this point the Commandos were also largely sheltered from the enemy fire.

Climbing along and up these gullies would appear to be their best course of action and perhaps their only way now of reaching the top to attack the battery. However, their progress was dogged by a series of obstacles. To begin with, the route was blocked by coils of Dannert wire, a type of razor-sharp barbed wire. The defenders had laced these coils with Teller mines on trip wires. A Teller mine was a German-made anti-tank mine which had explosives sealed inside a sheet metal casing and fitted with a pressure-activated fuse. Here they were used in a slightly different way against infantry and could be activated by a trip wire if a soldier moving up the gully walked into it. This was deadly and nervous stuff for the Commandos.

The ideal way to get over the Dannert wire was to use sections of tubular ladders which the men had trained with extensively in readiness for the operation. Unfortunately, all of the ones they had brought on the raid were on board one of the LCPs that had not made it to the beach. In the end Captain Wills decided that their best course of action was to try and get up the most accessible of the two gullies and in order to do this he set his men to work cutting a path through the wire with wire cutters. It was a painstaking process, being mindful to mark the positions of the mines as they went. Inch by inch, foot by foot, the men cut a path and slowly forced their way up to the summit of the cliff.

As the men eventually emerged over the top of the cliff they were once again subjected to heavy fire from a Spandau machine gun in a position nearby that had the opening to the gully completely covered in its sights. Captain Wills was wounded when a bullet ripped through his throat, knocking him to the ground in a pool of blood. Corporal 'Banger' Hall raced to his aid and attempted to drag him under cover but Wills was having none of it, and before he eventually lost consciousness he ordered Hall and the others to get on with the battle.

With Captain Wills incapacitated, Captain Geoff Osmond assumed command in the field, knowing that the only way forward was to clear the immediate opposition. Corporal Hall, who had also served with the Duke of Cornwall's Light Infantry before volunteering to join the Commandos, charged the enemy machine gun position and single-handedly put it out of action, first with hand grenades followed by the swift use of his Commando knife.

Lieutenant Edward Vincent Loustalot of the US 1st Ranger Battalion then attempted to attack a second machine gun post but sadly with a very different outcome, as he was hit and killed outright having already received three wounds while crossing the beach and climbing the gully. This apparently made him the first soldier from the United States of America to be killed in action in Europe during the Second World War.

Roughly fifteen minutes after the initial five LCPs had landed on Yellow Beach I, a sixth craft came ashore, on board Lieutenant Leonard William Druce in charge of another small group of thirteen Commandos. This now brought the number of those ashore to 115, consisting of ninety-six Commandos, six US Rangers and a few Free French troops who were there to act as guides and translators. Similar to those first craft which made it on to the beach, their LCP was not protected by the dim light of dawn and approached in broad daylight. Because of this they landed under the full gaze and fire of the enemy on the top of the cliffs.

ML346, although damaged, was still in the area and able to provide covering fire as the Commandos came ashore, just as they had done earlier as the first group of craft unloaded their passengers. This certainly helped to keep the enemy occupied and permitted the men to exit from the LCP and cross the beach to the base of the gully that Captain Wills and his men had earlier opened a path through up to the top of the cliff. They followed the same route and eventually emerged at the top where they met no resistance as the enemy machine gun nests had already been cleared by their comrades ahead of them. The sight of bodies littering the battlefield must have given them some indication of the intensity of the fighting that had gone before. Moving forward across the countryside they set off towards the battery and hoped to link up with any survivors from the first wave.

By the time Lieutenant Druce caught up with the rest of No. 3 Commando, now led by a barely conscious Captain Wills, the Germans had brought lorryloads of reinforcements up from

Dieppe and were strengthening by the minute. Others were arriving on bicycles. The Commandos on the other hand were losing men to the heavy fighting who could not be replaced. Faced with this dire situation Captain Wills was left with little choice but to give up the mission of attacking the Goebbels battery and instead make an attempt to retrace their steps back to the gully and from there climb back down to Yellow Beach in the hope of being evacuated.

In order to get back to the gully the Commandos had first to cross a lane which the Germans had by this time well covered by snipers. The men had to take it in turns to sprint across to the other side, attempting to dodge the bullets as they went. Not everyone made it, including a few of the US Rangers in the party who were cut down and wounded as they crossed. Unfortunately because of the nature of the situation, none of the soldiers who fell on the lane could be rescued, or their rescuers would themselves be cut down. So the wounded Rangers and Commandos had to be abandoned and left for the Germans to take prisoner and hopefully attend to.

Back out at sea, things were beginning to get even hotter when one of the armed German trawlers, the *Franz*, returned to the fray and closed in on the beach behind the waiting LCPs with ML346 and LCF1. From here the German ship was able to fire on the rear of the Allied vessels waiting to evacuate their Commandos. They were also in a position to open fire on the gully down which the Commandos were now descending. ML346 quickly returned fire on the enemy vessel with such ferocity that it was put out of action with most of those aboard killed. It went out of control and eventually ran aground on the beach and was boarded by Royal Navy personnel from ML346, who in spite of being under heavy fire from the Germans on the cliff top were determined to capture the trawler's colours and take them as a battle trophy. They managed to achieve this just before the ship finally burst into flames and exploded.

Meanwhile, the Commandos continued to battle their way back down the gully towards the beach, sustaining more casualties as they went. Captain Wills had to be carried down on the back of one Private John Lerigo, whose strength had been honed through hours of hard training on ropes on the assault course at the Commando Basic Training Centre at Achnacarry on the banks of the River Arkaig. On eventually reaching the beach their position remained precarious, as the enemy still controlled the high ground and could fire indiscriminately down on them from their cliff top positions.

The situation was becoming hopeless, and it was evident that the few remaining LCPs were unable to come any closer to the beach in order to pick up survivors. By now Captain Wills was probably unable to make any decisions and it seems Captain Geoff Osmond decided that the best course of action was to work their way west along the beach where they might eventually link up with some of the Canadian troops who should by now have come ashore on Blue Beach at Puys. Hopefully, from there the survivors could be evacuated. But the Germans along the cliff tops, of which there now seemed to be hundreds, were able to pick them off with rifle fire and stick grenades as they trudged along the shingle.

The Commandos were eventually forced to take shelter in a cave they happened upon where they finally surrendered when the German infantry descended onto the beach and began to fire in at them. In the area of Yellow Beach I, thirty-seven men were killed that day and eighty-two men captured. Only one man got away, Lance Corporal Sinclair, who escaped by swimming out to one of the flimsy wooden LCPs which was already being driven further away from the beach by enemy fire.

The last of the seven LCPs to survive the encounter with the German ships was LCP15, commanded by Lieutenant Henry Thomas Buckee, RNVR. This was one of the landing craft detailed for Yellow Beach II. On board were more soldiers of No. 3 Commando, eighteen in total, comprising three officers and fifteen other ranks, under the command of Major Peter Young MC, who was Lieutenant Colonel Durnford-Slater's second-in-command. They were in fact the headquarters party of this part of the attacking force. In spite of a situation which had left them as the only part of the force destined for Yellow Beach II, they quickly conferred and decided to carry on with their part of the operation, which was to land slightly to the west of the battery and attack it from the opposite side to those landing on Yellow Beach I.

At 04:10 Lieutenant Buckee and those with him found themselves safely shrouded by the shadowy twilight before dawn and were unobserved from the shore. It was still an hour before Captain Wills and his party would come ashore to the east of them. However, in the unfolding story it is better to relate the story of Yellow Beach II at this point, as they were to progress slightly further with their objective than those at Yellow Beach I.

Buckee spotted the gap in the cliffs on Yellow Beach II, which was his intended target for landing. He pointed it out to Major Young and said that his orders were to put them ashore at this location at all costs. Major Young replied that his orders were to go *ashore* at all costs. Undeterred by events, Lieutenant Buckee managed to steer his vessel skillfully into the beach and did so with five minutes to go before the launch of the main assault. If Major Young and his small band of brothers were going to put the Goebbels battery out of action by themselves and prevent them from attacking the ships at Dieppe, there was no time to lose.

Lieutenant Buckee had managed to navigate his LCP to within fifty yards of the spot where the Commandos had rehearsed to exit the beach during training. Here they were to climb a steep gully to the top of the cliffs, which, similar to the one on Yellow

Beach I that Captain Wills and his men had conquered, was blocked with coils of Dannert wire piled approximately ten feet high and again interlaced with mines. Beyond the wire the gully contained further obstacles. Barbed wire was pinned to the cliff with stakes. However, one massive positive was the fact that unlike Captain Wills and his men, Buckee's LCP had reached its intended spot in the dark and without being detected by the enemy or attracting their fire.

Having alighted on to the beach and seen their LCP move away from the shore, Major Young and his men took time to take stock and review their situation. They decided to limit what they were going to proceed with to their objective, particularly in terms of weapons. They reviewed their arsenal and decided they would be unable to take everything and had to prioritise, keeping only what would be essential for the task in hand. Among their weapons was a cumbersome three-inch mortar which they chose to leave on the beach along with its bombs. This left them armed with ten Mark III .303-inch Lee-Enfield service rifles, a Bren gun, six Tommy guns, three pistols, and a two-inch mortar with six bombs. Thus armed, they began to cut their way through the wires and slowly make their way up the gully, still undetected.

Like Captain Wills' party, they had no tubular ladders to climb over the obstacles, but they made no attempt to cut their way through with wire cutters. Instead, they found that they could make an improvised ladder using the wooden stakes that the Germans had used to hold the barbed wire in place. Surely the Germans would have been more than piqued to see this improvisation. That said, it was certainly not an easy task and made for a very difficult climb. However, still undetected by the enemy, Major Young and his men eventually scrambled to the top of the gully and out on top of the cliff, although the men were sporting numerous cuts and bruises from their ordeal and their uniforms were covered with rips.

On eventually reaching the top of the cliff, Major Young scanned the sea with his binoculars. He was relieved to observe ML346 and some of the other LCPs negotiating Yellow Beach I. It was now roughly 5:10 and what he could see was Captain Wills and his party coming ashore. He could see and hear that they had made contact with the enemy, but he was unaware of the true gravity of their circumstances and assumed that they would be in a position to forge ahead with their part of the operation and attack the battery from the other side.

Up until this point, as Major Young and his men were the only Commandos to have made it to Yellow Beach II, it must have seemed almost impossible to them that they would be able to attack the battery by themselves and no doubt thoughts of turning back had entered all of their minds. Now however, in the knowledge that other Commandos were also ashore and proceeding with the task to the east, they were given the confidence to continue. Major Young rallied his men and gave them a short speech about the implications of what could happen if they didn't knock out the battery and, suitably inspired, they began to move inland towards their rendezvous point, although as they were the only troops to have made it to their beach and beyond, there could be no RV.

Not far from the cliffs and on their way towards the battery, the party found cover in some woods. Major Young divided his troops into three groups and then went ahead himself with runners to make a reconnaissance of the terrain in front of them. He decided that the best course of action was to make for the further cover afforded by the village of Berneval-le-Grand, where he hoped to meet up with any other Commandos who might have made it that far. The situation suddenly became more critical; they could hear the guns of the battery roar into action and begin to fire on the ships now lying off Dieppe. More correctly, it seemed that only one of the guns was firing on the ships. Why this was the case is unknown, but possibly the other guns had been put out of action by Allied air strikes earlier.

Moving off again they came upon the road which led from Dieppe to Berneval-le-Grand and marched along it towards the village, still unseen by the enemy, remarkably. On the way they scaled a telegraph pole and cut the wires connecting the area to Dieppe. They also encountered a young French boy on a bicycle who was trying desperately to locate a doctor as his mother had been injured during an air strike, when British aircraft had missed the battery with their bombs and hit the village instead. The boy gave them clear instructions on how to get to the battery and informed them that it was garrisoned by about 200 men, undoubtedly an exaggeration of the true figure, which was probably around 150.

On reaching the village of Berneval-le-Grand, Major Young and his group found themselves in a scene of chaos after six British Hawker Hurricane fighter bombers of No. 175 Squadron had recently attacked the battery and hit houses in the process. Members of the French Fire Brigade known as Sapeurs-Pompiers, were desperately fighting fires in these dwellings. In spite of this, Major Young and his men were met with friendliness by the people in the village who were out of their houses, particularly children and young men, who once again were keen to direct them to the exact location of the battery.

As they continued through the village towards their target, they suddenly found themselves caught in the fire of a Spandau machine gun located on top of the church tower. They took immediate cover and tried to engage the enemy post with their rifles. However, these were not able to reach the tower with their fire, but they at least helped to keep the Germans pinned down until the two-inch mortar could be deployed. This made all the difference and after firing a number of their mortar bombs, the machine gun nest took a direct hit and was silenced.

Moving on again, they finally reached the perimeter of the Goebbels battery which had recently been hit by bombs from the Hawker Hurricanes of No. 175 Squadron. The place was in some disarray but still functioning. The Commandos crept forward and positioned themselves within 200 yards of their objective. It was clear that a full frontal assault on the battery was out of the question as it would have meant certain death for so few men; they were outnumbered by about ten to one. Instead, the Commandos engaged their target with small arms fire while others cut further telephone wires to disrupt communications.

Through sniping, Major Young and his men tried to prevent the enemy from shelling the ships at sea. It was a plan that seemed to work well, as each time there was any sign of movement from within the battery they opened up with their rifles. This evidently annoyed the Germans to such an extent that they attempted to turn one of their guns around and fire at almost point-blank range on their attackers. Luckily for the Commandos, the Germans were unable to sufficiently depress the muzzle of the gun and its shells whistled harmlessly over the heads of Major Young and his men, to burst somewhere deep in the French countryside.

Although they were not in a position to attack and destroy the guns at the Goebbels battery, the sniping of Major Young and his Commandos managed to harass and distract the battery to such an extent that it caused the gunners to fire wildly and there was no known instance of this battery sinking any of the Allied ships off Dieppe.

Hopelessly outnumbered, as well as being almost out of ammunition, Young finally gave the order to withdraw after a couple of hours. They retraced their steps back down the gully, withdrawing in the manner they had practised in training so many times, followed by enemy soldiers all the way. One Commando happened to stand on a landmine which they had missed during the ascent, but he survived and was able to continue with assistance.

When they arrived back on Yellow Beach II they found Lieutenant Buckee and his LCP waiting. They also found the three-inch mortar they had left on their arrival. They quickly set it up and turned it on their pursuers with great effect, firing until all its bombs had been used.

Lieutenant Buckee had lain off for three hours under fire while waiting for the Commandos to return. The men waded out and all of them managed to make it off the beach and safely back to England. The official report of the incident stated: 'it (the attack) was not crowned with success, but there is no doubt that the sniping tactics employed by Major Young and his men greatly interfered with the handling of the battery for upwards of an hour and a half, during the crucial period of the main landing.' Both Lieutenant Buckee and Major Young were later awarded the DSO for their actions.

6

ORANGE BEACH

As No. 3 Commando landed on the eastern flank of Dieppe to assault the Goebbels battery, No. 4 Commando would be responsible for eliminating the Hess battery (813) on the western flank to prevent its guns from firing on the Allied boats in front of the town and harbour. The Hess battery consisted of six 150 mm (5.9 inch) guns situated in a concrete emplacement some 1,100 yards inland from the cliffs and at the southern edge of the commune of Varengeville-sur-Mer, which is roughly five miles west of Dieppe. The emplacement was protected by two rows of barbed wire and several machine gun posts. There was also an anti-aircraft tower nearby that could defend the battery from a ground attack if required. It was manned by the 813th Army Artillery Troop and British intelligence had estimated that the strength of the battery was between 120 and 175 men, supported by two infantry companies stationed nearby.

The plan was for No. 4 Commando to land on two sections of beach codenamed Orange I and Orange II. Orange I was in front of Varengeville-sur-Mer and was overlooked by a chalk cliff. Similar to the situation on Yellow Beach, there were gullies leading to the top of the cliff. Before the war there had been steps in the gullies that bathers could take to go down to the beach but these had been removed by the Germans and the gullies had been filled in with barbed wire and other obstacles. The second beach, Orange II, was at Quiberville about one and a half miles further west at the mouth of the River Saane. This offered access to the top of the cliffs from where the slopes came down to sea level at the river mouth. Being an obvious landing place, the Germans had protected it by building a pillbox manned with a machine gun with an arc of fire covering the lowest point. The opening was also protected by lines of barbed wire. It would be easier to move inland from Quiberville than it would be from Varengeville-sur-Mer, as the Commandos would not have to climb any cliffs, but the downside was that it was further away from their objective.

The plan was for four troops from No. 4 Commando, being A, B, C and F troops, along with the headquarters troop and attached specialists, to be divided into two groups. Group One under the command of Major Derek Mills-Roberts, previously of the Irish Guards, would land at Orange Beach I. The group would be made up of C Troop, a section from A Troop, the mortar detachment and some of the specialists. They were given the daunting task of scaling the steep cliffs in front of Varengeville-sur-Mer. Having reached the summit they were to establish a fire base in some woods that were situated in front of the battery. Here they would wait, ready to support the assault of the battery by Group Two who would be coming up from Quiberville.

Group Two, commanded by Lieutenant Colonel Simon Lovat (15th Lord Lovat) formally of the Scots Guards, would land at Orange Beach II and in the first instance would take out any beach defences established there, notably the previously mentioned pillbox and barbed wire. B and F Troops would then move inland along the course of the River Saane from where they would take position and assault the battery from the rear, simultaneously from two separate directions. The rest of A Troop would be the reserve, positioned between the two beaches. After the attack, Group Two would withdraw through Group One and be picked up by the waiting LCAs on Orange Beach I, having descended the gullies that had already been cleared by Group One on their ascent.

No. 4 Commando made the crossing to Dieppe on board the troopship HMS *Prins Albert* from Southampton having been seen off by Lord Mountbatten in person. They had arrived at Southampton from their camp in Weymouth where they had trained for the mission, including carrying out exercises at Lulworth Cove in Dorset. At full strength they numbered just 252 officers and men, but on this occasion they were supplemented by a number of soldiers from the US 1st Ranger Battalion.

At the appointed place and hour the Commandos transferred into their assault landing craft which were then lowered into the sea for the final assault on the beaches. They sat on hard wooden benches looking to the front with their weapons between their legs. Once all the LCAs were in the water they swept forward in exact formation, led in by an MGB. For some time, nothing was to be seen except the faint wake of the rushing craft, but then they sighted three darkened ships between them and the shore and had to alter course slightly to avoid them. What they did not know was that these were the silhouettes of enemy craft and when suddenly the sky to the east was lit up by shell and tracer, the darkened ships moved off to join the battle against No. 3 Commando's LCPs and escorts. They were completely unaware of the presence of No. 4 Commando in their own waters.

The Commandos alighted successfully from their landing craft at around 04:50, only three minutes behind schedule, which was quite remarkable considering the detour they had to make to avoid the German ships. Once ashore, the men of Group One under Major Mills-Roberts, having received no interference from the enemy thus far, raced over the shingle and made their way to the foot of the cliffs at the back of a very short beach. Here the cliffs towered over them on top of which somewhere was the battery.

In the first instance they were confronted by a series of three gullies through the rocks, which could potentially take them to the top. After giving the situation due consideration they decided to attempt to scale the one on the far right as it appeared to offer the easiest route. Having said that, any of the three would have been difficult to climb, considering the obstacles the Germans had placed in them.

The main problem with trying to climb their chosen gully was it was severely choked up with barbed wire. However, unlike No. 3 Commando, Mills-Roberts and his men had brought Bangalore torpedoes to the party. A Bangalore torpedo was basically an explosive charge placed within tubes and would normally be used by combat engineers to clear paths through obstacles such as wire or heavy undergrowth. It could clear a path of between three to four metres wide through wire obstacles, but obviously made a huge din when exploded, so could give the game away.

No. 4 Commando placed two of these in position and exploded them just as cannon-firing Hawker Hurricanes of No. 129 Squadron flew fortuitously overhead to attack the battery. The considerable noise of the attacking aircraft mingled with the noise made by the exploding Bangalore torpedoes confused the enemy and did not give their position away.

After they had successfully blown a path through the barbed wire, it was relatively easy to scale the cliffs and emerge at the top of the gully, not far from the front of the battery and still completely undetected by the enemy. Lieutenant D. C. W. Style and his men were in front, closely followed by Major

Mills-Roberts with the mortar section under the command of Lieutenant J. F. Ennis. At the top of the cliffs there were some woods which they entered and pushed through almost to the other side, until they reached a position so close to the battery that they could hear its garrison talking and the words of command being given to the German gunners.

At approximately 05:45 the battery began to open fire on the main landing force at Dieppe taking everyone by surprise. This was roughly half an hour before Group One was expected to be in position and because of it, Major Mills-Roberts was compelled to respond by speeding up his attempts to get the guns of Group One into action as soon as possible. At 05:50 the Commandos were in a position to open fire on the battery with their mortars, Bren guns and sniper rifles and laid down a fierce onslaught of lead.

With only the third shot from a two-inch mortar, Troop Sergeant Major James Dunning aided by Privates Dale and Horn dropped a bomb right in the middle of the battery, which landed among the cordite charges and shells stacked alongside the guns ready for use. There was a massive, blinding explosion and the battery did not fire again.

The German gunners made every attempt to put out the fires that resulted from the explosion but found themselves being fired upon by snipers of Group One positioned at the edge of the woods and elsewhere. In particular, Lance Corporal Richard Mann, who had painted his face and hands green for camouflage purposes, had crawled to a position in some bushes which were about 150 yards from the battery, a position from which he could cause maximum damage. His shooting was deadly and equalled only by that of Gunner Thomas McDonough, who fired about sixty rounds from an anti-tank rifle against the enemy positions, killing and maiming many of the defenders.

While this was taking place, Lord Lovat and Group Two, which formed the larger part of No. 4 Commando, had come ashore at Quiberville to begin their part in the operation. Unlike Group One, their landing did draw the attention of the enemy because of course the Germans had a pillbox positioned for such an eventuality to guard the beach. The soldiers in the pillbox were immediately aware of the approaching Commandos and opened up with their machine gun, temporarily pinning the attackers down.

Lord Lovat was only too aware that time was of the essence if they were to stop the battery firing on the approaching ships. What he didn't know was that Group One had already succeeded in silencing the enemy guns, which wasn't actually part of the plan. First and foremost, he had to deal with the pillbox on the beach and he therefore took the decision to split his force up, detailing A Troop to stay behind and eliminate the pillbox and any other German defences in the near vicinity. While they were doing this and consequently keeping the German gunners occupied, he and the rest of his men would slip around the pillbox and continue to their objective.

Having completed their task, A Troop was then ordered to act independently and not try to follow the rest of the group to the battery, instead they would make their own way towards Orange Beach I for evacuation with the rest of the Commandos on completion of the mission. In point of fact, having dealt with the pillbox, A Troop became aware of an approaching German patrol which had obviously been drawn down to the beach by the sound of the action there. They laid in wait, ambushed and killed the members of the patrol before finally moving on to their evacuation point.

The rest of Group Two, which now mainly comprised of F and B Troops, followed the river for a short distance before cutting over land for a couple of miles to the rear of the battery, running most of the way and only stopping while Lord Lovat detailed parties to cut any telephone and telegraph wires they came across.

The group finally reached a few scattered farm buildings to the south-west of some woods that were themselves just to the south of the battery. Here Lord Lovat established his small headquarters consisting of himself, his adjutant Captain Michael Dunning White, four clerks from the orderly room, three signallers and a couple of runners employed to take messages to all parts of the group. Although the job of the clerks was to carry out administrative duties they were still first and foremost Commandos and had undergone all the necessary training to operate as such. They were armed with Thompson sub machine guns.

The men of B and F Troops would approach the battery from two different directions. B Troop would come in from behind the anti-aircraft tower, which would need to be tackled if it was currently occupied by the enemy. As they drew close, they could see a few German soldiers moving around on the tower, so three Commandos were sent to deal with them, which they did with their Commando knives. While in the process of neutralising the tower, B Troop also stumbled across an enemy machine gun post, which they quietly put out of service.

At 06:15, scouts from F Troop noticed that there was a group of around thirty-five German assault troops, who were part of the battery's garrison, that were getting prepared at the rear of a farmhouse to deliver a counter-attack on Major Mills-Roberts and his fire base in the woods to the north of the battery. Without hesitation, F Troop charged the group at bayonet point, killing several and dispersing the rest, without suffering any losses to their own number.

After both B and F Troops were finally in position to begin their attack on the battery, they waited until a pre-arranged strafing of the site was carried out by the Royal Air Force. Once this had been done, Group One increased their rate of fire in order to occupy the enemy while Group Two made their attack from the south.

At 06:30 Lord Lovat fired a flare from a Very pistol into the sky, which was the signal for the assault to begin. On seeing this, Mills-Roberts ordered his men to cease firing, in the knowledge that B and F Troops would now be charging into the complex and he didn't wish to accidentally hit any of the Commandos with stray bullets. As the attack went in, the job of B Troop was to attack and enter the battery buildings to put them out of operation, while F Troop would seek to destroy the guns themselves.

During the charge both troops came under heavy fire from the defenders and the two men leading F Troop, Captain Roger Pettiward and Lieutenant John McDonald, were killed while Troop Sergeant Major William Stockdale was wounded. Born in 1906 and educated at Eton and Christchurch, Oxford, before the war Roger Pettiward had been a celebrated painter and comic artist. He used the signature of Paul Crum on his cartoons, many of which were published in popular periodicals of the day, including *Punch*.

It was for this action that the already wounded twenty-four-year-old Captain Patrick Porteous, who was acting as the liaison officer between the two groups was awarded the Victoria Cross. With the two officers dead, he took command. Before joining the Commandos, Porteous had served in the Royal Regiment of Artillery and at Dieppe had been made up to acting major. The following citation was published in a supplement to the *London Gazette* on 2 October 1942, giving details of the action which led to the award.

The King has been graciously pleased to approve the award of The Victoria Cross to: Captain (temporary Major) Patrick Anthony Porteous (73033), Royal Regiment of Artillery (Fleet, Hants.). At Dieppe on 19 August, 1942, Major Porteous was detailed to act as Liaison Officer between the two detachments whose task was to assault the heavy coast defence guns. In the initial assault Major Porteous, working with the smaller of the two detachments, was shot at close range through the hand, the bullet passing through his palm and entering his upper arm. Undaunted, Major Porteous closed with his assailant, succeeded in disarming him and killed him with his own bayonet thereby saving the life of a British Sergeant on whom the German had turned his aim. In the meantime the larger detachment was held up, and the officer leading this detachment was killed and the Troop Sergeant Major fell seriously wounded. Almost immediately afterwards the only other officer of the detachment was also killed. Major Porteous, without hesitation and in the face of a withering fire, dashed across the open ground to take over the command of this detachment. Rallying them, he led them in a charge which carried the German position at the point of the bayonet, and was severely wounded for the second time. Though shot through the thigh he continued to the final objective where he eventually collapsed from loss of blood after the last of the guns had been destroyed. Major Porteous's most gallant conduct, his brilliant leadership and tenacious devotion to a duty which was supplementary to the role originally assigned to him, was an inspiration to the whole detachment.

On reaching the battery and capturing the surviving members of the German garrison, demolition experts from F Troop destroyed the guns with pre-formed charges and by 06:50 all six had been blown up. Meanwhile, B Troop searched the battery buildings for intelligence material.

Before vacating the site, the Commandos gathered the bodies of their fallen comrades and laid them beside the now useless guns they had helped to capture. The Union Jack was run over the British dead. Then, taking their seriously wounded with them and escorting prisoners, both troops withdrew through the fire base.

Both Commando groups made it to Orange beach I where the LCAs waited offshore, in spite of being fired upon by the enemy. The re-embarkation began at 07:30 with the men having to wade out to the boats because of the fast-ebbing tide. Some of them were up to their necks in water. Many of the wounded were ferried in a collapsible boat. The withdrawal was successfully completed and by 09:00 No. 4 Commando was on the way to England. They crossed the Channel without incident, arriving at Newhaven docks at 17:45 the same day.

For their part in the raid Lovat was awarded the DSO and Mills-Roberts the Military Cross (MC). The cost to the Commando was at first thought to be twenty-three dead but six were only severely wounded and were eventually reported to be prisoners of war.

No. 4 Commando's assault on the battery was the only successful part of the whole operation. The War Office claimed it to be 'a classic example of the use of well-trained infantry'. In February 1943, the War Office issued an infantry training pamphlet using the attack as its inspiration stating that this was done 'in order that all may benefit from the story of a stimulating achievement'.

Simon Lovat would become more famous for his heroic exploits on D-Day. He was tall, dashing and handsome, and in the movie *The Longest Day* Hollywood got it absolutely right in casting the actor Peter Lawford to play him. Churchill once said of the tall Scotsman he was 'the handsomest man that ever cut a throat'. After Dieppe, Churchill spoke with Lovat about the need for more training in special operations and gave the go ahead for the formation of the 1st Special Service Brigade, with Lovat as its inaugural Brigadier.

7

BLUE BEACH

The attacks made by Nos. 3 and 4 Commandos on the outer flanks were just the first of a number of operations to put out of action any artillery batteries in the Dieppe area which could hinder the main assault in front of the town as it came ashore. The plan included attacks on other batteries located in the inner flanks; there were also guns near the village of Puys, to the east of Dieppe and Pourville-sur-Mer to the west.

The Royal Regiment of Canada was detailed to land on Blue Beach at Puys together with three platoons from the Black Watch of Canada and a detachment of Royal Canadian Artillery. From the beach their job was to move inland, to capture another heavy battery of similar strength to the one faced at Berneval-le-Grand, and then capture a headland overlooking the eastern beaches of Dieppe on which the main assault was to be delivered. The battery in question was (B/302) Puys Battery (Rommel) armed with four 155 mm (6.1 inch) guns, and three 88 mm (3.46 inch) guns.

Having captured the headland and satisfied themselves that the Germans were no longer able to operate from here, they would then move west towards Dieppe itself, to link up with the Essex Scottish Regiment near to the port entrance, who would be landing on Red Beach. The men of the Royal Regiment of Canada would not return to Blue Beach after their mission and would instead be evacuated from the main assault area in front of Dieppe at the close of the operation. Nothing would go quite according to plan.

In command of the Royal Regiment of Canada was Lieutenant Colonel Douglas Cato. His plan was to land his force in three waves. The first wave would consist of three of the four infantry companies in the regiment. The second wave would have the remaining infantry company and the battalion's headquarters company (including himself). And finally, the third wave would be made up of a force of specialist troops which included the men from the Royal Canadian Artillery who were tasked with taking over and destroying the guns of Rommel battery, and the men of the Black Watch who would be used to cover the eastern flank. Similar to all stages of the operation so far, success would depend on surprise and speed.

The Royal Regiment of Canada had sailed across the English Channel from Portsmouth aboard the landing ships infantry HMS *Princess Astrid* and HMS *Queen Emma*, before transferring to their LCAs for their final approach to Blue Beach. In the darkness, there appears to have been some confusion and precious time was lost in getting the landing craft to form up on the MGB that was detailed to escort them to their landing zone. Because of this confusion, the flotilla set off about twenty minutes behind schedule and a smoke screen that the Royal Air Force had laid to hide them during the assault had already lifted.

John Barron was serving as a private soldier in the Royal Regiment of Canada at Puys and remembered this part of the operation. He had also been on the boats that were preparing to set out for Operation *Rutter*, so was surprised when they were told they were still going to Dieppe after it had already been cancelled once. He felt sure that in the month that had passed since *Rutter,* the Germans would have been aware that Dieppe was the intended target and would of course now be ready for them when they arrived.

Within a half an hour after we left the Channel port of Portsmouth we knew that we were going to Dieppe. Most of us felt like hurling ourselves overboard and swimming back to England. We didn't think too much of going into a battle zone where it had already been scrapped as far as we were concerned. So it was kind of a surprise to us, a shock too. As far as we knew, the plans for the raid had been discovered about a month before that, when we were supposed to go the first time, back around July. We were surprised on the boats by the (German) aircraft coming in and bombing and strafing and we were taken off the ships and sent on leave. Now, much to our surprise and horror, we were told that we were going into Dieppe after all and we didn't think very much of that at all.

It was a beautiful hot sunny day when the sun finally did arise. And as far as I can remember, it was very warm and I don't mean just from the action, I mean the weather was warm. And the Channel was very calm at that time and no swell of any kind.

As far as I can remember, we didn't have any camouflage on at all, just straight uniform and no markings on it of any kind. All markings had been removed so that they couldn't tell what divisions or regiments we came from. But we got the signal to load into the assault landing craft and we went swarming down the netting on the sides of the ship and loaded into the assault landing craft. And then we, with some difficulty, got into different flotillas to make the run into shore. And at one point, one of the flotillas got mixed up a bit and there was a man hailing everybody, trying to get the flotilla together and a very loud voice, through a loud hailer, which was very alarming because there were U-Boats out in the Channel and we were afraid that we would be discovered.

It is perhaps a surprise to learn from John Barron's interview that following the cancellation of Operation *Rutter* the men were permitted to go on leave. In view of the secrecy that should have been maintained at this time, you would think that all of those concerned would have been confined to barracks until the task was complete. With only a month between the two raids and men meeting local people and no doubt local girlfriends, one misplaced comment in the wrong ear could have easily given the game away, especially after the Germans had discovered the task force formed up for *Rutter*. Because of this they would surely have had agents in the area asking questions.

John Barron's account is verified by Louis Pantaleo. Louis was also serving with the Royal Regiment of Canada and was likewise aboard the ships back in July and recalls going on leave after the operation was cancelled: 'I wish they would tell the truth about it. Dieppe, we were supposed to make it a month before we did. And we all knew the word Dieppe, and then they sent us on leave. It sounds as if they purposely gave the secret out. The Germans were really prepared for us. And they knew where we were going.'

The flotilla heading for Blue Beach, the 10th LCA Flotilla, was under the direction of Lieutenant Commander Harold Wilkinson Goulding DSO RNR, who was perhaps the man using the loud hailer. Apparently he knew this coastline intimately, and before this and previous missions he had been employed by Combined Operations headquarters to train the Commandos in things like the deployment of landing craft, navigation, and seamanship skills, so he was quite an important figure in the overall scheme of things.

He was the senior landing officer for Blue Beach and from a report recommending him for promotion by his then commanding officer, a Captain Chambers said of him:

He is an outstanding officer; a great leader; a good organiser; handles men well. His great knowledge of every part of the French coast has been used to great advantage in night raiding by landing craft. In a great many raids he has personally led in the craft. This officer is very strongly recommended in all ways as being fitted for higher rank. Very loyal, keen and hardworking. Has an exceptional energy.

Lord Mountbatten personally endorsed this by adding: 'I fully concur. This officer is outstanding and fully worth immediate promotion.'

Captain Hughes-Hallett, the naval force commander at Dieppe, tried to explain what had happened to cause the mix up and delay in front of Puys in the supplement he wrote in *The London Gazette* on 12 August 1947:

The landing on Blue Beach was delayed for fifteen minutes, on account of time lost when the boats were forming up. This was due to MGB315 (Lieut. J. I. Lloyd, RNVR) (whose role was to remain with HMS *Queen Emma* and escort her back) going ahead and getting mixed up with the Landing Craft from HMS *Princess Astrid,* who mistook her for MGB316 (Act. Temp. Lieutenant Commander T. N. Cartwright, RNVR) whose role it was to lead in these landing craft. Although the landing subsequently took place according to plan, I fear that the fifteen minutes' delay must have been partly responsible for the very heavy opposition which the troops immediately encountered after landing, and which apparently pinned them down on the beach area throughout the day.

Eventually, Lieutenant Commander Goulding managed to get all of the boats in the flotilla sorted out with the LCAs supporting the regiment's first wave being escorted to Blue Beach by Cartwright in MGB316. They followed a course which took them past the piers of Dieppe Harbour. This must have been a very anxious passage but thankfully the enemy, who surely must have seen their silhouettes in the dim light, did not pay them any attention. It is thought that they might have mistaken them for one of their own convoys, most probably part of the one that had engaged the boats of No. 3 Commando, which was of course known by the Germans to be in the near vicinity and expected at Dieppe. Due to this stroke of good luck, the harbour lights were turned on and the Germans did not open fire on them.

Having successfully passed Dieppe Harbour the boats approached the small beach at Puys a short distance to the east and the landing craft carrying the first wave from the Royal Regiment of Canada touched down and hit the shingle at approximately 05:06, by which time the sun was up and they were in full view of the defenders ashore.

Puys was nothing more than a very small settlement with a cluster of houses sitting at a point where the chalk cliffs came down to the sea behind a narrow pebble and stone beach. The cliffs then rose gently to both the east and west of the settlement, with more houses built along the ascending slopes. At this point the beach was about 300 yards wide and between 100 and 250 yards deep, depending on the tide. At the back of the beach, in front of the seafront houses, was a low sea wall that the Germans had defended by building a number of pillboxes with interlocking fields of fire. They had also covered the wall with rows of barbed wire. Behind this, a road led inland to the main village. The beach itself was divided into two unequal parts.

As the initial landing craft touched down and the first elements of the Royal Regiment of Canada rushed ashore, they were immediately met by withering fire from the enemy positions which, according to survivors, appeared to be ready and waiting for them. Although they had passed the piers of Dieppe without making contact with the enemy, here they would not be so lucky. Undoubtedly, with the unfolding situation further east regarding No. 3 Commando, the defenders would have been alerted to a possible attack by now and their thorough training to repulse a beach assault would have kicked in. As the first troops landed, they were greeted by a hail of bullets from the pillboxes and other enemy positions along the seafront and even from the cliffs overlooking the beach and village.

Lieutenant Alasdair Ferguson was second in command of the 10th LCA Flotilla. During the approach to the beach, he could feel the hull of his craft scrape the bottom as enemy fire poured down from the cliff, hitting the boat. Having touched down, he ordered 'Down ramp' and urged the troops on board to head for the beach. He later recalled how these soldiers were shot down before they even cleared the ramp and their bodies blocked the way of others coming off behind them.

Led by their officers, most of whom became casualties in the first few moments ashore, the men rushed up the beach but had nowhere to go, as their way ahead was blocked by the low sea wall topped by barbed wire. At best, all they could do was take shelter behind the sea wall, unfortunately having to leave their wounded crying out in pain on the beach behind them. Here they attempted to keep their heads down and out of the line of fire while the surviving officers and NCOs attempted to regroup their men as best they could.

The situation worsened when the third wave landed behind them shortly afterwards. By this time, if the plan had worked, the men from the first wave should have been up into the village and off the beach, but instead they were stuck behind the sea wall, where the men from the third wave were now piling up behind them and finding it increasingly difficult to find any shelter whatsoever. Even for those who did manage to get behind the wall, it provided little or no protection as it was covered by the line of fire from the strategically placed pillboxes. Because of this, the casualties were swiftly beginning to mount. The second wave had landed slightly to the west so had not exacerbated the problem at this location.

Although the German fire was devastating, it later transpired that only around fifty German soldiers were positioned to defend the beach at Puys, who belonged to the 571st Infantry Regiment, so they were greatly outnumbered. The difference of course between the two sides was that the defenders were dug in and protected by concrete fortifications with machine guns and cannons, whereas the Canadians were caught out in the open with little more than rifles until they could get a foothold and bring up better weapons for deployment.

If any of the troops were going to make it off the beach, either to continue with their mission or just to escape the relentless fire from the enemy pillboxes and other positions, they would have to blow some paths through the barbed wire along the top of the wall. Together, Captain George Graham Sinclair and Lieutenants William George Rogers Wedd and William Clark Patterson set about successfully doing this with Bangalore torpedoes.

However, the pillbox which had them in its sights continued to take casualties and hindered their progress, so Lieutenant Wedd took it upon himself to try and neutralise it. He climbed through a break in the wire caused by one of the Bangalore torpedoes and then rushed the pillbox through an onslaught of bullets and though hit several times, managed to reach the structure and throw a hand grenade through its fire slit. There was an explosion inside which must have killed or seriously wounded all of the occupants. Certainly, its guns did not fire again. Having achieved this remarkable feat of heroism, Lieutenant Wedd fell to the floor riddled with bullets.

Lieutenant Wedd was posthumously mentioned in despatches and was also posthumously awarded the Croix de Guerre. His actions were also recommended for the award of the Victoria Cross, although this did not transpire. A citation printed in the *Canada Gazette* on 9 February 1946 read: 'For gallantry of the highest order, Lieutenant Wedd gave his life at Dieppe in August 1942 when he advanced under intense fire through many obstacles to put a pillbox out of action.'

Meanwhile, a gap was made in the wire by Captain Sinclair, who before the war had been a lawyer in Toronto. The gap was near a flight of steps leading off the beach through a gully and Lance Corporal Leslie Ellis volunteered to slip through the gap and go up the steps and along the gully to scout ahead. Having successfully done this, he used the cover of the undergrowth to press on until he eventually reached the top of the hill. Here he came into contact with the enemy and engaged them with his rifle using the protection of what appeared to be a deserted sniper pit. He eventually withdrew and got safely back to the beach, to report that the gully was not a suitable route for the rest of the men to take as the Germans had it completely covered.

In the meantime, the second wave, which included the HQ Company with the commanding officer, Lieutenant Colonel Cato, had landed on the extreme right of the beach to the west of the sea wall under the cliffs. They were also met by heavy fire and immediately began to suffer losses. After considerable delay, for their Bangalore torpedoes had been lost, some of them, led by the colonel himself, cut a path through the wire, scaled the cliff and cleared the enemy out of some houses situated at the top.

They were only a small party of six officers and fifteen other ranks, some belonging to the Royal Canadian Artillery, including Captain G. A. Browne, who was there to act as forward observation officer. It was his job to radio coordinates to the destroyer HMS *Garth,* in order to direct their supporting fire onto enemy targets once identified. However, they soon found themselves cut off as the Germans had positioned a machine gun to cover the gap they had made in the wire. This meant that no one was able to pass up or down without being hit.

Back on the beach itself the well-fortified German forces were holding the remaining Canadian soldiers behind the sea wall. They were unable to move forward, or retreat to their landing craft. They were completely pinned down and the whole regiment was being slowly but surely annihilated, man by man.

Captain Browne of the Royal Canadian Artillery later described the situation facing the regiment:

Owing to the heavy and accurate fire of the enemy, the Royal Regiment of Canada was changed in five minutes from an assault battalion on the offensive to something less than two companies on the defensive, pinned down by fire from positions they could not discover. Notwithstanding this situation, the men followed their leaders smartly whenever they could and when, as was mostly the case, it was impossible to move, they lay still under the heavy fire of mortar bombs, watching for orders from their platoon and section commanders.

From his interview with *The Memory Project* of Historica Canada John Barron gives us a vivid understanding of how desperate the situation had become on Blue Beach behind the sea wall.

We made the final run in and everybody ran off the boat and there were very heavy casualties running up the beach. One man on the side of me was killed and then he just fell to the deck right to the sand or the gravel and I threw myself down and then things got a little bit hot, so I picked myself up and ran for the wall.

I was only able to fire my Bren gun and throw smoke grenades and hand grenades. But apart from that, I don't know that I ever hit anything. I just fired a lot of lead towards the shore, over the top of the wall and then sprayed bullets all over the place. So I imagine I hit something, I don't know what though. But I can't actually say that I really killed any enemy soldiers or anything, or did any real damage. I do know that my smoke grenades helped three of our chaps get back over the wall again. They had gone over and they were stuck there, so had to wait until the smoke came over and fortunately, I threw smoke in the right direction and they got back over because of it. So that did help in that respect. But apart from that, I don't think I did anything too much, really. Except take up space and fire a lot of lead.

Also on the beach sheltering behind the sea wall was Louis Pantaleo:

I landed with the anti-tank rifle. I got on the beach and I flopped on the beach in the prone position to fire the anti-tank rifle. And I couldn't hit anything. The clips were in the way. So I had to stand up to aim at the blockhouse that was on top of the cliff. ... apparently, I did some damage to the German morale.

David Mann was another soldier serving with The Royal Regiment of Canada at Puys. He provides us with further confirmation of the terrible scenes that took place on Blue Beach that day.

During the night, we went about halfway in the Channel on the mother ships and then put in the landing craft and went the rest of the way in the landing craft. We were supposed to land under the cover of darkness. But unfortunately, we were a bit later, the sun was up and the enemy seemed to be waiting for us. When we came out of the smoke, we were right in sight of the shore and the sun was up. And as soon as we came out of the smoke, of course, they started firing at us. The platoon I was with was the reserve platoon but the first thing I saw, really, there were three of us in the front position in the landing craft, lieutenant and his batman and I was the platoon runner. And, when we come out, we were, oh, awful close to the shore and they had dropped the ramp, the two fellows on either side of me, they made a mad jump and went in over their heads. I hesitated just long enough and when I jumped, I landed only up to my ankles in the water. And all hell broke loose.

There was very little beach. There was a sea wall and then a very steep cliff and that's what we were up against. And grenades and shell fire was just pouring at us. And you could see a whole line of people lined up in front of the sea wall just where they fell. They fell when they hit the beach actually, it was just like shooting fish in a barrel.

The group with Lieutenant Colonel Cato in charge moved westward along the cliff top, using the cover afforded by some trees and a wall. Their only hope now was to try and make contact with the Essex Scottish Regiment, which they hoped had by now been able to land on their beach and penetrate into Dieppe. It wasn't the Essex Scottish that they stumbled into but a strong enemy patrol, which they avoided by slipping into some woods near an anti-aircraft battery, where they took measure of their situation as the colonel decided what to do next.

Throughout the landings on Blue Beach the Royal Navy did their utmost to ease the situation using two support craft to give covering fire until their guns were silenced by enemy action. Further out to sea, the destroyer HMS *Garth* shelled the headland on the right flank, which was also attacked by cannon-firing Hawker Hurricanes of No. 32 Squadron.

It soon became apparent that the landing on Blue Beach and the mission of its troops had failed and all that was left to do was to try and rescue as many men from the beach as was possible. A succession of efforts was made to withdraw the troops with a number of landing craft going in under heavy fire. But the situation was almost hopeless. One landing craft, loaded with men, received a direct hit as it was moving out from the beach and capsized with all the men on board tumbling into the water. A number of them clung to the bottom of the craft and were later rescued by a daring effort on the part of another naval craft.

David Mann described what happened when the landing craft returned to try and evacuate some of the troops:

> They sent in two landing craft to pick up wounded and you wouldn't want to see what happened with that. One landed right by, I got hit right away and one landed right in front of me and I said to myself, "Am I bad enough to get on that?" because I could still manoeuvre. I said, "No, I'm not bad enough." And it didn't even stop, it just dropped them back right off again and the one over, about 100 yards over, it was a big crowd made a run for that one from under the shelter of the sea wall. And they ran out into the open and that you wouldn't want to see. They just opened up and gave it all they had and bodies in the water, a big red stain in the water and that only got out about fifty, 100 yards and it sunk. So there was no more attempts to pick up wounded.

Ultimately, the German fire proved too intense for the landing craft and those that survived were forced to move away leaving the men of the Royal Regiment of Canada to their fate. Any prospect of the regiment either capturing the Rommel battery or the headland was now impossible. Although the troops on Blue

Beach surrendered at around 11:00, the colonel's group managed to hold out in the woods on the hill until 16:20 in the afternoon.

According to John Barron, even the act of surrendering wasn't as straightforward as you might expect:

> We surrendered three times and the third time, we made it stick. It came from headquarters apparently and we just stood up and put our hands up in the air and that was it. That was the end of the battle for us. Although there were still a lot of bombs going off and shells being fired and so forth all around. But in our little corner, that was the end of it for us.

Louis Pantaleo also remembers surrendering and couldn't believe it after all the training they had done for this back in England:

> It was a general surrender and I was in that general surrender. Somebody, I don't know who it was, gave the order that we put our hands up and just surrender. And we did. And we walked off the beach. I couldn't believe my ears. I couldn't believe they were going to surrender. But I surrendered with the rest. All that training we had and … for a half hour of fighting. No, it was a very bitter pill to take.

Of the 556 men of The Royal Regiment of Canada who set out for Blue Beach at Puys, 200 were killed outright and 264 captured. The rest, by some miracle, managed to scramble into LCAs and make it off the beach before the boats finally withdrew. Another twenty-seven soldiers later died of their wounds. It was the heaviest toll suffered by a Canadian battalion in a single day during the entire Second World War. Their failure to clear the eastern headland would allow the Germans to continue to defend the Dieppe beaches with firepower from both sides and nullify the main frontal attack.

8

GREEN BEACH

While most of the Royal Regiment of Canada was being pinned down on Blue Beach behind the sea wall at Puys, the second inner flank attack to the west of Dieppe was being implemented by the South Saskatchewan Regiment, followed by the Queen's Own Cameron Highlanders of Canada. The objective of the South Saskatchewans was to land on Green Beach near the village of Pourville-sur-Mer, which sat at the mouth of the River Scie. They were to occupy this former fishing village (which had become a fashionable resort in north-west France prior to the war) then move quickly inland to seize another battery (Hindenburg battery), which consisted of captured French 75 mm guns now being employed by the Germans alongside their own light artillery pieces. They were also to take and hold a defensive position at Les-Quatre-Vents Farm, which the Germans were using as a temporary barracks, and to seize the headland overlooking Dieppe to the west. As well as this, they were to carry out a raid on a German coastal radar station that stood on top of the cliffs about halfway between Pourville-sur-Mer and Dieppe.

The South Saskatchewan Regiment under the command of Lieutenant Colonel Charles Cecil Ingersoll Merritt had sailed from Southampton aboard the infantry landing ships HMS *Invicta* and HMS *Princess Beatrix*. Charles Merritt, who would play an important role on Green Beach that day, was born in Vancouver in British Columbia in 1908. His father, Captain Cecil Mack Merritt, had been killed at the Second Battle of Ypres on 23 April 1915. He entered the Royal Military College of Canada at the age of sixteen and graduated with honours. He was commissioned into the Seaforth Highlanders of Canada (a Militia regiment) in 1929. Merritt read for the Bar and became a barrister in 1932 and practised law in Vancouver until he was mobilised at the outbreak of the war, when he was promoted to the rank of major. In December 1939, he sailed for England. In the next two years he held a variety of staff and regimental appointments and attended the war staff course at Camberley in June 1941. From GSO2 of the 3rd Canadian Division, in March 1942, he was promoted to command the South Saskatchewan Regiment barely two months before they moved to the Isle of Wight to train for the Dieppe raid. The brevity of his time with the regiment would not hinder his remarkable leadership skills on and around Green Beach.

The Queen's Own Cameron Highlanders of Canada, under Lieutenant Colonel Alfred Gosling, had arrived directly from Newhaven aboard their LCPs. Tragically, Alfred Gosling, as will be seen, did not have a chance to make the same type of impact on his regiment that Merritt would make on his.

The South Saskatchewans arrived aboard their landing ships to a point somewhere off their destination beach undetected and uninterrupted by enemy activity, which enabled the men to climb over the sides of the ships, down the netting and into their assault landing craft ready to make their final approach to Green Beach. The first of them landed successfully on the shingle at Pourville-sur-Mer at 04:52, which was five minutes behind schedule. Although they didn't encounter quite the severe levels of opposition when they reached Green Beach that the Royal Regiment of Canada had done at Puys, they still approached the shore under dogged enemy fire.

Serving with the South Saskatchewan Regiment on Green Beach that day was Paul Henry DeLorme:

> I experienced two grenade explosions, one on the ship going to Dieppe and quite a few boys got killed from this grenade. I was lucky to just get some shrapnel through my mouth. I was able to just spit the shrapnel out but I had a big lip the rest of the time when I landed at Dieppe. We (The South Saskatchewan Regiment) landed at Dieppe at a little village called Pourville-sur-Mer, about three miles south of Dieppe. The Germans, by this time, they were all over the place and we never made it back.

Some of the landing craft had drifted slightly to the west of where they should have been because of the strong tide, which meant that they came ashore at the wrong spot. It was only a matter of a few hundred yards, but it would make a huge difference because they had landed on the wrong side of the River Scie and would have to cross the river from west to east by the closest available bridge before they could even begin to carry out any of their tasks.

It was the job of A Company of the South Saskatchewan Regiment to capture the all-important headland to the west of Dieppe and destroy the Hindenburg battery, while a small detachment would slip away to make their attack on the radar site. Thankfully, A Company had landed on the correct side of the River Scie on the beach to the east of Pourville-sur-Mer. Here, similar to Puys, they were faced by a low sea wall at the top of the beach that was crowned by barbed wire. Luckily, they were not subjected to the ferocity of enemy fire experienced at the former. Because of this they were at least able to move up the beach in numbers and were soon able to scale the wall and its barbed wire by using the tubular ladders they had brought with them.

Having tackled the sea wall, A Company was in a position to proceed towards the high ground in order to attack the battery and protect the main assault on Dieppe. The Germans had other ideas and had the whole area well covered with pillboxes, the inhabitants of which were firing their machine guns relentlessly at the invaders. Following the training they had undergone in England, the men soon dealt with the initial couple of pillboxes in a rapid and professional manner, allowing them to continue their advance up the hill.

Their next obstacle was a natural one as they became slightly bogged down in an area of marshland, but they were soon able to move around this without taking too much of a detour and continued on their correct route under the cover of a smoke screen. Then at around 06:00 they found themselves halted by fire from a German roadblock in the form of further pillboxes, which waited for them up ahead and which proved to be a much more serious hindrance than either of the pillboxes already dealt with, or the marshland. Because of the terrain and the clever positioning of the enemy defences they were unable to outflank the German positions and had effectively come to a halt.

Very heavy fighting ensued as A Company attempted to get around the enemy position and special mention is made of Private Charles Edward Sawden, who rushed one of the pillboxes and single-handedly put it out of action while killing all six of its German occupants. Sawden, a Yorkshireman from Bridlington who had emigrated to Canada, paid for this achievement with his life.

About forty minutes after the South Saskatchewan Regiment had landed, a subsequent wave of assault craft carrying the Queen's Own Cameron Highlanders of Canada swept on to Green Beach. It was broad daylight by now and as the wooden LCPs came thundering up to the shingle, Pipe Major Alex Graham was playing *The Hundred Pipers* on a small forward deck of a landing craft to spur his comrades on and continued to do so during the entire landing process. Again, most of the craft landed on the wrong side of the river. (*The Hundred Pipers* is a Scottish song and jig attributed to Lady Carolina Nairne and popularised from 1852 onwards. It takes as its theme events during and after the Jacobite Rising of 1745, so could stir the blood of the Scots and their Canadian descendants. It was also the official march of the regiment's B Company.)

When the Queen's Own Cameron Highlanders of Canada came ashore they were met by a great volume of fire from an already stirred up enemy and suffered a tragic misfortune at the very outset of the battle, as their commanding officer, Lieutenant Colonel Alfred Gosling, was killed as he jumped on to the beach from the LCP. He was hit in the head by a bullet, becoming the battalion's first casualty. Under their second in command, Major Andrew Thompson Law, the regiment moved briskly forward into Pourville-sur-Mer to continue with their objective, which was to capture an enemy airfield a few miles inland at Saint-Aubin-sur-Scie and destroy its facilities, thus preventing it from being used as a forward operating base by the Luftwaffe to attack Allied ships in the Channel.

While the Camerons were coming ashore and A Company of the South Saskatchewans were striving to meet their objectives, B and D Companies of the regiment, who had landed on the wrong side of the River Scie, had to somehow make good their attack on Les-Quatre-Vents Farm by first crossing the river. They marched into the western half of Pourville-sur-Mer heading for the nearest bridge, which was clearly marked on their maps.

However, on reaching the bridge, the South Saskatchewans discovered that the German defenders who were now alerted to their presence had reinforced it with machine guns, mortars and anti-tank guns. The Canadians attempted to cross the bridge but were stopped dead in their tracks as the Germans opened up with everything they had. Their advance had come to a grinding halt.

Theodore Jack Bennett was a signaller in the South Saskatchewan Regiment working in Lieutenant Colonel Merritt's headquarters company. He recalls the time between their landing and reaching the bridge in Pourville-sur-Mer.

We were supposed to come into Pourville beach, Green Beach. There was a river down there, a bridge across the river, the River Scie. And they landed us, the Navy landed us all on the wrong side of the river and it was supposed to be a 50-50 split. And that's where the thing was, we couldn't get across the river, we couldn't get across the bridge. It's the unknown. Sure, you're scared. But you know it's got to be done, discipline, that kind of stuff. But inside you're scared.

We got in and landed and ran right up the beach, slogging in those doggone stones. We got to the far wall. And fire was opened up against us and over the far wall, and we were told to get up into the town. And we got up and there was a spot that was vacant. I'd say it used to be a garden, but there was just grass and that, and they set up headquarters there.

It's just gleaming light and I ran up that beach, right up to the wall, before the first shots were fired. Then they started being fired. But we got up and we got inside, and we were at regimental headquarters. And we're squatted down and I'm trying to get headquarters (on the radio), but couldn't get anything. And suddenly, *wham*! And the next thing I know I'm laying on my back, I got dirt all over me, and there's cries, and just cries and groans and moans and everything else.

I looked at Henderson. He was there and he's down on his face with a pool of blood under his face about darn near as big as a dinner plate. I said, "Where are you hit?" He said, "In the face, in the eye." And I looked over at Keith Marsh and he was lying back on the radio set and he coughed once and coughed up blood, so I knew he was in trouble. So I went to him (Henderson) first because Henderson was able to talk and Marsh was dead, four feet away. And Henderson and I got out my dressing, which I wasn't supposed to do, but he's lying down on his face, so I got out my first field dressing and I gave it to him, and he said, "Are you in communication?" And I said, "No." He said, "I'll put this on myself, you get into communication."

Well, there's an officer behind me, what is he called? Anyway, the different regiments had an officer that they worked together, type of thing, they had to do. And, anyway, I turned there and I said, "Where are you hit, sir?" He said, "In the back." I said, "I'll turn you over, I'll see what I can do." And he said, "Don't touch me, I can't feel my legs and my back's broken, I think. Call for a stretcher bearer." So I start yelling, "Stretcher bearer! Stretcher bearer!"

I looked around and I found the piece of my antenna that had been sheared off. I pulled the old piece out and I took the thing off and I had a couple of spares, and I got it working again but still nothing from headquarters at all.

Just then Colonel Merritt came along and looked around and he said, "We've got to separate you guys." And he said to Henderson, "Can you still work a set?" and Henderson said, "Yes, sir. I can work the set." And he said to me, "You, Sigs, (Signaller) you come with me." That's when I started to follow him around.

We got to one place and he said, "We've got to get across that bridge. You stay here." Thank God. I think I'm here today because he told me to stay there. He went out and he went on that bridge and tried to get guys across, and by God the boys were trying and it was just a slaughter. Just a slaughter.

With the battalion's dead and wounded piling up on the bridge, Lieutenant Colonel Merritt, the commanding officer, attempted to give the attack impetus by repeatedly crossing the bridge himself, in order to demonstrate that it was feasible to do so. Apparently, he took off his steel helmet and while nonchalantly swinging it by his side crossed and re-crossed the bridge four times under fire from what must have been a very confused enemy and didn't get a scratch.

It did the trick and with renewed purpose the men around him eventually fought their way over the bridge, with some swimming across the river or using makeshift rafts to bear down on the enemy from the rear. So having finally cleared the bridge, B and D Companies of the South Saskatchewan Regiment under Merritt could now continue with the next part of their plan, which was to capture the temporary barracks at Les-Quatre-Vents Farm.

The approach to the farm was covered by several pillboxes that would have to be dealt with first. Small groups were detailed to tackle each of these in turn with Lieutenant Colonel Merritt taking charge of a number of the subsequent attacks himself, while one of the assaults was led by Major McTavish. All of the pillboxes were eventually captured and special mention is made of the bravery of one Private Oliver Fenner, who apparently – possibly inspired by Merritt's earlier antics on the bridge – walked coolly up to a number of enemy positions firing a Bren gun from his hip like a movie star. German prisoners were now mounting up and sections of men were detailed to watch them and in due course escort them back to the beach for evacuation to England for interrogation.

As the attack on the farm continued, the Queen's Own Cameron Highlanders of Canada had their own objective: to attack, capture and destroy the airfield a few miles inland at Saint-Aubin-sur-Scie. From Pourville-sur-Mer they pushed down the valley of the River Scie but since Les-Quatre-Vents Farm was still under attack by Lieutenant Colonel Merritt and his men, they decided to stick to the west side of the river to avoid becoming caught up in any crossfire around the farmhouse. They pushed on through woods towards their objective, some three and a half miles from the coast.

Meanwhile to the east of Pourville-sur-Mer, a small detachment of eleven men from A Company of the South Saskatchewan Regiment had slipped away from the main group that was still pinned down by the German road block to carry out their own mission, which was to gain access to a German radar station on the cliffs. Having located the site, they were to capture and interrogate its occupants, in an attempt to discover more about the performance capability of the German radar setup.

This was a Freya radar station, operating a system that was named after the Norse Goddess Freyja. During the course of the Second World War, over a thousand of these sites were constructed. At this point in the war the Freya radar system was definitely more advanced than its British counterpart, Chain Home. It had a much smaller antenna system, one that was easier to rotate, move and position, and it also offered higher resolution, allowing it to detect smaller targets.

In order to understand the internal workings of this radar site and to interrogate its technicians, the Canadian section was accompanied by a British radar specialist. This was Flight Sergeant Jack Nissenthall of the Royal Air Force, who had worked extensively with British RDF and knew its capabilities inside out. It was thought that he would be able to apply his own understanding and knowledge of the subject while examining the enemy's equipment and while interrogating its operatives.

Jack Nissenthall was born in Bow, London, in 1919, and was the son of Jewish immigrants. From an early age he had shown a great interest and aptitude in electronics and wireless and took a position with EMI in 1935 at the age of sixteen, firstly at the EMI factory in Hayes, Hillingdon, and then at their main retail outlet in Tottenham Court Road. At the same time, he was enrolled at the Regent Street Polytechnic studying advanced electronics. In 1936, Jack was effectively headhunted by the RAF and given an apprenticeship, which involved him working during his free time at the experimental radar station at Bawdsey Manor in Suffolk, thus involving him at a critical period in the developing work of Robert Watson-Watt, the pioneer of RDF (Radio Direction Finding), which later became known as radar.

On the outbreak of war, he volunteered for service in the RAF but his request for flight duties was refused and instead he was posted to RAF Yatesbury where he was assigned to the first RDF training school in Britain. Thereafter, he was posted to various radar installations across the country. His skills and his abilities were increasingly being recognised by higher authority, as indicated by his suggestions for technical improvement of equipment being regularly accepted without question. By early 1942, with the rank of sergeant, he was stationed at Hope Cove in Devon, where he had been instrumental in establishing a pioneering ground-control intercept (GCI) facility.

Since being rejected for aircrew service due to the value of his technical knowledge Nissenthall made it known that he was prepared to be involved in special assignments where his knowledge would be of use. He would often give up his leave to pursue further training, including taking the commando course. In early 1942 Nissenthall was ordered to report in person for an interview at Combined Operations headquarters in Whitehall, where he met Air Commodore Victor Tait, who was RAF Director of Signals and Radar, and was asked to volunteer for a dangerous assignment.

Nissenthall volunteered to take part at Dieppe even though he was apparently made aware that because of his own sensitive knowledge of Allied radar technology, which the Germans would be keen to ascertain, his Canadian bodyguards were under strict orders to kill him if it seemed likely that he would be captured at any point. As a secondary measure, Nissenthall was himself issued with a cyanide pill to take as a last resort, if he was threatened with capture and his bodyguards were already dead themselves.

After the war, Lord Mountbatten claimed to author James Leasor, when being interviewed during research for the book *Green Beach,* that if he had been aware of the orders given to the escort to shoot him rather than let him be captured, he would have cancelled them immediately. If he had been captured Nissenthall would have been very badly treated by the Nazis as he was a Jew and he apparently refused to remove his Jewish identity discs, wishing to live and die with the sign of his people.

As it turned out, the radar station was much more heavily defended than anticipated, so none of the group actually managed to gain access to it. The best Nissenthall could do was to crawl up to the rear of the station under enemy fire and cut all the telephone wires leading to it. This forced the crew inside to resort to using radio transmissions to talk to their commanders. These transmissions were subsequently intercepted by listening posts on the south coast of England. Owing to this single act, the Allies were able to learn a great deal about the location and density of German radar stations along the Channel coast, all of which helped to convince Allied commanders of the importance of further developing radar jamming technology.

Of the small unit that set out for the radar site, only Nissenthall himself and one other would make it safely back to England. Because of the nature of his task at Dieppe and despite his extreme bravery, he received no official recognition for his part in the operation, or awards. He did, however, become part of the team set up to work on radar jamming technology and in that way contributed to the Allied victory in no small measure.

In spite of the courage shown by the South Saskatchewans and their success in neutralising pillboxes, their progress had been slow on all fronts. This was partially due to the earlier error when landing on the wrong section of beach but also because of the heavy resistance they met from the enemy. It was apparent that the overall operation was not going according to plan as the troops of A Company, having taken the headland, were supposed to link up with Churchill tanks arriving from Dieppe. However, because of the heavy resistance they were experiencing around the roadblock they were unable to complete their allotted task and capture the high ground and no tanks arrived over the horizon to come to their rescue.

When the signal came to say it was time to withdraw back to the beach, A Company had not put the Hindenburg battery out of action or taken the headland; B and D Company's had not captured Les-Quatre-Vents Farm and its garrison; and the Queen's Own Cameron Highlanders of Canada had not reached their target airfield at Saint-Aubin-sur-Scie. While the Camerons did manage to penetrate further inland than any other troops that day, they were also soon forced back as German reinforcements rushed to the scene. None of the objectives in the Green Beach sector had been achieved.

For seven hours, the South Saskatchewan Regiment found themselves embroiled in very heavy fighting and accounted for very many of the enemy. However, the German mortar fire was incredibly accurate and well maintained, causing them grave concerns during their withdrawal. On the way back to the beach some of the men were also picked off by German snipers. These were well-trained, dedicated individuals, who were cool enough to lie quiet until the Canadians had passed them and then swing round to open fire on them from the rear.

During the withdrawal, losses were particularly heavy in C Company of the South Saskatchewan Regiment, which formed the rearguard because their positions were vulnerable to German fire bearing down from the headland, which their comrades had failed to take. Thus the enemy was able to dominate not only the village of Pourville-sur-Mer itself, but also the beach from which the withdrawal would have to take place. They also had the slopes to the east covered, down which the remnants of the South Saskatchewan Regiment would have to come in order to be evacuated.

During the continued evacuation, casualties were carried down and placed under the cover of the sea wall, their movement being directed by the beach master, Lieutenant Commander Redvers Michael Prior DSO RN and the assistant beach master, Lieutenant R. D. Millar RNVR, both of whom showed utter disregard for their own safety and both of whom were wounded. At 10:45, landing craft came up to the beach to take off the troops. They were met with heavy mortar fire, and one was hit and capsized.

Others, however, took men on board and cleared the beach successfully, and later a second wave of landing craft appeared and attempted to do the same. In order to reach them, the soldiers would have to cross around 200 yards of open ground and then wade or swim through 150 yards of water, while under enemy fire. The state of the tide made it impossible for the craft to come any closer to the shore without the risk of being stranded.

Don Wolfe served with the Queen's Own Cameron Highlanders provided an account of what happened to him that day while trying to make it back to the landing craft:

We went to England in 1940. My first battle was 18-19 August 1942, which was the Dieppe raid. They won't admit it, but to me, it was suicidal. How I got back, I'll never know because what happened was this. I tried to swim with my army boots and my gaiters and I couldn't kick to stay afloat. So what I did, I had to go up and down in about eight feet of water, because they (the Germans) had machine guns firing on the water... I went up and down until I got my shoes off. Once I got my shoes and my gaiters off, then I swam out in the Channel and they picked me up with a landing craft. So this is how I survived the Dieppe raid.

But as far as I was concerned, it was suicidal. You should have seen it. They (the Germans) were waiting for us on the breakwater. So as soon as we got off the landing craft, boy, it was murder. Like I said, when we landed at Dieppe, there was a town on the right-hand side of Dieppe they called Pourville. Now, Pourville, that's where we landed. So my battalion or my brigade, the 6th Canadian Infantry Brigade and the 2nd Canadian Infantry Division, we went in the farthest of anybody.

Heavy losses were incurred over that open stretch of sand and water. The work of the stretcher bearers at this time was very gallant, as was the conduct of Captain W. A. Hayter, the Medical Officer of the South Saskatchewans who had established three Regimental Aid Posts. He moved from one to another as the opportunity arose or necessity directed, until he too became a casualty.

At about 11:30 Lieutenant Colonel Merritt and Major Claude Orme collected some men and attacked some machine guns to the west of the beach, silencing their fire. By noon, most of the troops had been re-embarked and only a few remained. These were formed into a rear guard and held the perimeter under the command of Lieutenant Colonel Merritt, aided by Lieutenant Commander Prior.

Theodore Jack Bennett, the signaller in the South Saskatchewan Regiment, recalls Lieutenant Colonel Merritt's continued coolness in face of the enemy:

He (Merritt) came back and we got the news that the Queen's Own Cameron Highlanders of Canada couldn't complete their thing and they were coming back to us. So Colonel Merritt gave orders, "We'll hold the perimeter of the town until they get back." And that's what we did, and we were going along from place to place. And then the Camerons came through us and then Merritt started to yell, "Every man for himself! Pass it on – every many for himself! Get back to the beach! Not you Sigs, you stay with me."

So Henderson and I stayed with him and he had two guys, bodyguards, and we worked our way slowly back to the beach. We crossed the beach. It was a funny thing, there were some houses. There were about six of them, but they were all joined together and in-between their front lawns were stone walls. And we got in there and then there was the road, and then there was the sea wall down to the beach.

And there was a sniper up the east way from us. You could hear the guys calling, "Can you see him? Where is he?" And they couldn't see him and that, and Colonel Merritt said to me, "Are you in communication?" I said, "I can't get a thing, sir." He said, "Get out in the open and try." Now, the only open was the road. And it's funny how your mind goes. I figured sure I was going to get shot and I thought I'm not going to get shot in the back. I turned and faced the direction where the sniper was, and I had time to press the button and say, "Hello Southam, hello." *Whack*! And he shot my antenna off right here, above my ear. And I flopped, grabbed the broken thing... I guess I looked stupid, but I said to Merritt, "I couldn't get through." He gave me a big smile and said, "Nice try Sigs, close it down." So we closed it down.

So he said, "We'll wait until everybody's over and then we'll go." And he wouldn't go back to the beach until there were no more guys running across that road. He wouldn't desert his men. And then he said, "Okay, this is it. Spread out, run like hell, get over the fire, the sea wall." So away we went.

Well, I got this brand-new wireless set and so I ran right down into the Channel and I was in about my waist and then I took the thing apart. It was easy to get apart, I threw the radio part over here, threw the battery pack in another direction, threw the microphone another way, and threw the earphones another way.

Just then a couple of landing craft came in and they weren't making it to the beach, but they were picking guys up. So I went swimming out and that was bad. You'd see a head beside you and it would go down, and a patch of red would come up. There's not a thing you could do. And anyway, I got about fifteen feet from the blessed boat and I'm waving and yelling and they turned away. I had to come back. And I swam back and I was just about beat. And I can remember staggering up the beach. The next thing I knew, I hear a voice say, "Don't try and give him any water, he's water-logged!" And I came around and I'm laying huddled right up beside a guy from the SSR. And I said, "Jeez, how did I get here?" He said, "I pulled you in, you were out like a light." So I thanked him very much. We were behind a rock. That dang rock had more bullets bounced off it than you could shake a stick at.

Lieutenant Colonel Merritt and a few other men continued to hold the perimeter until their ammunition was exhausted and they were forced to surrender at about 15:00, but their action had enabled many men to be taken off who would have otherwise remained behind and been taken prisoner. They lived to fight another day.

For his exemplary leadership and valour that day Lieutenant Colonel Merritt was awarded the Victoria Cross. His citation in *The London Gazette* on 2 October 1942 included the following:

From the point of landing, his unit's advance had to be made across a bridge in Pourville which was swept by very heavy machine gun, mortar and artillery fire: the first parties were mostly destroyed and the bridge thickly covered by their bodies. A daring lead was required; waving his helmet, Lieutenant Colonel Merritt rushed forward shouting "Come on over! There's nothing to worry about here."

He thus personally led the survivors of at least four parties in turn across the bridge. Quickly organising these, he led them forward and when held by enemy pillboxes he again headed rushes which succeeded in clearing them. In one case he himself destroyed the occupants of the post by throwing grenades into it. After several of his runners became casualties, he himself kept contact with his different positions.

Although twice wounded Lieutenant Colonel Merritt continued to direct the unit's operations with great vigour and determination and while organising the withdrawal he stalked a sniper with a Bren gun and silenced him. He then coolly gave orders for the departure and announced his intention to hold off and 'get even with' the enemy. When last seen he was collecting Bren and Tommy guns and preparing a defensive position which successfully covered the withdrawal from the beach.

Lieutenant Colonel Merritt is now reported to be a Prisoner of War. To this Commanding Officer's personal daring, the success of his unit's operations and the safe re-embarkation of a large portion of it were chiefly due.

Throughout both the initial assault and the evacuation of Green Beach, covering fire had been provided at frequent intervals by the Royal Navy and many attacks were made by squadrons of the RAF against enemy positions on the high ground. The fire of HMS *Brocklesby* was also very effective during the withdrawal and her guns silenced some of the numerous machine gun and mortar positions which by then had been brought into play. All of this was of considerable help during the extraction of the troops and many men were rescued. Unfortunately, the RAF by now were unable to help out on Green Beach as they were fully engaged over Dieppe to support the main beaches in front of the town, and Green Beach had come under fire from increasing numbers of German bombers, some of which were armed with flame thrower equipment.

Despite the bravery and dedication of Lieutenant Colonel Merritt and his rear party, the death toll on Green Beach was devastatingly high. In just a few short hours, eighty-four men of the South Saskatchewan Regiment and seventy-six of the Queen's Own Cameron Highlanders lost their lives. Their sacrifice is commemorated on the Pourville Memorial.

9

WHITE AND RED BEACHES

The principal reasons for all of the preliminary landings we have so far described on Yellow, Orange, Blue and Green beaches was to neutralise the fire of all the various enemy batteries around Dieppe, to enable the main assault on the town and harbour to go ahead as smoothly as possible. If these objectives had been realised it would of course also mean that the Allied forces would now hold the headlands to both the west and east of Dieppe. This situation would mean that the Allies would dominate the area and any remaining enemy forces would be trapped down in the town itself. They would have captured or silenced all known enemy positions circling the town, as well as the barracks from which reinforcements could be supplied and the nearest airfield and radar site. This would leave the enemy still capable of mounting a defence, but their movements would be severely restricted to within the confines of the town itself.

Of course, none of this had actually happened and although Lord Lovat and No. 4 Commando had successfully taken out the Hess battery at Varengeville-sur-Mer, all of the others, Goebbels battery at Berneval-le-Grand, Rommel battery at Puys, and

Hindenburg battery at Pourville-sur-Mer, remained in operation. More alarmingly, the Germans still held both of the headlands where there were numerous other gun positions. What this meant was that when the main forces came ashore, the troops and the vessels escorting them would be at the mercy of the defenders who would be looking directly down on them from all vantage points.

In view of this unfolding scenario you would think that those in charge on the ground would have considered abandoning the whole mission, or at least rethinking it. It must have been obvious at this point that it was doomed to failure. Nevertheless, the attacks went ahead as planned, as it seems that Major General Roberts and his staff on the headquarters ship HMS *Calpe* were not made fully aware of the situation, either through confused reporting or the complete failure of communications systems. We saw in the last chapter, for instance, how the signallers of the South Saskatchewan Regiment were unable to raise anybody on their radio sets. There might also have been cases of false reporting, with the Germans themselves possibly feeding the Allies incorrect information. This is hinted at by Captain Hughes-Hallett, the naval force commander when talking about the situation on Blue Beach in the supplement he provided to *The London Gazette*:

At about 05:30 I was informed that a signal had been received stating that no landing had taken place on Blue Beach, and I reported this in my situation report made at 06:12. Actually there is some reason to suppose that this report was of German origin but the whole of the events that took place ashore at Blue Beach were obscure, although it was clear from the very outset that the troops were held up.

The main thrust to capture both the town of Dieppe and its harbour was to be made by the Essex Scottish Regiment and the Royal Hamilton Light Infantry. The Essex Scottish under the command of Lieutenant Colonel Frederick (Fred) K. Jasperson would land on Red Beach to the east and the Hamilton's under Lieutenant Colonel Robert (Bob) Ridley Labatt, on White Beach to the west. Both of these, which were effectively stretches of the same beach, sat just to the west of the main piers at the entrance to the harbour. It was the task of these two regiments to seize the beaches, thus enabling the tanks to land and push through the town. They would then hold their positions while the specialist teams came ashore to carry out the demolition of the port and other facilities.

At the point where the Canadians were to land, the beach was roughly 1,700 yards long between the west breakwater of the harbour to the east, and cliffs to the west upon which nestled the Vieux Chateau, an imposing castle dating from around 1188. This had commanding views of the coast and Channel and had previously been used as a barracks by the French. The Germans had taken it over to use as their headquarters in the area. Although the defence of the wider area was that of *Generalleutnant* Konrad Haase and the 302nd Static Infantry Division, the town itself was the responsibility of *Oberstleutnant* (Lieutenant Colonel) Hermann Bartelt, and from the chateau he could control the actions of roughly 1,500 troops.

On 20 July 1942, Haase had issued an order which demanded 'the highest degree of watchfulness and readiness for action'. This was to be of particular importance during three periods of what were considered to be favourable tide and moon for the Allies; 27 July to 3 August; 10 August to 19 August; and 25 August to 1 September. The Germans evidently knew a raid was coming at some point, so Bartelt would have been mindful to make sure his men and defences were at the ready at these identified periods of opportunity.

The Germans had also fortified many of the other buildings along the seafront in preparation for this suspected attack. For instance, they were occupying the resort's casino, which was another substantial building that stood close to the seafront and which had been particularly heavily defended by them. Many of these buildings had been armed with various calibres of guns sitting in concrete emplacements.

At the back of the beach there was a sea wall, beyond which was a promenade with a seafront road called the Boulevard Marechal Foch. Between the boulevard and the town was an esplanade containing grass and ornamental gardens, on the other side of which ran the Boulevard de Verdun. All of this is still there today and the green area between the two boulevards is called The Esplanade de Dieppe. In 1942, the sea wall and the garden areas would have been covered in barbed wire and other obstacles. The seafront houses and hotels really begin along the other side of the Boulevard de Verdun and the Germans had occupied and fortified all of these. These buildings formed a defensive line so that any troops making it off the beach and onto the esplanade would be caught in the open and subject to fire from these defended properties, with guns having overlapping arcs of fire designed to cover every possible approach. Openings into narrow streets were blocked by tank obstacles, often large concrete blocks similar to the dragon's teeth that had been established all around the south coast of England to hinder the progress of German tanks if the Wehrmacht had attempted an invasion of Great Britain in 1940. Behind these tank obstacles were well placed anti-tank guns and their crews.

Part of the Essex Scottish Regiment had sailed out of Southampton on HMS *Prince Leopold*, the remainder setting off from Portsmouth aboard HMS *Prince Charles*. The Royal Hamilton Light Infantry sailed from Southampton aboard HMS *Glengyle*. Once in position off the coast of France the troops boarded their LCAs that had been lowered into the water from davits, which were like small cranes. The two regiments assaulted their respective beaches simultaneously as planned, with the Essex Scottish hitting Red Beach to the east and the Hamiltons on White beach to the west.

To coincide with the landing of the LCAs, the destroyers out at sea put down a short but intense bombardment directed at the buildings suspected to be housing German defenders, especially those along the Boulevard de Verdun, which was effectively the German front line. However, it was a very short bombardment and as the ships ceased firing, around sixty Supermarine Spitfires and Hawker Hurricanes flew over the beach to fire cannon shells into the same buildings. At the same time, squadrons of Douglas Bostons and Bristol Blenheims appeared over the eastern headland to lay a smoke screen. This temporarily shielded the troops coming ashore and smothered the town and harbour with a cloud of thick smoke.

Close fire support for the assault landing craft as they approached the beach was provided by motor gun boats and other assorted craft, which accompanied them as far into the shore as was possible, all the time under intense attack from enemy positions on the seafront, cliffs and caves in the headland to the east. These caves, which as previously noted had not been identified by Allied reconnaissance, hid guns of varied calibre, some quite considerable. There were anti-tank guns and machine guns that could be wheeled out of the caves in the cliff face and because they had not been identified, they had not been attacked by either the Naval or RAF bombardments, so they were completely intact, and in some ways proved to be the death knell for the entire operation.

For the MGBs and other small craft escorting the LCAs, this was a very hazardous undertaking, but they fired back at the enemy with considerable effect. All of these supporting vessels

Right: 1. A proud Canadian soldier: Sergeant Maurice Snook in the dress uniform of The Essex Scottish Regiment in 1937. Like all of the Canadians at Dieppe, he was a professional soldier before the war as conscription was not introduced until later. His regiment would land on Red Beach. (Photo: courtesy of Historica Canada/ Maurice Snook)

Below: 2. Don Wolfe (far right), heading to Halifax in Nova Scotia with other members of the Queen's Own Cameron Highlanders of Canada in 1940, where they would catch a ship to England. Two years later they would land on Green Beach at Pourville-sur-Mer. (Photo: courtesy of Historica Canada/Don Wolfe)

3. Jack McFarland who served with the Royal Hamilton Light Infantry is pictured here during training in England, circa 1940. His regiment would land on White Beach and he would be involved with the fierce fighting around the casino. (Photo: courtesy of Historica Canada/Jack McFarland)

4. Canadian troops exercising with landing craft on the Isle of Wight prior to the raid. (Creative Commons Attribution 4.0 International licence. Attribution: Department of National Defence Library and Archives Canada PA-113243)

5. Personnel of the Royal Canadian Army Medical Corps during a training exercise in England before the raid. (Creative Commons Attribution 4.0 International licence. Attribution: Department of National Defence Library and Archives Canada PA-113242)

6. This photograph is believed to show soldiers of the Queen's Own Cameron Highlanders of Canada in the act of going ashore during the raid, heading for Green Beach at Pourville-sur-Mer. (Creative Commons Attribution 4.0 International licence. Attribution: Department of National Defence Library and Archives Canada PA-113245)

7. A German MG34 medium machine gun emplacement at Dieppe in August 1942. (Creative Commons Attribution-Share Alike 3.0 Germany licence. Attribution: Bundesarchiv, Bild 101l-291-1213-34/Muller, Karl/CC-BY-SA 3.0)

8. In the foreground of this photograph taken at Puys you can clearly see the remains of a German gun emplacement which had the beach here completely covered by its fire. It was here on Blue Beach that the Royal Regiment of Canada landed and a monument at the bottom right of the picture has a plaque containing the words: 'On this beach officers and men of the Royal Regiment of Canada died at Dawn 19 August 1942 striving to reach the heights beyond. (Photograph copyright Christine und Hagen Graf/reproduced under the terms of the Creative Commons 2.0 Generic Licence)

9. This photograph shows some of the naval craft that took part in Operation *Jubilee* with MGB 321 nearest the camera. (Creative Commons Attribution 4.0 International licence. Attribution: Department of National Defence Library and Archives Canada PA-171080)

10. A Dingo scout car is seen abandoned on Dieppe beach immediately following the raid. Note how the vehicle's wheels have sunk into the chert. (Creative Commons Attribution-Share Alike 3.0 Germany licence. Attribution: Bundesarchiv, Bild 101l-362-2211-04/ Jorgensen/CC-BY-SA 3.0)

11. The bodies of Canadian dead who had served with the Royal Regiment of Canada on Blue Beach can be seen behind the sea wall at Puys. You can see the slit of a German gun emplacement to the centre left of the picture, from where it would have been able to shoot all along the wall. (Creative Commons Attribution-Share Alike 3.0 Germany licence. Attribution: Bundesarchiv, Bild 101l-291-1230-13/Meyer; Wiltberger/CC-BY-SA 3.0)

12. A landing craft is on fire on Dieppe's main beach with the bodies of dead Canadian soldiers in the foreground. To the right of the picture you can see one of the concrete gun emplacements that covered the beach with its fire. (Creative Commons Attribution-Share Alike 3.0 Germany licence. Attribution: Bundesarchiv, Bild 101l-291-1229-12/Meyer; Wiltberger/CC-BY-SA 3.0)

13. Canadian wounded lie on the beach in front of an abandoned Churchill tank after the raid. A landing craft is on fire in the background. (Creative Commons Attribution-Share Alike 3.0 Germany licence. Attribution: Bundesarchiv, Bild 101l-291-1205-14/Koll/ CC-BY-SA 3.0)

14. A Douglas Boston aircraft of the RAF taking part in Operation *Jubilee*. Their main role was to put down smoke screens. (Creative Commons Attribution 4.0 International licence. Attribution: Department of National Defence Library and Archives Canada PA-183771)

15. Paul Dumaine, who served at Dieppe with Les Fusiliers Mont-Royal, painted this representation of the raid in 1944, while he was a prisoner of war. (Photo: courtesy of Historica Canada/Paul Dumaine)

16. Two landing craft mechanised pictured next to one of the destroyers shortly after the raid. The one on the right is LCM2, which is empty of its troops. The one on the left still has a Bren Gun carrier and men on board and it is unclear whether these men didn't make it to the beaches or have been evacuated.

17. German troops examine one of the abandoned Churchill tanks of the 14th Canadian Tank Regiment that managed to make it off the beach and into Dieppe. (Creative Commons Attribution 4.0 International licence. Attribution: Department of National Defence Library and Archives Canada C-029878)

Left: 18. A Canadian soldier is seen here with a captured German soldier in England following the raid. (Creative Commons Attribution 4.0 International licence. Attribution: Department of National Defence Library and Archives Canada PA-210156)

Below: 19. British Commandos who took part in the raid returning to England on its conclusion. (Creative Commons Attribution 4.0 International licence. Attribution: Department of National Defence Library and Archives Canada PA-183776)

20. Bedraggled Canadian soldiers who took part in the raid following their return. (Creative Commons Attribution 4.0 International licence. Attribution: Department of National Defence Library and Archives Canada PA-183775)

21. Lord Lovat (left) is pictured with some of his men from No. 4 Commando after the raid. (Creative Commons Attribution 4.0 International licence. Attribution: Department of National Defence Library and Archives Canada PA-183766)

22. Wounded soldiers being evacuated after the raid. (Creative Commons Attribution 4.0 International licence. Attribution: Department of National Defence Library and Archives Canada e010869432)

23. Soldiers who took part in the raid on Dieppe, disembarking from a Royal Navy destroyer in England, probably at Newhaven. (Creative Commons Attribution 4.0 International licence. Attribution: Department of National Defence Library and Archives Canada PA-183765)

24. Another picture of wounded men arriving back in England after the raid. (Creative Commons Attribution 4.0 International licence. Attribution: Department of National Defence Library and Archives Canada PA-183773)

25. Crewman with a Douglas Boston aircraft of the Royal Air Force, which was used in the raid on Dieppe. (Creative Commons Attribution 4.0 International licence. Attribution: Department of National Defence Library and Archives Canada PA-183774)

26. This photograph was taken at the Stalag VIIIB prisoner of war camp at Lamsdorf, circa 1942. Maurice Snook can be seen in the top row, far right. Similar to Maurice, most of these men would probably have been captured at Dieppe. (Photo: courtesy of Historica Canada/Maurice Snook)

27. The telegram that Jack McFarland's mother received advising her of her son's location as a PoW. (Photo: courtesy of Historica Canada/Jack McFarland)

28. Armand Emond is pictured on the left, with fellow prisoners of war, René Cardinal and Roland Langlois. They are seen cutting wood in Poland in 1944, one of the many jobs prisoners were expected to do for their German captors. (Photo: courtesy of Historica Canada/Armand Emond)

29. The Canadian war cemetery at Vertus Wood near Dieppe. Note how the headstones are placed back-to-back in double rows, which was the norm for a German war cemetery, but unusual for Commonwealth War Graves Commission sites. (Photo: courtesy of Historica Canada/ Theodore Bennett)

Above: 30. A happy ending: the wedding of Paul and Joan Dumaine on 4 July 1945. They got engaged prior to Paul's departure for England and subsequent capture at Dieppe. After his release she was given permission to travel to England where they were married. (Photo: courtesy of Historica Canada/Paul Dumaine)

Left: 31. A monument on Dieppe seafront which commemorates the soldiers of Les Fusiliers Mont-Royal who fought and died here. As the monument points out they were a regiment of mostly French Canadians. (Photograph copyright Frederic Bisson/reproduced under the terms of the Creative Commons 2.0 Generic Licence)

were hit and one (LCF2), under the command of Temporary Lieutenant Eric Leslie Graham RNVR, was eventually disabled with all of her guns put out of action. Graham, her captain, was killed and the only surviving officer, Temporary Surgeon Lieutenant Miles Patrick Martin, took command, remaining on board until the vessel finally sank. Martin was rescued from the sea and taken aboard HMS *Calpe,* where although wounded himself, he immediately set to work with the other surgeons on the ship aiding the wounded until they eventually returned to port. For his actions Martin was awarded the DSO.

Captain Hughes-Hallett also praised Lieutenant Graham in his supplement in *The London Gazette,* writing: 'The work of L.C.F. (L) 2 (Lieut. E. L. Graham, R.N.V.R.) in supporting the main landing, calls for special mention. This vessel closed in to provide point blank range, and gave most effective support. She was soon disabled, and her captain killed, but her guns were fought until one by one they were put out of action, and the ship herself was finally sunk.'

Albert Kirby served in the Royal Canadian Navy during the war and earlier described the training he had undergone to be a proficient member of the three-man crew of a small landing craft assault. He goes on to describe the moment that all that training turned to reality as he came into Dieppe to unload the soldiers:

I mean, I could sit and talk about it and say, "Oh, I loved it." But the fact is, I was scared to death. And I was glad when we got back. We left the place without losing anybody on board our landing craft. You know, like we did, we made this landing in a veritable hail of machine gun fire and yet, every soldier that we had on our landing craft got off, was still running when we backed off and left. And although we had a number of dents and holes in our landing craft, they're made of armour-plated steel, so for the large part, bullets didn't go through them, but they made big dents in them all over. And so it was a frightening thing but we backed off and waited, the plan was to wait. We landed them at something like 05:00 in the morning and the plan was to pick them up at, I think it was 07:00 or 08:00 in the evening?

As the assault landing craft carrying both the Essex Scottish Regiment and the Royal Hamilton Light Infantry hit the beaches, they lowered their ramps on to the shingle at the water's edge and the men aboard rushed out and advanced towards the seafront. These landing craft touched down between 05:20 and 05:23, so only slightly behind schedule. They were immediately met by a fierce torrent of bullets from the promenade, casino and elsewhere. The Germans were by now fully prepared and had manned every conceivable position and vantage point.

Arriving immediately at the cessation of the naval and aerial bombardments that had hit the buildings along the front of Dieppe, the Canadians were expecting the enemy to be heavily mauled and with much of their armour put out of action, or at least a little subdued at the very least. This was not the case. The enemy guns had hardly been affected by these attacks and after rallying in their aftermath, the Germans were soon back at their posts with deadly effect. Also, the smoke screen which had been laid on the eastern headland was quickly lifting so the guns in the caves that looked directly down on the beach had been wheeled out of their encasements and now also had the troops well in their sights as they were coming ashore.

The Essex Scottish who attacked on Red Beach, which was the closest to the guns on the eastern headland, suffered the worst in those opening moments and many of the men were mown down as they alighted and made a frantic rush up the beach towards the cover of the sea wall that divided the beach from the promenade. Similar to the Royal Regiment of Canada at Puys, most of the men who made it to the relative safety of the sea wall became pinned down and could advance no further, as bullets were landing all around them, or among them. The wall was surmounted by barbed wire which would have to be destroyed if any advance from this position was to be attempted, but the Germans had its entire length well covered from their pillboxes.

Coming ashore that day with the Essex Scottish Regiment was Wilson Howard Large:

We went to Bognor Regis and that's where we got our orders to go to Dieppe. We went aboard the ships, the first time in July, and we were sailing out and then they cancelled it, bad weather. And, the first time, we cheered like the devil, when they said we were on our way over. But the second time, when they told us, well, we're on our way again, there wasn't a cheer. It was just silence.

We landed in the daylight, or in the early sunrise. And they were just bombarding us. They knew we were coming, because the big guns were going and the smaller guns were going, and the machine guns were going, and everything. The noise was something. Then we hit the beach and hit the water, and we got in. Some of us got in – some of us got hit right in the water.

We got in and got up to the wall. The engineers were with us and they drug about ten foot-long pipes they called Bangalore torpedoes. They're filled with explosive, and they threw them up on top of the barbed wire. And they ignited the one, and it started slipping back towards us, and one of our fellows by the name of Everett McCormick from Leamington (Ontario), he reached up and was pushing it back and it kept coming. And he stood there and held it, and got himself blown up. He should have had a decoration. You know, his family should have got it. He was just a little fellow, too. Yeah. So that was my first real blow. I mean the shooting and that, it was going on and that, but it didn't bother me like that... I saw the others being hit, but to get blown right up, that sort of got to me for a bit.

While the Essex Scottish was being pinned down behind the sea wall on Red Beach, to their right the Royal Hamilton Light Infantry fared only slightly better on White Beach. Jack McFarland remembers what was occurring on White Beach at approximately the same moment:

We were so confident that our intelligence was correct. Intelligence told us that the only defenders were a bunch of old German soldiers, almost like home guard. We had no idea we were facing people that had just come back from Russia. We had a good trip across the English Channel. We had good escorts and minesweepers, so we had no problem crossing the Channel. We had no trouble getting off the mother ship into the assault crafts. We climbed down the rope ladders into the assault craft and took off. And it was a nice bright morning. I imagine we were about ten miles offshore, to save the noise from the mother ships and keep them off the radar.

So as we approached the coast, it was pretty light. We could see aircraft over the town of Dieppe. So it was pretty light when we touched down. And we were under heavy fire; I would say anti-tank guns that were knocking out the landing craft. One boat about two boats over from where I was got hit head-on before we touched down. I don't think anybody survived that.

Landing craft will sit low in the water and the centre part is open from the motor right to the bow where the door is that goes down. I was in the centre aisle, there were three aisles, I was in the centre one. When I got off the boat, I jumped over two guys that were already hit. Now, I don't know whether they were dead or what, but they were down on the ground anyhow.

And I had taken, because one of the fellows in the platoon asked me to take the Bangalore torpedo to help blow the wire, because he was a little smaller than I was. So I took it and I had to go down to ground because the corporal had the other half of the Bangalore and I had to wait until he was in the position and called me. And he set the Bangalore off, we put it together, he set it off to make a hole in the wire.

Having alighted from their landing craft and made their way to the cover of the sea wall, most of the Essex Scottish Regiment was unable to advance any further for quite some time, although a small party did manage to cut their way through the wire and subsequently move into the town. One of these was Wilson Howard Large:

About twenty of us made a dash for the houses, and seven of us made it. Yeah. The rest were all piled up all along the way. And then we went inside and a German patrol came in the building, and Sergeant Leopold just said, "Wait until I say fire." And the seven of us fired our guns, the Bren gun and rifles, right down the hallway. They'd come in and they were laughing and that. Oh. And he said, "Fire." And then there was no more laughing, not even a moan. We got the whole patrol.

Oh, and that's when they finally said, "Howard, look at your foot." And the blood's just squirting out of it. So I had to cut my laces with my bayonet, got my foot out, and put my field dressings on it and I had to put a tourniquet on it – I used my knife and scabbard and my rifle sling, and put a tourniquet on my leg. So I couldn't move very well. So I went down to the basement of the house and it was a dirt floor. So I went down there and I took the rest of my grenades and I buried them in the floor, and, waited.

The infantry were of course supposed to be supported by the Churchill tanks of the 14th Canadian Tank Regiment (Calgary Regiment), but because of a navigational error the LCTs were running late and none of them reached the beach before 05:35.

This was critical because the LCTs also carried some of the parties of Royal Canadian Engineers whose task it was to destroy beach, tank and other obstacles in their path, in order for both the infantry and the tanks to proceed into the town.

In spite of all this, one group from the Royal Hamilton Light Infantry led by Captain Anthony (Tony) Champain Hill, who was the second in command of B Company, managed to get over the sea wall and through the barbed wire to make a determined attack on the casino, which was not only heavily defended itself but was also protected by pillboxes. Teams of men from the Hamiltons targeted and blew up these pillboxes using Bangalore torpedoes, which allowed a party of Royal Canadian Engineers who had come ashore with the first wave, led by Lance Sergeant George Alfred Hickson, to approach the casino and lay demolition charges.

Hickson's group had been charged with destroying the main telephone exchange in the Post Office, but finding the fire on the beach too heavy to move directly to his target, he assisted the infantry in their task of attacking the casino. Using explosives, he blew his way through the walls to reach a large concrete gun emplacement. Then another charge blew in the steel door, killing a gun crew of five. He then destroyed a six-inch naval gun and two machine guns after infantry had cleared the post.

Jack Clifford McFarland, serving with the Royal Hamilton Light Infantry, was one of the men who attacked a German machine gun post in the vicinity of the casino:

The bunch I was with, we were told to head for the casino and try to get over the wall... The casino wasn't our objective, so we looked out and it was a gun post, the Germans had a gun post to the, I guess the west of the casino. And it was knocked out and we took over that. Every time you tried to get over the wall, you had a casualty. And this was mounting terribly. We were to the left of the casino going in and we never got past there. Well, we just tried to pick off the Germans we could see. From our vantage point, we couldn't see many.

With the casino captured and now firmly in Allied hands, Captain Hill led a small party of men into the town, followed by Sergeant Hickson with another group, while a third went forward under Lieutenant Llewellyn Clarke Bell. They eventually reached the Church of St Remy, but being unsupported by their tanks, they were unable to go any further until back-up arrived.

Captain Denis Whitaker of the Royal Hamilton Light Infantry recalled a scene of carnage and confusion, with soldiers being cut down by German fire all along the sea wall while his commanding officer, Lieutenant Colonel Labatt, desperately tried to use a broken radio to contact Major General Roberts. For his leadership at Dieppe Labatt would be awarded the DSO.

On leaving military college in 1923, Labatt was commissioned as a militia officer with the Royal Hamilton Light Infantry. At the time of the regiment being mobilised in September 1939 he was the regiment's second in command. He became the CO on 2 April 1940 and commanded the regiment until he was taken prisoner at Dieppe. His citation for his DSO stated:

Lieutenant Colonel *Labatt,* by his personal leadership, courage and initiative, contributed in full measure to the action in which his unit participated at Dieppe 19 August 1942, and from which he did not return. After the landing he quickly established his HQ on the beach and in person directed the attack of the battalion. For several hours he was in constant first hand touch with the situation and his direction of the companies was responsible for considerable success in forwarding the advance and in the destruction of enemy positions. In addition to these duties he was entrusted with control of the Brigade in a wireless message received from the commander who had become a casualty. Colonel Labatt stayed in the thick of things, under heavy fire, all through the engagement. He was in the rear guard of the withdrawal, and was last seen standing over his adjutant, evidently badly wounded, prepared to defend him. Colonel Labatt was apparently unwounded, but was not among those who reached the evacuation craft. All ranks of the unit have paid tribute to the worth of his leadership and the inspiration of his example.

It was now 05:35 and to the huge relief of all those soldiers pinned down on the beach behind the sea wall, the first wave of landing craft tanks finally appeared off the shore and came thundering up on to the shingle. As well as the Churchill tanks of the 14th Canadian Tank Regiment (Calgary Regiment) they were of course carrying specialist teams of Royal Canadian Engineers, sappers who were needed to clear paths through the streets of the town, destroying any obstacles that stood in their way.

As the LCTs approached the beach they came under intense fire from several angles, as although the guns around the casino had been silenced, most others were still in full operation. All of the craft in the first wave were repeatedly hit but still managed to deliver their cargoes on to the beach. For some of the LCTs, the landing was anything but simple and one of them took four attempts to beach before it finally succeeded. During these attempts the craft in question lost three helmsmen as each in turn fell victim to enemy fire. The gallantry shown by all the crews was of the highest order, as against all the odds they pressed on until the job was completed.

Eventually, all but two of the tanks the first wave transported were able to make it out of their landing craft and onto the beach, which itself caused further immediate problems. The reason was that several of the tanks found their movement extremely restricted and several of them got uncontrollably bogged down by the shingle, which was made up of large pebbles known as chert. As for the LCTs themselves, in the process of successfully landing their cargo, one of them was sunk and one remained aground on fire.

As the tanks that had come ashore tried to move up and off the beach the second flight of LCTs eventually came in behind them but didn't arrive for another half hour, and as they approached the water line they were subjected to an even fiercer reception than the first wave. Again, each craft was relentlessly subjected to a pounding from all types of shells coming from the front, the east and down from on top of the cliffs and caves. One of the ships from this wave was crippled so badly, it sank before it even managed to reach the shore.

Another of the craft made two attempts at trying to put her tanks down and most of her crew was either killed or very seriously wounded in the process. Because of this situation Sergeant Thomas Badlan of the Royal Marines took charge of the vessel and under continued heavy fire, kept a cool head and managed to steer the craft up on to the beach. Badlan was a member of the beach provost party under the command of Lieutenant Colonel Robert (Bobbie) Granville Parks-Smith RM, who was on the staff of Combined Operations headquarters. Parks-Smith had himself been mortally wounded and lay in the hull of the boat. For his actions Badlan would be awarded the Distinguished Conduct Medal (DCM). On board the vessel in question was Brigadier Sherwood Lett, the commander of the 4th Canadian Infantry Brigade, who was in overall charge of the three components of the brigade, the Essex Scottish Regiment, the Royal Hamilton Light Infantry, and the Royal Regiment of Canada, and as such was obviously keen to get ashore with his men.

At Dieppe the Canadian 14th Canadian Tank Regiment (Calgary Regiment) was the first tank regiment of the Canadian

Army to go into battle in any war. They had the further distinction of being the first tank regiment of any army to be engaged in an amphibious assault during the Second World War. They were under the command of Lieutenant Colonel John Gilby Andrews, his second in command being Major John Begg. When John Andrews was promoted to Lieutenant Colonel he was only thirty-two years of age and at the time was one of the youngest men of that rank in the Canadian Army, with only two others known to have been younger than him. So he was evidently a very gifted and highly rated officer. He took command of the battalion on succeeding Lieutenant Colonel G. R. Bradbook MC, who had recruited the battalion and brought it to England. Bradbook had been posted to other duties with Middle East Command.

Lieutenant Colonel Andrews' own tank, a Churchill Mk II, was in the second wave of LCTs but unfortunately just as he was about to go ashore the ramp chains of the landing craft in which he was travelling were cut by enemy gunfire and the ramp fell prematurely into the water. His tank was just going through the door as this occurred and fell into eight feet of water and sank from view. It is thought that the tank's waterproof cover ripped during this incident, which is why it sank so speedily. All that could be seen of it was Andrews' commanding officer's pennant which was flying from the wireless mast and remained there for the remainder of the day.

Eyewitnesses reported seeing some of the tank's crew escape from the turret but were unsure whether Andrews was one of them. These men were subsequently picked up by a motor launch that immediately put out to sea, but it had only gone a very short distance when it received a direct hit from one of the shore batteries and burst into flames. The men on the boat were seen to leap into the sea. Lieutenant Colonel Andrews was not seen again and was initially reported missing, but after the raid it was confirmed that he had indeed been killed. In his absence, Major Begg, a veteran of the First World War, took command of the battalion for the rest of the operation.

In total, twenty-eight tanks managed to get out of the LCTs and on to the beach. Two of these sank in deep water, including of course the CO's tank, while twelve more became bogged down in the chert, or had their tracks damaged by the shells from enemy guns, leaving them stranded. In particular, one anti-tank gun along the seafront was doing a great deal of damage and having crippled one of the Churchills as it came out of its landing craft, it was spotted by the crew of a second tank coming up behind it. The crew turned their turret to towards the enemy target, fired their six pounder gun, and put the German menace out of action.

George Edmund 'Jim' Marchant was in a Churchill tank as it came into Dieppe aboard a landing craft tank – number thirteen.

I think what happened at Dieppe was unavoidable. Hindsight is easy to come by, and it's easy to find fault in the things when things are all over. But certainly, we've made mistakes, everybody makes mistakes. But it tested us as troops, and we fulfilled our obligation to do the best we could under horrendous conditions. I was prepared probably a little less than most of the troops because I was on a special course when the training at the Isle of Wight took place. And I joined the regiment just shortly before they went to Dieppe properly, and I was devoid of the training that the chaps on the Isle of Wight had. I went over on a tank landing craft, TLC13. I remember the number exceedingly clearly because I went aboard in the evening and in the morning, when we were just leaving dock, one of the chaps looked at me and he yelled at me from a troop ship nearby and he looked down on us in this little tank craft and he said, "You're not coming back, Marchant." And I said, "Why would you say that?" He said, "Look at the number on your ship." Well, I couldn't, I was inside this boat and it was TLC13.

And they said, "You're in 13, you're never going to make it." I said, "Oh, don't worry about that," I said, "I'm not superstitious." Unfortunately, I was the only one that did come back...

There were three Churchill tanks on that boat plus a Jeep that was tied to the last one. And when we went ashore early in the morning, the ramp went down too early, actually, it was shot down, I believe, by the enemy and it splashed down into the water. And the first tank went off because they were already sealed in, waterproofed, and the first tank went off and we never heard from him again, he went under the landing craft and we went right over him, pinned the three of them in the tank and the next two went off the same way. The third one got on the beach, but it was totally devastated, the tracks were blown off it.

But we weren't able to land properly, there was no proper landing as such. We got ashore as best we could, so to speak, but it was very disarrayed. Sitting in the boat, in the bottom of that tank landing craft in these three Churchill tanks, waiting to take off, waiting for the ramp to drop, we were coming under fire from the shore, from the cliffs. And the enemy were shooting at our tank, at our vessel at that point in time, and the British sailors on that landing craft jumped to the Oerlikon gun at the back of that boat, it's a heavy anti-aircraft gun, and the British sailor, this is the part that really caught my heart, jumped into that saddle that he was put in and he opened fire on the enemy and about as fast as he opened fire, they shot him out of that seat. And as he came out of that seat, another man without any word or instruction, another man leaped to that seat, got into that saddle and grabbed the gun and started firing again. That happened three times. The third time, the gun was totally demolished – it was the end of it. But I actually watched three men voluntarily, without any instruction, without any solicitation, without any urging, climb into that saddle and open fire on an enemy they couldn't even see, just firing into the cliffs. And they didn't have a chance, they didn't have a chance.

But remarkable courage these men had. If I learned anything out of it, I learned to be grateful. And the smallest man could be the biggest friend in the world.

Several of the tanks did eventually manage to struggle slowly up the shingle and climb over the sea wall and through the barbed wire, making their way onto the promenade. Here they discovered a number of tanks from the first wave that were still waiting for the parties of sappers to arrive to remove the tank obstacles which seemed to block every exit from the esplanade and gardens. Without these obstacles being dealt with, the tanks were unable to go any further.

In total, fifteen Churchills made it up onto the promenade and were creating a bit of a traffic jam because there was still no sign of the Royal Canadian Engineers. The reason for this was that the casualties among them had been so heavy that there simply were no specialists now available to tackle any of the tank blocks that had been placed at the end of the narrow streets leading from the Boulevard de Verdun into the town. If any of the tanks were going to advance, they would have to do it by themselves. On realising that the situation was not going to improve, one group of tanks decided to crack on and turning right, attempted to attack the German defences on the western headland. At the same time another group tried to break through into the town itself.

One of the tanks, commanded by Lieutenant A. B. Patterson, did manage to smash completely through a house and got into the town around the blocks that way, followed by two more. Other Churchill's simply went up and down the esplanade firing at whatever defences they could identity until their ammunition was finally exhausted. Although these tanks were able to do considerable damage to the positions they could locate, they were unable to give the type of support to the operation that the planners had hoped for. The problem of course being that many of the German anti-tank defences, particularly the artillery in the caves, had not been identified or tackled at the start. The fact that they were concealed within the caves also made it almost impossible for the tanks themselves to accurately locate and engage them. Also, the naval and aerial bombardments had not been sufficient to eliminate the anti-tank units that waited behind the road blocks on the Boulevard de Verdun. It was not a great baptism for the concept of using tanks during an amphibious assault and had little or no effect on the success of the operation itself.

In the supplement he wrote for *The London Gazette*, Captain Hughes-Hallett, the naval force commander, gives what is perhaps an overly positive and not totally accurate account of what actually happened:

Meanwhile the main landings on Red and White Beaches took place punctually and according to plan, with the exception that the leading wave of LCTs approached from too far to the westward and were about ten to fifteen minutes late in touching down.

The air support and the smoke-making aircraft on the east cliff, were accurately synchronised, and the destroyer's fire, both on the houses along the front while the boats were going in, and subsequently on the east and west cuffs, appeared to be as effective as could be expected. No losses of landing craft took place during the initial landing, but it did not appear to the officer in charge that the troops were able to capture the strong points along the front after landing. However, the LCTs on going in encountered very heavy opposition, and I consider that theirs was a notable achievement in landing twenty-eight out of thirty tanks dryshod. The heavy damage and casualties in the LCTs were undoubtedly due in a large measure to the relatively long periods they remained on the beach, waiting for the miscellaneous troops that they were carrying in addition to the tanks, to disembark.

Among those miscellaneous troops which Captain Hughes-Hallett mentioned was the mortar platoon from the Calgary Highlanders, commanded by Lieutenant Jack Reynolds. They were attached to the landing force but stayed offshore after the tanks on board their LCT (codenamed Bert and Bill) landed. Sergeants Lyster and Pittaway from his platoon were both mentioned in despatches for their part in shooting down two German aircraft. Serving in the mortar platoon of the Calgary Highlander was Amos Wilkins:

I had an older brother that went to join and they wouldn't take him. But if he'd got in, it's possible that I would not have gone, because my dad was a man with no fingers and he was farming three quarter-sections of land, somebody would have had to stay home and help him and it would probably have been me. So having had that experience, I never criticise anybody that didn't go until I know why they didn't go. I could have got an agricultural deferment in five minutes. And don't ask me why I went because that question is not answerable. It really isn't. To say I was patriotic – Hell, I didn't even know how to spell the word at that time.

I guess to some extent, I feel we were conscripted by our conscience. Jack and Joe were going, you know, and maybe I'd better go, too. And there were those that hadn't had a decent job throughout the Depression, and it was an opportunity to get a bit of money and a place to sleep and eat. And after a while, it grew. And we were all caught up in something that was much bigger than we were.

I had a kind of a unique career. I joined here (Calgary) in 1940, went over in 1941, was in Dieppe in 1942. And after that, I was made a sergeant in the spring of 1943. I was called in and told that I was to apply for a commission, which I did and was accepted. I was one of the only ones who had ever done it with a Grade 8 education. I never went to high school.

I was at Dieppe and, well, we never landed – we were manning anti-aircraft guns. But on the approach to the beach, there was a piece of shrapnel took the top of a man's head off, a piece of his skull as big around as that glass. If I live to be 200, I'll always be able to see that laying there on the bottom of that landing craft.

We (The Calgary Highlanders) actually got to shore and unloaded a platoon of infantry, three tanks, and a bulldozer. I was a member of a special outfit, what they called a three-inch mortar platoon. And we were supposed to go in after the beachhead was established. But what happened, we couldn't get in. The Navy boys, manning the anti-aircraft guns, they were all down and our officer decided that we should maybe go up and see what we could do. So some of us did. And we manned the anti-aircraft guns.

Two of our sergeants shot down a German plane. But we were right there and we were in and out of the beach several times picking up the wounded. It was, I guess, scary, but I was fortunate in a way. I was a corporal at the time and I've always thought that, to have responsibility in a case like that, is not a bad thing, because it takes you out of yourself. You have other people and other things to think about. And I've always felt that way all my life, in an emergency. If there's something that you can do for somebody else, it takes – you know, the poor guy at the back of the end of the line, he doesn't really know what's going on and he gets pretty nervous. And that's been a philosophy of mine, all my life.

I don't believe that there are any real rules for war. War is a battle for existence. It's not a prize fight. It's not a hockey game. There are no real rules. We do not here (in Canada) trumpet our victories like they do in some countries. We've just kind of allowed it to fade away. I see it in the (Royal Canadian) Legion and you know, we're gradually running out of members because young people don't find it all that fulfilling to join the Legion – too many other things to do. And that is not a bad thing. I'm happy that my children grew up not having to worry about going to war. And I hope my grandchildren and my great grandchildren – but no, it's a hard question to answer. But it was something I guess that had to be done.

Blocked from going any further because of the tank obstacles and debris in the streets, all of the tanks that had made it into the town were eventually forced to return to the beach, where they would shortly provide fire support for the now retreating infantry. None of the tanks managed to return to England and most of their crews were either killed or captured.

At this point, the main attacks on Red and White beaches fared little better than those elsewhere along the front. Most of the troops were pinned down, going nowhere, and certainly in no position to complete any of their objectives. It was time for decisions to be made at the top as to whether to continue with what was quickly turning into a disaster, or to pull out and save what men and resources that could be saved.

10

THE RESERVES GO IN

It was now 06:30, which was roughly an hour after the first Churchill tanks had landed in front of Dieppe and aboard his command ship HMS *Calpe,* the military force commander, Major General John Roberts and his staff were aware that there had been a number of problems with the initial landings and that things were not developing according to plan but they were not acquainted with the severity of these problems and they did not seem to appreciate just how bad things had become. So, giving the situation due consideration, Roberts was of the opinion that if he was to use his reserves at this point, it would give the attack renewed impetus and put it back on to a firm footing once again, even though he would be using them not necessarily for the purposes for which they were intended.

Because of continuing problems with the radio sets that had been issued to the troops ashore, Roberts had so far received no word from either No. 3 Commando, or the Royal Regiment of Canada. They were of course detailed to attack and suppress the Goebbels battery near Berneval-le-Grand and the Rommel battery near Puys respectively. What he had no way of knowing was that neither of these attacks had succeeded and both batteries were still in enemy hands, so all he could do was assume that they were still in the process of being captured. On the other hand, according to the limited information available to him, the situation at Pourville-sur-Mer, where the South Saskatchewan Regiment and the Queen's Own Cameron Highlanders of Canada were engaged, appeared to be fairly promising. It was also known that No. 4 Commando was successfully engaging the Hess battery at Varengeville-sur-Mer. So all in all, there were enough positives to assume things were going in the right direction, albeit slowly.

Major General Roberts could not see for himself the situation on the beaches in front of Dieppe from the bridge of HMS *Calpe*. This was due to the lingering smoke screen that had been laid by the Royal Navy destroyers and aircraft of the RAF to help shield the attackers as they came ashore. It was impossible to get visual confirmation of the situation on any of the landing beaches.

As the man in overall charge of the operation, any decisions about how to proceed were ultimately his to make, and in his own mind he felt certain that if Lieutenant Colonel Jasperson and the Essex Scottish Regiment could be reinforced without delay, they would be able to press on and take the vital eastern headland, which was so crucial to the success of the entire mission. His thinking was further supported by the knowledge that the Essex Scottish now had tanks to back them up, for he had just received a message to say that the Calgary Tanks were indeed ashore. He therefore based his decisions on the assumption that his troops still held the initiative and came to the conclusion that the time was right to send in his first reserve troops, which consisted of Les Fusiliers Mont-Royal, a famous French Canadian Regiment here under the command of Lieutenant Colonel Dollard Menard.

Les Fusiliers Mont-Royal had travelled directly from the port of Shoreham aboard the LCPs that would deliver them to the beaches and had been nervously waiting aboard them at the rear for the word to go. As they waited, they could hear the sound of the desperate battle being fought ahead of them. The waiting was finally over. Major General Roberts issued the order for them to go and they steamed ahead in twenty-six landing craft, immediately coming under heavy fire as they emerged through the smoke into the battle zone from the still strong enemy positions on the seafront, cliffs and caves. Two of the LCPs were hit and sunk on their way to the battle while the remainder touched down on the beach at around 07:05.

They soon discovered that the fire on the beaches was still as fierce as ever, and instead of helping to relieve the Essex Scottish Regiment they immediately became bogged down with them. They were expecting to see the troops from the initial thrust clear of the beach and attempting to take the eastern headland, but instead found them pinned down behind the Dieppe sea wall. Rushing off their landing craft, the Fusiliers that were not immediately hit by enemy fire attempted to take cover where they could find it. Some crouched behind the burning remains of Churchill tanks that were stranded on the shingle, others simply falling into the folds of the beach itself, or behind the bodies of already fallen comrades. The commanding officer, Lieutenant Colonel Menard, was already among the wounded.

Some of the LCPs had drifted too far to the west because of a strong wind pulling the tide in that direction. They had completely missed both White and Red Beaches and come ashore to the west of the casino on a small stretch of shingle and rocks below high and extremely sheer cliffs. They found themselves cut off from the rest of the regiment, with no room to deploy because whichever way they moved, the Germans had them covered with heavy machine guns and mortars positioned above them on the cliff tops. Not only were they unable to move from the spot but they found it impossible to even attempt to engage the enemy who they simply could not see. One by one the men on this beach were either killed or wounded and at around 12:00 they were left with no option other than to surrender.

Elsewhere, some members of the regiment fared a little better. One group under the command of Captain G. Vandalec had landed close to the casino, which was of course now in Allied hands. From here they pushed on and attacked some of the properties along the Boulevard de Verdun where the enemy still had considerable fire power.

A second group under Sergeant Pierre Dubuc, which also came ashore opposite the casino, was able to penetrate further into the streets of the town. With eleven men, he turned east and reached the Basin du Canada, part of Dieppe's inner harbour. The group fought its way step by step, from house to house, and in doing so destroyed a German machine gun post that was dominating a street corner. When they finally arrived at the edge of the dock basin, the group killed or wounded all the enemy personnel that could be found on the barges and other small craft that were sheltering there. They then pressed on until they encountered superior German forces, by which time their ammunition was exhausted and they were forced to surrender.

Their German captors made them take off their clothes and once they were stripped down to their underwear, they were lined up facing a wall and left in the charge of a single German soldier. In the first instance they of course feared the worst but after the other Germans had left, they realised that they were not going to be shot. Thinking quickly, Sergeant Dubuc distracted the sentry's attention and as soon as he turned his head the other members of the group fell upon him and killed him. The group speedily set off in their vests and underpants and attempted to retrace their steps back through the streets of the town towards the beach. They split up in order to do this and while some did manage to make it back a number did not, although what happened to them is unsure.

Sergeant Dubuc was one of those who did get back to the beach and there he found his commanding officer, Lieutenant Colonel Menard, seriously wounded. It was now about 11:00 and the evacuation from the beaches had already begun. Sergeant Dubuc took it upon himself to try and get Lieutenant Colonel Menard onto one of the landing craft that was coming back into the beach to pick people up. Menard ordered him to leave him where he was, but Sergeant Dubuc disobeyed and got him safely onto one of the LCAs. Still in his underpants, he then went to the aid of a badly wounded corporal, managing to haul him onto a landing craft before finally pulling himself onto the boat and collapsing with exhaustion and no doubt relief. He returned to port in England and for his bravery and devotion to duty he was subsequently awarded the Military Medal.

A number from the regiment Les Fusiliers Mont-Royal who survived the battle that day were interviewed about their experiences for Historica Canada's *Memory Project*, including Arthur Fraser, and the following is the transcript of his contribution. It is interesting to note that the first person he encountered on the Dieppe seafront was an officer of the Scottish Essex, surprised that the reserves had been sent in as he had been trying desperately to send messages to Major General Roberts and his staff on HMS *Calpe*, to tell them it was pointless to do so, but none were getting through; another example of the problems that everyone experienced with their radios in each zone of the raid. Arthur remembered that some of the tanks landed after the Fusiliers, but we have already established that the tanks had already come ashore before the reserves went in. We know that all of the LCTs landed well behind schedule and some had been delayed because of navigation errors, so it is quite likely that at least one of these did arrive on the beach even after the reserves had been sent in.

August 19, 1942, we land at 7:00 in Dieppe, in France. We were the last battalion to land at Dieppe. It was a raid. A raid is that you attack and then when the raid is finished, you're supposed to come back. But we never came back because the raid was finished at 11:30 in the morning and the ones that survived were taken prisoner of war for the duration of the war.

We were all on small boats, all our battalion was, there was some 500-odd people on small yachts. When we landed at Dieppe, we landed in a straight line. And when I landed, I passed one officer and that officer told me that, "I asked the headquarters on the boat, not to send you because this raid is lost." But at the time, we didn't know why, probably they didn't get the message. I've read books saying that the Germans were blocking the zone. So of course, whatever was said on the beach, never reached the headquarters on the boat.

So we landed and when I jumped off the boat and looked around, and I saw so many dead soldiers or wounded, I was really surprised to see that. I was in a three inch mortar section. I had three bombs and I would go through my three bombs, and that was it. On a raid like that it goes so fast on the front that you see one thing and the fellow next to you sees other things. It was all mixed up.

There was a Churchill tank that landed after us. They should have landed … before us but they landed after us. These were big Churchill tanks that weigh seventy tons. And some sunk in the Channel, that was what we crossed, it was the English Channel. And one of these boats landed on the beach. I went on that boat and I saw so many wounded there. And then the German artillery started to shoot at us but it didn't last too long. The Commandos were supposed to destroy the German artillery. They did succeed in destroying some of the guns but not all of them.

Another member of Les Fusiliers Mont-Royal was Roland Gravel, who also recorded his memories. Roland talks about meeting

German soldiers who were not based in the area but were there for training purposes. Earlier we also heard that there were German soldiers in the area who were resting from the eastern front. Perhaps these were the same group of men and if so, they would have considerably bolstered the defences of Dieppe and made the enemy strength greater than had been anticipated.

What happened on August 19, 1942, is that we attacked Dieppe in the morning, the first troops landed at 05:30 and then everything was over between 12:30-13:00 in the afternoon. We unloaded at 07:00 in the morning. My company was directly in the middle of the town so, like everything else, we mopped up the beach and started fighting with the enemy, unfortunately, without us knowing that there was an accumulation of Germans who just happened to be training in the area around Dieppe, so they sent all of those Germans to the town of Dieppe... The dead were everywhere, and naturally there were also a lot of wounded. We surrendered with a white flag at approximately 12:45-13:00. We felt two things; the first was not having achieved all of the objectives we had set out to achieve and the second was joy for being alive, those of us who remained. Those were the two feelings we had.

Jacques Nadeau, was also with Les Fusiliers Mont-Royal:

We were in East Lancing which was the name of the base. The commander (Lieutenant Colonel) Dollard Menard got us together and said, "Boys, tomorrow morning we'll be in Dieppe!" We started whooping; we were happy since we were tired of training. We left the port of Shoreham in a line, and when we set off, we went north-east and eventually met up with the other units. Some were arriving from Newhaven and others from Portsmouth and then all of a sudden the convoy was formed. We had thirteen groups in total and there were 252 craft. Us, the Canadians, we numbered about 4963 if I remember correctly. Then the craft had to go where they were supposed to be, and we departed east across the Channel. It was a spectacular day. It was a hot day. There was hardly any wind and the sea seemed more or less like oil, it was still. We were told not to talk or to smoke and to rest as much as possible since the next day was going to be busy. We, Les Fusiliers Mont-Royal, we had to get off last since we had to protect the retreat of all of the other units who, after having finished their work in the various locations they had to go, were coming back via Dieppe. We would return to our ranks to board again. And we would have waited for the very last people to board before boarding ourselves. But that's not exactly what happened. I was the last to board since the bikes were in the rear on a little ramp that measured approximately eighteen to twenty-four inches wide. I spent the night there, but fortunately the sea was calm. The ship landed on the shore and remained stuck there in the shoreline. Then all of the guys got off. It took more time for me because of the ramp that was there and I had to go around to the front to jump off. Towards the front of the ship there was less water. Where I was, there was over twenty feet of water and I would have certainly disappeared in an instant what with my size and all. Then the commander of the ship pushed me with the tip of his machine gun trained on my back and I thought to myself, if he pulls the trigger, I'm gone. So I threw the bike into the ocean and I jumped out after it. I leaned over to try to find the infamous bike but I couldn't see it anywhere and I thought to hell with it, I'll find another one in Dieppe. While I was in the water, the Germans were firing at us. Bullets were hitting the water; I could see them go by. One of them hit my steel helmet, but fortunately the double layer decreased the speed and I was able to get out of the water and hit the ground. Eventually, towards 14:00, we surrendered and everything stopped and we couldn't hear anything except for the wounded crying out. Then the

Germans came down to the beach. There was a great big guy, I can still see the way he acted. He would approach a body on the ground and using his foot, he would turn the body over to see if the person was dead. If so, he would move on to the next body. I was playing dead, and I had my left hand, no my right hand, under my chin. So when he got to me, he put his foot under my right armpit, and since I am very ticklish, I jerked. So he said to me, "Komme komme mein liebe," which means, "Come, come my dear"! He said to me, "The war is over for you." So I got up and took off my gear and went to meet up with my friends who were waiting under the escarpment. Many were wounded and thirsty. So I asked one of the German guards, I gestured to him, showing him the water bottles belonging to those that were dead. He gestured back indicating that I could go and retrieve the bottles, so I did in order to give them to those that needed water. Then we walked up the escarpment, they made us climb up to a place called the circus. Once we got to the top, they made us line up in rows of five and then they counted us. One German would start counting from the left, and another from the right, because when they were done counting the 200-300 of us, they had to report to an officer with the same number. But when the German walked by me and touched my shoulder to count me, I called him a pig. He stiffened and stopped right in front of me and we spent several seconds that felt like minutes just staring at each other. Then we heard a shout from in front and he had to continue on his way but his eyes were like daggers when he looked at me. Even today, I don't like talking about it.

Finally, Paul Dumaine, who also came ashore with Les Fusiliers Mont-Royal, recalled his experiences. Paul's story is slightly more uplifting amidst all this despair.

I have to tell you about this; because it wasn't all war, there was also love. I met a young woman, who I became engaged to.

We didn't want to get married because the war was going strong and I could have been hurt or killed. So we said that we would wait until after the war to get married. So I asked her to marry me. She was young. One day, I left for Europe. I arrived in Dieppe. On August 19, 1942, we arrived in Dieppe. My fiancée had no idea where I was. The battle was poorly organised. We lost everything we had to lose. I was injured and then taken prisoner.

Over there, the beaches are made up of little round pebbles. You walk and you roll. The tanks couldn't advance. The little stones would get caught in the tracks and they would break and remain stuck. All of the tanks were on the beach. A couple of them ventured into the town but then they came back. Most of them were stuck on the beach. They could still shoot but they couldn't advance.

They had trouble getting messages out. The ships at large received a message that the town was occupied by the English-Canadian regiments, but that was wrong. They had said that only a few men had advanced that far. They understood that the entire regiment was in the town. As it was occupied, they told Les Fusiliers Mont-Royal, the reserve unit, to go in. They received the order to advance. We landed in broad daylight. We got there and the beach was ablaze. The battle was full-on. Everyone was getting killed and falling down all over the place, it was terrible.

I collapsed after an hour. My head was injured. I stayed a long time there just doing nothing. I couldn't walk. It was like I was paralysed. I was bleeding and I wanted to get up. I wanted to go wash myself off in the ocean. I wanted to get up, but I couldn't. My legs were paralysed from the shock of my injury. I had to drag myself on my elbows to the ocean. I washed my head with water. There was a great big boat called a tank landing craft; a boat that carried tanks. The doors opened and the tanks came out.

One of them had foundered on the beach. It was there and it was burning. It was there on the beach and it wasn't moving any more. We used it as a shelter to hide from the Germans. The injured went and sat at the back of the boat to avoid getting shot at. I went there right away. I had nothing left, no weapons. I stayed there for a while.

All of a sudden, I saw a German. He was an airman, and his plane had been shot down. He was making his way towards us on a little rubber raft. He arrived ashore and came towards me with his arms up yelling, "Kamerad! kamerad"! He thought we were going to kill him. He came and sat beside me. He took some photos out of his pocket and he showed me his wife and children. He wanted to soften my heart so that we wouldn't kill him. He said, "fräulein, fräulein" for his wife and "kinder" as he showed them to me. I didn't pay him any attention; I couldn't speak German. He stayed there until the end of the battle.

When I got back in 1945, I married my wife. It was the most beautiful thing of the war. I suffered during the war, but my most beautiful memory was marrying her. After I'd been taken prisoner, I was released. I was ill. When I got to England, I stayed in hospital for a month. She learned from others that I was in England. She was still in the army then. The colonel called her to his office and said, "Joan, I have some good news for you," She thought that it was news from her parents. "Your fiancé is in England, at Aldershot. I know that you would like to see him," She said Yes, yes, yes. "I am giving you a pass. Get dressed in civilian clothes and go see him." I was lying in my bed. They said to me, "Dumaine, you have a visitor." She was there. It had been three years. When I saw her, she was so beautiful. I took her in my arms.

In spite of sending in Les Fusiliers Mont-Royal to reinforce the Essex Scottish Regiment in an attempt to finally capture the eastern headland, which was so important to the outcome of the battle for both sides, it still remained firmly in enemy hands. Having committed his first reserves, perhaps Major General

Roberts felt he had now gone beyond the point of no return and he would have to send in further reinforcements to try and salvage something from the situation. So, shortly after 07:00, Roberts took the decision to reinforce again, this time by using No. 40 Commando Royal Marines.

It seems that Roberts was still not totally aware of the desperate situation facing the troops on Dieppe beach and he remained optimistic about securing a final victory. So, what did he actually know? Apparently by this time he had been informed that No. 4 Commando had indeed destroyed the heavy battery at Varengeville-sur-Mer. He had also been informed that the Queen's Own Cameron Highlanders of Canada had proceeded through Pourville-sur-Mer on the way to their objective, with the village itself now in the hands of the South Saskatchewan Regiment. He was further encouraged to learn that the seafront casino which had been so heavily defended by the Germans had been captured. And he knew that several other buildings which the enemy had been using as fortifications behind the promenade were on fire and had most likely been destroyed.

Unfortunately, even now the smoke from the earlier naval and aerial bombardments still lingered in the air, so the commander still had no way of actually seeing for himself what was happening on the beaches. He could hear the spluttering and rumbling of the battle but could see nothing. He was certainly not aware that both the Essex Scottish and now Les Fusiliers Mont-Royal were simply pinned down on the beach behind the sea wall and had been unable to subdue the eastern headland. He assumed they were still maintaining their assault. So, weighing everything up he decided with his staff that as the casino had been captured and some of the tanks were known to have made it over the esplanade, there was still a very good chance that they might seize the town and harbour with one last concerted effort. There was a reasonable prospect he thought, or so it appeared, that the Royal Hamilton Light Infantry, if reinforced, would be able to capture the western headland. No. 40 Commando Royal Marines was accordingly sent in to help them do so. No. 40 Commando was under the leadership of Lieutenant Colonel Joseph Picton-Phillips.

Sending them into the battle at this point with the aim of helping to take the western headland was effectively an admission on the part of Roberts that there was something drastically wrong with the whole situation in Dieppe. The original plan for the Royal Marines Commandos was to use them in a more specialist role. They were supposed to sweep into the harbour on the fast motor boats manned by the Fighting French and once there, destroy as much of the dock and its facilities as they could in the time available. They would also ransack port offices searching for any official documents. So to use them now as back-up troops for the Royal Hamilton Light Infantry would suggest that Roberts was willing to sacrifice that phase of the overall mission.

Similarly, the mission for Les Fusiliers Mont-Royal had also been changed, as they were originally meant to wait until the operation was over and then form a defensive perimeter through which all the other units could withdraw. Instead, they had now been used as assault troops to help capture the eastern headland, which would ultimately weaken the ability of the perimeter to hold once the operation was over and the troops were being withdrawn.

Because of this change in their role, the Royal Marines Commandos now had to be collected from the Fighting French chasseurs in which they had been taken to Dieppe and transferred into landing craft detailed from the boat pool. This pool had been established, in accordance with the plan, as soon as the landings had taken place. Landing craft returning from the beaches would wait in the pool, protected from the fire of the enemy by continuous smoke screens laid at frequent intervals by the destroyers. It took some time to collect enough landing craft and it wasn't until about 08:30 that No. 40 Commando was ready to make for the shore.

As the landing craft moved forward, the RAF's air umbrella was still very much in evidence with swarms of Supermarine Spitfires circling overhead at anything between three and ten thousand feet, keeping all enemy aircraft well away from the Allied boats. Over land the situation in the air wasn't quite as comfortable as the German anti-aircraft batteries were proving to be a real cause for concern. There were lulls followed by periods of extreme activity, when the guns opened up as waves of Allied fighter bombers flew in low over Dieppe, roughly once every twenty minutes, in order to renew their attacks on the German shore defences along the seafront.

At this point it was getting very hot and the sea was still calm. The boat pool had drifted slightly to the west because of the tide and lay offshore somewhere between Pourville-sur-Mer and the D'Ailly Lighthouse. From this scene of seeming summer serenity, the Royal Marines Commandos moved forward in their landing craft through the smoke, which at first afforded them cover. Fire support for their landing was provided by the gunboat HMS *Locust* backed up by two motor launches and the Fighting French chasseurs.

At the point at which this small fleet pierced through the last of the smoke screens, enemy guns of all descriptions were waiting for them, which opened a murderous fire. This was returned with Bren guns from the deck of the landing craft fired by several of the soldiers aboard, including Marine Les 'Brad' Bradshaw, who was afterwards singled out for his bravery. He stood and fired his gun through a torrent of bullets from a position that provided him with no protecting cover whatsoever. For his actions, Bradshaw would receive the Military Medal. But he was just one of a number who acted similarly.

The men who alighted from the first few landing craft were under the command of Lieutenant Kenneth William Ridley Smale, who, with two non-commissioned officers and the remains of his platoon, engaged the enemy with Bren guns from behind a stranded LCT. For bravery, endurance and inspiring devotion to duty during operations in the raid on Dieppe he would be awarded the Military Cross.

At this stage not all of the landing craft had reached the shore and others were still approaching under very heavy fire. One of these carried the commanding officer of No. 40 Commando, Lieutenant Colonel Picton-Phillips. As he came through the curtain of smoke he could see for himself that the beach and seafront were a long way from being clear of the enemy as he had been led to believe, but instead they had the beach completely swept by their concentrated fire. The whole seafront was littered with the burning wrecks of landing craft and Churchill tanks. Realising that the situation was not what the military force commander had visualised from aboard his headquarters ship, Picton-Phillips took it upon himself to stop the landing of any more of his men.

Picton-Phillips put on a pair of white gloves so that his hands could be more easily seen by his Marines. He then stood up on the forward deck of the landing craft he was in and gesticulated frantically to the rest of the boats to put about and return back into the smoke and hopefully, its relative safety. The other craft saw the figure gesticulating and immediately understood his meaning and began to turn away. Having potentially saved 200 of his men from death or capture, he was then himself hit by a bullet and fell mortally wounded to the deck and died a few moments later.

According to the original plan, a smaller unit belonging to No. 30 Commando would go into Dieppe along with No. 40 Commando with their very own, quite separate agenda.

Their job was to locate and steal a new German 4-rotor Enigma code machine, along with its associated code books and rotor setting sheets. The Naval Intelligence Division (NID) had planned this part of the raid, which was termed a 'pinch', with the intention of passing this material to cryptanalysts at Bletchley Park to assist with the Ultra project.

Bletchley Park was the centre of British code-breaking where scientists and mathematicians would intercept and try to decode enemy radio messages. This was hugely important work as the messages often related to Allied convoys bringing supplies moving to Britain from North America and directed the movement of German submarines in trying to stop them. The British had succeeded in breaking into the three-rotor Enigma machines and were successfully cracking the messages. However, that would all change on 1 February 1942, when the Germans introduced the four-rotor Enigma machine and Bletchley Park found itself back to square one. This is where the newly formed No. 30 Commando came in.

This unit was in part created by the novelist Ian Fleming, who after the war would find fame as the author of the James Bond books. Prior to Dieppe, he was employed as a personal assistant to Admiral John Godfrey, the head of British naval intelligence. Together with other naval intelligence specialists they created a unit of Commandos specifically designed for covert intelligence gathering. They became No. 30 Commando but were originally known as No. 30 Assault Unit (30AU). They were tasked to go into Dieppe harbour as part of No. 40 Commando so that their own involvement would be kept secret.

Their primary target was the Hotel Moderne, situated close to the main harbour, which British intelligence had identified as the German naval headquarters and control centre in Dieppe. They had reason to believe that one of the new Enigma coding machines had been established there.

The unit travelled to Dieppe aboard HMS *Locust* and would transfer to the chasseurs in order to enter the harbour with the Royal Marines Commandos. Unfortunately, when Major General Roberts changed the task of No. 40 Commando and they had to now support the Royal Hamilton Light Infantry, the situation also changed for 30AU. They would also be sent into the main beach instead of the harbour on the landing craft, but through the actions of Picton-Phillips, they failed to reach the shore.

While all of this was going on, Ian Fleming himself waited patiently aboard HMS *Fernie* with instructions to return to England and Bletchley Park as soon as any material discovered by 30AU was in his hands. Of course, this never actually came to pass and much of what is known about Dieppe's Enigma pinch comes from the research of Canadian historian David O'Keefe and his book *One Day in August*.

Back to the battle itself; it was now obvious that neither of the two headlands to the east and west of Dieppe could be captured in the remaining time allotted to the operation and still allow for a successful entry into the town and harbour. Major General Roberts now had no other option open to him but to issue the order to withdraw any troops that were able to get away: it was now 09:40 and the order to withdraw, *Vanquish*, was reluctantly given for 10:30, amended to 11:00.

11

BATTLE ABOVE THE BEACHES

It is important to dedicate a chapter to the part played by the RAF and other Allied air forces during Operation *Jubilee*. An excellent book by Norman Franks describes the air operations over Dieppe as *The Greatest Air Battle*. He is probably correct in that description, as for Fighter Command the raid would certainly be their biggest challenge since the Battle of Britain.

Since the summer of 1940, RAF Fighter Command had spent much of its energies undertaking intensive fighter sweeps across the English Channel and the French and Belgian coasts in an attempt to lure the aircraft of the Luftwaffe into combat in substantial numbers in order to shoot down as many of their fighters as possible. As far as Fighter Command was concerned, the overall situation in the west would change drastically when Germany invaded Russia and opened the eastern front. A large percentage of their aircraft, both fighters and bombers, were transferred east, which gave the RAF fewer targets. It was known that before a second front in the west could take place the Allies needed to put the Luftwaffe virtually out of business, so it was important for their air battles to continue over France. This had another adverse effect for the Allies as it meant that their aircraft were kept in England, achieving very little at a time when they could have been used to great advantage in other theatres, notably in the Middle East and Far East.

It was hoped that the raid on Dieppe would stir things up a bit and cause the Germans to rethink their position. Surely if an important sea port on their Atlantic Wall was threatened or even captured, they would be compelled to send enough aircraft back to the west to counter the threat. Their leaders would have no option but to consider that such an attack was as a result of the Allies opening the second front, so they would have to meet it accordingly and try to stop it before it got off the beaches. So the RAF very much considered the raid on Dieppe as being the opportunity for them to wage a conclusive battle of attrition with its adversary, here in the west.

On the evening of 18 August 1942, at airfields all over the south and south-east of England, aircrews from a number of countries including Britain, America, Canada, France, Belgium, Norway, Czechoslovakia, New Zealand and Poland, were summoned to briefings and issued with their final orders. They were informed under strict security that in the morning they were to provide air support as some 6,000 troops, mainly Canadians, would be landed on the French coast at Dieppe from an armada consisting of around 237 vessels. Once the shock had abated and turned to excitement, each unit began to go through its own individual set of instructions.

During the course of the operation the brunt of the work fell on No. 11 Group Fighter Command, whose normal responsibility was protecting the air space of London and south-east England. They would field no less than forty-four squadrons flying variants of Supermarine Spitfires, which included five Polish, two Czechoslovakian, two Norwegian, one French, One Belgian, five Canadian and three Eagle Squadrons, which were made up of

American citizens serving with the RAF. It also employed eight squadrons flying Hawker Hurricanes; three flying Hawker Typhoons; and one Canadian squadron flying the Douglas Boston. There were six squadrons from RAF Army Cooperation Command, four British and two Canadian. Four of these flew the North American P-51 Mustang, the other two Bristol Blenheims. No. 2 Group RAF Bomber Command contributed three squadrons using Douglas Bostons. The United States Eighth Army Air Force also contributed four bomber squadrons using the Boeing B-17 Flying Fortress and three fighter squadrons flying Spitfires. Several sources also state that a Bristol Beaufighter squadron was deployed, but I can find no further details as to the identity of the unit.

This was the largest gathering of Allied aircraft since the summer of 1940. The Allies were making a huge statement of intent and in some ways taking a mighty risk, as the German resources they would be facing were unknown. But they were confident that they had read the signs correctly and they would take to the skies with a massive upper hand and win air superiority over the beaches of Dieppe.

During the night of 18 August, a few squadrons from Fighter Command, together with units supplied by Coastal Command, flew protective sweeps across the Allied ships as they headed out across the English Channel bound for France. First and foremost, the job of the fighter screen, or umbrella, during the mission was to protect the ships and the troops as they came ashore, to win that all-important air supremacy over the invasion beaches. This was of course not a real invasion, but the idea was to test the feasibility of gaining air supremacy during an amphibious assault, with the task of keeping all enemy aircraft completely away from the Allied armada and the force as it landed.

As the mission progressed through the night, at airfields in the south of England most of the Allied air crews slept to be fresh for the challenges of the following morning. In Europe, the German defenders of the Atlantic Wall had no indication that a raid was about to take place. Yes, it is true to say that the Germans were expecting an attack at some point as all their intelligence pointed towards it and they were on a general state of high alert, but they did not know exactly when it was going to come, or where. Quite fortuitously, even though the Luftwaffe pilots were in that official heightened state of readiness, on 18 August, this had been somewhat relaxed. In fact, the men of *Luftflotte 3*, the German air fleet which operated in the area, had been stood down in order to attend dances with the girls of the Women's Auxiliary Air Signals Corps. So as the Allied pilots slept, many of their German opposite numbers were having a party.

On the morning of 19 August 1942, the pilots of No. 11 Group Fighter Command were awakened at their various airfields at 03:00 and told to get ready for their allocated missions. The commander in chief of No. 11 Group, Air Vice Marshal Trafford Leigh-Mallory, was already waiting at his headquarters at RAF Uxbridge, where a map room would be his workplace for the duration of the operation and from where he would control the air operations over the Allied force. It was the same room from where Air Vice Marshal Keith Park had directed the defence of London and the south-east during the Battle of Britain two years earlier. During that conflict, Leigh-Mallory had been in command of No. 12 Group Fighter Command.

Leigh Mallory was something of a controversial figure who during the Battle of Britain was the instigator of the Big Wing, and as such had a very public quarrel with Keith Park. Park had accused Mallory of not doing enough to protect the airfields in the south-east with his aircraft, which were based more in the Midlands. Leigh Mallory had devised, together with Squadron Leader Douglas Bader, a massed fighter formation known as the Big Wing, which they used with little success to hunt German bomber formations over Britain, except for on a couple of occasions.

Leigh-Mallory was critical of the tactics of Park and Air Chief Marshal Sir Hugh Dowding, the commander in chief of Fighter Command, believing that they did not do enough to support his wing-sized formations. He then worked energetically in political circles to bring about the removal of Park from command of No. 11 Group, with false claims for the success of the Duxford Big Wing playing a part in this. Throughout the Battle of Britain, his lack of support for No. 11 Group contributed materially to the damage that the Luftwaffe was able to inflict on Park's airfields.

After the Battle of Britain, Air Chief Marshal Charles Portal, the new chief of the air staff, who had agreed with Leigh-Mallory, removed both Park and Dowding from their posts. Leigh-Mallory took over from Park as commander of No. 11 Group Fighter Command in December 1940. As a beneficiary of the change in command, Leigh-Mallory has been accused of fomenting a plot to overthrow Dowding, the man who had effectively won the Battle of Britain and saved Britain from invasion, but who never really received the recognition he deserved.

Leigh Mallory's second in command was Air Commodore Adrian Lindley Trevor Cole of the Royal Australian Air Force, known to his peers as 'King' Cole. He was aboard HMS *Calpe* with the naval and army force commanders, from where he would liaise with Uxbridge. He had joined the Australian army at the outbreak of the First World War, and later transferred to the Australian Flying Corps in 1916, flying with No. 1 Squadron in the Middle East and No. 2 Squadron on the western front. He became an ace, credited with ten enemy aircraft, and earned the Military Cross and the Distinguished Flying Cross. In 1921, he was a founding member of the RAAF.

From his map room at RAF Uxbridge Leigh-Mallory could see where his squadrons were at any time in the proceedings, but Cole would be in a position to advise in-theatre on things such as where and when to utilise smoke-screens on the beaches, or give updates on requirements for fighter cover or bombing runs.

Examining the part played by the Allied air forces during the operation gives us a good chance to summarise the events of the day thus far, as aircraft were involved at every stage. We know that the opening attacks of the day were carried out by No. 3 Commando against the extreme eastern flank where they were to tackle the Goebbels battery at Berneval-le-Grand. They were only partially successful and only a small party made it to shore at around 05:10 after running into an enemy convoy. However, they did manage to keep the battery diverted for almost two hours before withdrawing. During this part of the operation the RAF provided supporting attacks on the battery using two Douglas Bostons and six Hawker Hurricane 11Cs, which first strafed the complex at 05:30.

At the same time No. 4 Commando was tackling the Hess battery at Varengeville-sur-Mer to the west of Dieppe. As the first Commandos came ashore, which was around 04:50, two Spitfires of No. 129 Squadron attacked the battery's OP near the D'Ailly Lighthouse. Simultaneously, other squadron aircraft strafed the battery itself repeatedly. Also, cannon-firing Hawker Hurricanes attacked two flank batteries near Vasterival. At 06:26, in close co-ordination with the Commandos, Hurricanes delivered the final air attack on Hess and by 06:45 the guns of the battery finally fell silent.

Just as important as the attacks on the batteries at Berneval-le-Grand and Varengeville-sur-Mer were the inner flank attacks on the headlands to the east and west of Dieppe as, ultimately, whoever controlled the high ground would dominate the battlefield. As we already know, both of these attacks were doomed to failure despite the intervention of the RAF.

At Puys the main undertaking of the Royal Regiment of Canada was to silence the Rommel battery on the eastern headland. The first troops came ashore at around 05:06 under the protective curtain of a smoke-screen laid by RAF Bostons. More Bostons of No. 88 Squadron attacked the battery itself at 06:45 but their efforts had no effect on the guns, which continued to operate while the Royal Regiment of Canada found themselves pinned down on the beach subjected to murderous fire from the battery and other supporting troops. They were finally forced to surrender despite the assistance of Hurricanes from No. 32 Squadron that had hoped to give cover during their evacuation.

At Pourville-sur-Mer the tasks of the South Saskatchewan Regiment and the Queen's Own Cameron Highlanders of Canada were to capture the Hindenburg battery on the western headland and the barracks at Les-Quatre-Vents Farm. Again, despite the concerted support of the RAF, neither of their objectives were achieved, although many of the troops were successfully evacuated.

While all of these preliminary attacks were taking place, back in England the pilots who would make up the air umbrella during the main assault on the Dieppe seafront were getting prepared. At 04:30 the first two wings of the umbrella, based at RAF Kenley and RAF Northolt, took off and headed out across the Channel. Fifteen minutes later, many other squadrons from supporting bases were also airborne and on their way to join them over the fleet.

At 04:50 the twelve Hurricanes of No. 43 Squadron under the leadership of a Belgian airman, Squadron Leader Danny Le Roy du Vivier, came over the beaches in line abreast to carry out a low-level cannon strike on the enemy gun positions along the seafront, thus opening the main Dieppe assault. They had left their base at Tangmere at 04:25 in darkness. On their arrival over Dieppe the gunners of the 13th Flak Division caused severe damage to seven of their aircraft with two being shot down.

At 05:12 the Royal Navy destroyers offshore opened fire on the buildings lining the promenade. At the same time the Douglas Bostons of No. 226 Squadron laid smoke-screens as four squadrons of Hurricane 11Cs and 11Bs hedgehopped over the beach, spraying cannon fire and dropping 250lb bombs on the German positions. Although their efforts did keep the defenders' heads down, the few bombs they dropped hardly had any effect at all, and when they were gone the Germans got back into their positions and re-commenced fire. And of course, as we learnt in the last chapter, the smoke screen probably did as much harm as it did good, as it hindered the Allies as well as the Germans. That said, it was a necessary part of any such operation and the carnage that followed on the beaches was not the fault of the smoke-screen but the poor reconnaissance that the planners had made of the German defences beforehand.

As the RAF and Royal Navy continued their attacks on the seafront of Dieppe, the situation on the east and west headlands was still unresolved. Flight Lieutenant (acting Squadron Leader) John Scott led No. 614 Squadron's Blenheims to lay smoke on the east headland. A hit from a flak battery shattered his jaw. In spite of this injury, he continued with the mission and by 05:15 the air attacks on both headlands were in full swing. Scott was awarded the DFC. Spitfires and No. 88 Squadron's Bostons continued the attacks on the Rommel battery near Puys behind the eastern headland, on the Hindenberg battery near Pourville-sur-Mer on the western headland, as well as several other gun positions and highlighted targets.

Just before the main assault began, at 05:23 all supporting fire from the Allied navies and air forces came to an end in order not to interfere with the soldiers of the Essex Scottish Regiment and the Royal Hamilton Light Infantry as they alighted from their landing craft. The German defences were still almost completely intact. On the beaches all control of the situation was lost and with a few exceptions, the assault was pinned down behind the sea wall. However, with the beaches covered in smoke-screens and due to a monumental communications breakdown, the force commanders on HMS *Calpe*, including Air Commodore Cole, were totally unaware of the real situation for the next three hours or more and continued to act according to the plan, although deviating from it in accordance with their own understanding of events, notably in the use of the reserves.

The enemy forces in the area were represented by two fighter wings, *Jagdeschwader* 2 (JG 2) and *Jagdeschwader* 26 (JG 26), which between them had around 200 fighters, mostly the Focke-Wulf Fw 190. There was also a bomber wing in the area, *Kampfgeschwader* 2 (KG 2) flying mostly Dornier Do 217s. During the latter stages of the operation, aircraft from other bomber wings based in Northern France and Holland would also be brought into the fight.

Supermarine Spitfires and Hawker Hurricanes had combined with great effect to win the Battle of Britain against German fighters like the Messerschmitt Bf 109. But in the Focke-Wulf Fw 190, they were facing something much more formidable. It was powered by a BMW 801 radial engine which helped the FW 190 to lift larger loads than the BF 109, allowing it to be used as a day fighter, a fighter bomber, a ground attack aircraft, and to a lesser extent, a night fighter, so it was incredibly versatile. It had been designed by Kurt Tank at Focke-Wulf in the late 1930s and was well-liked by its pilots. Some of the Luftwaffe's most successful fighter aces claimed many of their kills while flying it. The Fw 190 provided greater firepower than the Bf 109 and, at low to medium altitude, superior manoeuvrability. It is regarded by most historians as one of the best fighter planes of the Second World War.

JG 26 was slow to respond to the initial attacks due to mist over their airfields. However, in the area where JG 2 was based (*I Gruppe* at Triqueville; *II Gruppe* at Beamont-le-Roger; and *III Gruppe* at Cherbourg-Maupertus) the sky was clear and the Luftwaffe was able to make its first sortie of the day, which was a reconnaissance to the north-west of Dieppe at 05:30. This was still more than an hour and half after the first contact was made with the Allied force at 03:48. At first, only a few German fighters were up. No. 71 Squadron shot one of them down, probably the first kill of the day.

Between 05:45 and 05:55, the Hornchurch and Biggin Hill Wings became airborne, while elements of their chief adversary, JG 26, at last joined the fray shortly after 06:00 as the fog in their areas began to lift. However, the Hornchurch Wing arrived too late to stop FW 190s of JG 26 engaging No. 174 Squadron in combat as they gave cover to Bostons in the area. Three of their Hurricanes were shot down, including the one flown by the CO, a French-born officer, Squadron Leader Emile Francois Marie Leonce Fayolle. His Hurricane IIB was also hit by flak, after which he eventually crashed and was killed.

Also entering the battle by this time was the 307th Fighter Squadron of the 31st Fighter Group of the United States Eighth Army Air Force. Lieutenant Samuel S. Junkin shot down a FW 190, thus scoring the first USAAF kill in the European theatre of operations. His own aircraft, a Spitfire VB, was damaged during the fight and he was forced to ditch in the Channel, from where he was rescued and returned to England. His reward was to be decorated with the Distinguished Flying Cross and the Purple Heart by Brigadier General Frank D. O. Hunter, the commanding officer of the United States Eighth Army Air Force Fighter Command.

At 06:10 the North Weald (Norwegian) Wing began to take off from its airfields to join the force. On reaching Dieppe, Captain

Bjorn Raeder became separated and went on to fight an epic action against eight FWs single-handedly. After his aircraft was damaged he was eventually forced to disengage over the Channel and managed to make it back to England where he crash-landed.

Meanwhile, Douglas Bostons were bombing several inland batteries and enemy positions, one of which being 256 battery near Arques-la-Bataille about four miles to the south-east of Dieppe. Just behind this attack, six Hawker Hurricanes went in to attack the chateau there, which was believed to be the headquarters of the German 110th Infantry Division. Unfortunately for them, it was not and four Hurricanes were lost, some crashing into the nearby commune itself, killing their pilots and eight civilians.

The situation on the main beaches was still unclear to the force commanders on HMS *Calpe,* prompting Major General Roberts to send in his reserves, with Les Fusiliers Mont-Royal beginning to land from around 07:05. The only cover given by the RAF during this period of operations was a Hurricane cannon strike on the east headland. Because the landing of the reserves went ahead almost on a whim of the force commander, there was no time for Air Commodore Cole to arrange any adequate air support via Uxbridge. The reserves, similar to the troops who had hit the beach before them, were soon pinned down by what *The London Gazette* would later describe as 'an inferno of fire'.

As for the great air battle with the Luftwaffe that Fighter Command had hoped for, by 07:00 there were still only about thirty German fighters in the air over Dieppe. Leigh-Mallory was greatly disappointed by the enemy's response. One of these fighters was a FW 190 flown by Oberleutnant Josef 'Sepp' Wurmheller of JG 2, despite the fact that he had a broken leg, which was in plaster. Engaging the enemy and reporting engine trouble he was forced to crash-land on a beach away from the fighting, from where he was recovered and taken back to his airfield. But that was far from being the end of his involvement that day and later he would be in the air again, when he went on to shoot down seven Allied aircraft.

19 August 1942 turned out to be Wurmheller's most successful day of the entire war as a fighter pilot. His seven victories were claimed during the course of four combat missions and were said to be six Spitfires and a Bristol Blenheim. The last of these was listed as his 59th victory. The very next day, 20 August, he claimed his 60th aerial victory, which earned him the German Cross in Gold, which he received on 21 August.

Above the English Channel, Hurricanes in support of MGBs scoured the surface of the water hunting for German F-boats. Similarly, on the enemy side, FW 190s of JG 26 searched out and attacked isolated Allied ships, although with much less success than they claimed. The Germans were also scouring the Channel for another potential Allied attack force. Their leaders were still taking the situation seriously and as far as they were concerned, Dieppe could have been just the inaugural action of a much larger operation, perhaps even the Allies opening the second front. They had no way of determining whether or not it was just a raid or the start of the real invasion. If it was something bigger, then certainly, other Allied ships would surely be approaching the French coast at other locations.

While all of this was taking place over Dieppe and the English Channel, tactical reconnaissance Mustangs flew deep into France looking for German reinforcements but found little evidence of any. One was flown by Pilot Officer Arnold Christensen, who was a New Zealander. He was flying a Mustang with the serial number AL977, of No. 26 Squadron. His wingman was Pilot Officer E. E. O'Farrell (flying AG463). Neither pilot returned from the mission. Their aircraft were two of five which their squadron were to lose that day. Both of these aircraft were shot down by machine gun fire from the ground. Christensen himself managed to dive into the sea and hoped to be picked up and taken back across the Channel. He was to spend the next two days adrift in a tiny dinghy before being washed ashore on the French coast and subsequently taken prisoner. He is also notable for the part he took in the Great Escape from Stalag Luft III in March 1944 and was one of the men recaptured and subsequently executed by the Gestapo.

Back at Dieppe, roughly every twenty minutes sections of Hurricanes arrived for ground support patrols over the town, attacking the seafront positions. Douglas Bostons would also make an appearance at longer intervals. At around 08:30 the first German bomber made its appearance, bringing the total number of Luftwaffe aircraft now brought to battle at around fifty.

By 09:00 the force commanders on HMS *Calpe* were beginning to become aware of the true situation on the beaches and the withdrawal order, *Vanquish*, was given for 10:30. However, Air Commodore Cole was forced to point out that the RAF's timetable only allowed for a maximum effort to cover *Vanquish* at 11:00. His point was made and accepted, so Cole informed Uxbridge at 10:04 that smoke-screens would be required over the main beaches for the evacuation starting from 11:00. These would have to last for a minimum of half an hour. At 10:10 the final attempt to soften up the indestructible headlands began and was kept up for thirty minutes by twenty-four Bostons and twenty-two Hurricane bombers. But as with most of the Allied air attacks during the day, the assault was too soon and too short and contributed little.

By 10:00 the German bombers had arrived in force and the Luftwaffe had committed over 100 aircraft to the battle over Dieppe at any one time to meet Fighter Command's challenge. With the job of air cover foremost, the RAF was soon paying a high price for maintaining its superlative and near-impregnable air umbrella over the main assault force. Losses to the British

Spitfire VBs were mounting as they were outclassed by the Fw l9os coming to bear, but by sheer numbers and determination they were stopping the German bombers from getting through to the ships or attacking the soldiers on the beaches. For all the victories of the FW 190s, the Luftwaffe was actually losing the air battle of Dieppe.

At 10:30, the American Army Air Force lent a hand. Twenty-two out of a force of twenty-four B-17E Boeing Flying Fortresses of the 97th Bombardment Group, 8th USAAF, escorted by four squadrons of Spitfires, carried out an accurate bombing of Abbeville-Drucat airfield as a diversion. During the run sixteen enemy aircraft were destroyed or damaged at their dispersal points, and the airfield itself put out of action for a vital two hours. More than that, the controllers of the whole of that fighter area appear to have been killed or wounded, for the control remained out of action until the evening, when a new and unfamiliar voice came on the air.

Ever since 10:00, Luftwaffe fighter reserves between Flushing in the Netherlands and Beaumont-le-Roger had been put on the alert, while bomber forces from Holland to Beauvais were steadily being committed to battle. So it seems that Fighter Command's ploy was working and fighters were being drawn into the battle from other areas.

Fighter Command's Typhoon Wing flew a diversionary feint to Ostend and from there moved towards Le Treport, making it seem that the Allies were everywhere. They ran into a group of Fw 190s and two Typhoons crashed when they failed to pull out of dives and their tails snapped off.

Although initially slow to respond to the raid, the German fighters were now really beginning to make their presence felt over the port itself, even though the Allied fighters did a sterling job of keeping them away from their ground and sea forces. Operating so far from their bases in England, the

Allies were considerably hampered. The Spitfires in particular were at the edge of their range, with some only being able to spend five minutes over the combat area. The raid on Dieppe was the baptism of fire for the latest Spitfire Mark IX, the only British fighter at that time which was regarded as equal to the Fw 190. Six squadrons (four British, two Canadian) flew the Mark IX at Dieppe.

In the end, some nine Spitfire squadrons were sent into the area to stop the bombers reaching Dieppe. The North Weald Wing on their second sortie shot down eight of nine unescorted Do 217Es. While returning back across the Channel one of the pilots turned quickly on an enemy aircraft after hearing the frantic words through his intercom 'Look out 190 approaching three o'clock!' He managed to get off a short but effective burst. What he had thought was a FW 190 burst into flames and dived inverted into the Channel and it was only at this point that he realised it was one of Fighter Command's Typhoons, R7815 of No. 266 Squadron. The pilot was killed.

As the withdrawal from the beaches continued the Allied air forces maintained their desperate fight to cripple the Luftwaffe in the west, but losses were mounting on both sides and only time would tell which side would be the ultimate victor over the beaches of Dieppe.

12

THE WITHDRAWAL

In the last chapter through our summary of the battle as seen through the part played by the Allied air forces, we have already touched upon the final evacuation of the remnants of the raiding force. Once it became quite evident that Operation *Jubilee* had failed, the best that the force commanders could hope for was to extract as many men as possible from the beaches before they and their equipment fell into enemy hands.

After much confusion and discussion between the various force commanders, *Vanquish* was timed to begin at 11:00. To coincide with the start of the evacuation, a curtain of dense smoke was laid between the two headlands and all along the main waterfront of the town, to shroud both the returning landing craft and the men they were coming to rescue. The smoke-screen was provided by Douglas Bostons flown by Nos. 411 and 226 Squadrons. It was certainly no easy task and was carried out under an immense onslaught of fire from the batteries of an enemy unsubdued and very much encouraged by their efficient repulse of the invading force, so were still fighting with great and even increased vigour.

To add further pain to the Allied evacuation, by now the Luftwaffe had brought in bomber reinforcements which were arriving in strength. They were in such numbers that the RAF's fighter umbrella began to falter for the first time and the German pilots were able to cut through them and bombard the soldiers on the beaches. Together with the German gunners on shore, the Luftwaffe bombers were beginning to turn the evacuation from Dieppe into a massacre of Allied personnel.

At 11:15 Hurricanes of No. 43 Squadron flew in and attacked the German positions on the east headland in an attempt to subdue the fire coming from that area. As of course much of this fire was coming from batteries concealed within and protected by the cave system on the headland, their attacks did very little to suppress them.

At around 11:20 a call came from the beach begging for more air support and more smoke because the German bombers were obliterating the soldiers there. The smoke was not sufficient enough to conceal them and the German pilots were picking them off at will. No more smoke was forthcoming, and HMS *Calpe* received further appeals from the beach for more smoke at 11:35 and again at 11:38. The desperate calls were to the effect that the beaches were under tremendous fire and evacuation was impossible under such conditions.

Air Commodore Cole relayed these messages to RAF Uxbridge, which in addition was becoming inundated with calls for more bombing runs. Consequently, Fighter Command sent off more Hurricane fighter bombers almost immediately, but to send more aircraft with smoke-laying capability wasn't quite so easy. The Bostons, which were the main aircraft designated to do this job, were still on their way back to England and it would take time to rearm them and get them out again.

At Pourville-sur-Mer, the remnants of the assault on the west headland were being evacuated under increasing attack from both shore and air. Here the survivors of the South Saskatchewan Regiment and the Queen's Own Cameron Highlanders of Canada came under constant attack from Fw 190s that strafed the beach and Junkers Ju 88s apparently using flame thrower equipment to attack the Allied personnel, which has been described as an early sort of napalm.

The RAF were unable to intervene and help protect the men stranded on Green Beach as they were already fully engaged over Dieppe at White and Red beaches, so were unable to provide any further cover. It is known that some German bombers, including Ju 88s, were fitted with backward firing flamethrowers intended not so much to burn enemy fighter pilots to death, but to blind them with black oily smoke. They did not produce much flame at altitude as it was too cold and the air too thin for the oil to burn well, but the unburnt oil did foul some windscreens. Perhaps at low level, used over troops on a beach, they could be more devastating.

At last the Hawker Hurricanes arrived over Dieppe at 12:00 and ploughed into the shore defences and for a while their attacks helped to keep down the heads of German gunners and allowed the Spitfires in the umbrella to tackle the dogged incursions of the increasing numbers of enemy bombers, which now included Junkers Ju 88s, Dornier Do 217s and a few Heinkel He 111s.

As the battle overhead continued to rage and the Allied aircraft seemed to be getting the situation under better control, the members of the Royal Hamilton Light Infantry who were still holding out in the casino took the opportunity to move back to the seafront under the leadership of Major H. F. Lazier and Captain John Currie. While they did this, detachments of the regiment and of Les Fusiliers Mont-Royal held the casino until everyone else had got out. Among the last to leave was Sergeant Major Dumais of the Fusiliers, who eventually withdrew his men to the beach and got them on board a landing craft. He himself was unable to climb onto the deck of the craft due to the weight of his equipment and remained behind to be taken prisoner.

Similarly, Captain Currie of the Royal Hamilton Light Infantry, who had led the evacuation from the casino, at first managed to get aboard one of the landing craft but jumped off again because he believed it was overcrowded. He then boarded another landing craft, which was bombed and sunk. He was wounded and also captured by the Germans.

Throughout the day and especially during the period of re-embarkation the work of the medical officers and orderlies with the Royal Canadian Army Medical Corps was said to be of the highest order. The number of wounded was incredibly high and many more than had been anticipated, so medical supplies quickly ran short on the beaches and large dressings in particular were more or less used up.

On White Beach many of the wounded owed their lives to the trio of Captain David Wesley Clare, a medical officer with the Royal Hamilton Light Infantry, Honorary Captain John Weir Foote, the Chaplain of the regiment, and the very aptly named Corporal Al Comfort. Clare's battalion had originally come ashore with thirteen men to dispense first-aid - two to each of the four companies in the regiment. However, most of these had quickly become casualties themselves leaving the three men in question to do what they could under immensely difficult circumstances.

Captain Clare and his helpers were finding it almost impossible to seek out and help the wounded where they lay on the beach because of the intense and accurate enemy fire. Instead, Clare established an aid post in the lee of a derelict tank landing craft that had floated in broadside to the beach. Largely it was up to the wounded soldiers on the beach themselves to somehow make their own way to the back of the craft and seek help, although all three men made dashes into the open to bring men in.

For his actions that day Captain Clare was awarded the Military Cross, the citation for which stated:

> Throughout the operation Captain Clare carried on his work without regard to his own safety, under heavy enemy fire. The rate at which casualties had to be treated on that day used up all the medical supplies available in a short time and Captain Clare was forced to improvise. At all times this gallant officer gave unstintingly of his efforts, far beyond the ordinary duties of a Medical Officer, while working under the most hazardous conditions. At the conclusion of the action Captain Clare refused to take his place on the last available landing craft leaving the beach because he believed that he was the only Medical Officer in the area and many men still needed professional care if their lives were to be saved.

Honorary Captain John Weir Foote was awarded the Victoria Cross. Foote was a Presbyterian minister who was born in 1904 and in later life would be a politician and cabinet minister. During the Second World War he was the only Canadian chaplain to be awarded the VC. His award was gazetted after the Second World War on 14 February 1946:

> The KING has been graciously pleased to approve the award of the VICTORIA CROSS to: Honorary Captain John Weir FOOTE, Canadian Chaplain Services.
>
> At Dieppe, on 19th August, 1942, Honorary Captain Foote, Canadian Chaplain Services, was Regimental Chaplain with the Royal Hamilton Light Infantry. Upon landing on the beach under heavy fire he attached himself to the Regimental Aid Post which had been set up in a slight depression on the beach,

but which was only sufficient to give cover to men lying down. During the subsequent period of approximately eight hours, while the action continued, this officer not only assisted the Regimental Medical Officer in ministering to the wounded in the Regimental Aid Post, but time and again left this shelter to inject morphine, give first-aid and carry wounded personnel from the open beach to the Regimental Aid Post. On these occasions, with utter disregard for his personal safety, Honorary Captain Foote exposed himself to an inferno of fire and saved many lives by his gallant efforts. During the action, as the tide went out, the Regimental Aid Post was moved to the shelter of a stranded landing craft. Honorary Captain Foote continued tirelessly and courageously to carry wounded men from the exposed beach to the cover of the landing craft. He also removed wounded from inside the landing craft when ammunition had been set on fire by enemy shells. When landing craft appeared he carried wounded from the Regimental Aid Post to the landing craft through very heavy fire.

On several occasions this officer had the opportunity to embark but returned to the beach as his chief concern was the care and evacuation of the wounded. He refused a final opportunity to leave the shore, choosing to suffer the fate of the men he had ministered to for over three years. Honorary Captain Foote personally saved many lives by his efforts and his example inspired all around him. Those who observed him state that the calmness of this heroic officer, as he walked about, collecting the wounded on the fire-swept beach will never be forgotten.

By 12:20 most of the men who had fought their way back to the main beaches had been got away by the crews of the landing craft, who, says the official report 'showed complete disregard of danger in their efforts to take off the troops'. And at 12:43 three

Bostons arrived and laid the final smoke-screen of the operation in the face of heavy AA fire from the shore.

Albert Kirby, who was serving on landing craft with the Royal Canadian Navy described what happened around the time of the evacuation. You get the sense when reading his story that perhaps not enough was done; some of the crews were ordered to abandon the men on the beaches and leave them to their fate.

Well, we went in at that time, at 7:00. We waited out in the harbour until our time to pick them up came and we went in, we drove in and we attracted such an immense fire from the enemy that it was apparent that we were never going to pick anybody up alive. So we were given a signal to turn around and go back out into the centre of the harbour again while the Air Force and the naval guns tried to settle the enemy down. So we waited for an hour or two out there and then we were told to go in again, it should be a good bunch better now. So we went in and it hadn't changed a bit, it was just as bad as it was the first time. So we were ordered to turn around and go back out again and then they sent us a signal to head back to England. So we headed back to England with nobody else on the boat but the crew. So we landed about thirty-five or forty soldiers there, but didn't pick anybody up at all, they were just left.

Albert Kirby goes on to talk about the general evacuation of the troops from Dieppe:

We were losing the battle and we were going to lose everything if we didn't get out of there. So they loaded them all back up and took them back out. I shouldn't say all because nine-tenths of them were captured or killed. But the one tenth that survived, they loaded them back up and put them on the ships and scooted back to England. And although we called it an utter failure, because we didn't actually accomplish anything and lost a great deal of men, in the papers they called it a great success because we landed there and came back.

Among the soldiers of the Royal Hamilton Light Infantry was Jack Clifford McFarland, who recalled what happened to some of the regiment during the evacuation from White Beach:

We headed for the beach. I saw one of our officers had been wounded and my buddy and I, he got a stretcher and I got a smoke bomb and we put that – the smoke bomb – between us and the Germans and put him on a stretcher and took him down to the beach. Some of the fellows were risking their lives putting these wounded people on the assault craft to take them back. So we handed them over to them because they had it organised. And he got back fortunately, but he was a paraplegic the rest of his life.

And then I went down the beach further where a tank landing craft was beached. It was on fire. And I got onto an assault craft there and got started back and sitting on the motor part, there was four of us sitting there, three of us got hit, one dead and the other wounded. And I thought that it had blown my arm off so I left the craft and went back onshore. Well, I didn't think I should head back to England. Then another guy and I set up a Bren gun and tried to keep the Germans off the beach while the other guys were going out on the assault craft. He loaded it and I fired it left-handed. Eventually, an officer or somebody grabbed what seemed to me to be a German airman that had parachuted down and was in our midst and got them to raise a white undershirt. And the Germans came down from nowhere. Where they all came from, I don't know. But all of a sudden, the beach was just loaded with them and they took us prisoner.

You will recall that in an earlier interview for *The Memory Project*, Wilson Howard Large described how he had come ashore on Red Beach with the Essex Scottish Regiment. He was one of a small group of soldiers who had made it over the sea wall and into some town houses where they had come face to face with a German patrol, the members of which they had killed in a fire fight. Wilson had been shot and made his way into the basement of a house to treat his wounds and hopefully be rescued later, when more of his regiment made it into the town. It didn't work out like that. The next people to happen along were the men of another German patrol.

All of a sudden, I hear a patrol coming, and I yelled that I was wounded, and all I got was gunshots coming down into the basement. And, so when they quit firing, I yelled again. And they fired again. They fired down there about three times. Then they came down – and got me out.

I'm sure it was another German patrol, but the thing is, when I got upstairs and they went to take me out, the dead bodies of the other fellows were there and one put the rifle right to my head, and I thought, this is it. And the one soldier just reached up and just grabbed a hold of the rifle and he said, in English he said, "This is my prisoner." So he made the other fellow help me, over the bodies, because I couldn't walk very well, and I'd lost my tourniquet from my leg. And they took me down to where they were taking the wounded out in front of this building – just put me on the lawn.

Oh, and on the way, a lady came out of the house, with a tray of beer, and offered it to us. And they handed me one before they took one themselves. Best beer I ever had.

Also serving with the Essex Scottish was Maurice Snook, but he had not made it into the town with Wilson Howard Large and was one of the men who remained pinned down behind the sea wall throughout the battle:

> I lay for nine hours behind a wall and then we got captured at 13:50 in the afternoon, the Germans got us, took all our weapons away from us and marched us into town. When we got into town, a nurse there, Sister Agnes, took care of the wounded Canadians and a German pulled his pistol and said to her, stop working on the Canadians and do my men or I'll shoot you. And with that another guy pulled his pistol out and said, if you shoot her, I'll shoot you. So she finished her job.

By 13:00, most of those who could be evacuated had been, but Captain Hughes-Hallett, the naval force commander, decided to make another effort to rescue any others who could make it. He sailed the *Calpe* as close to the shore as was possible, emerging through the smoke that still shrouded the shoreline. This brought the ship into full view of the enemy who opened up on the craft relentlessly, mainly from machine gun posts on the Dieppe breakwater. There was no sign of any further troops waiting for evacuation so the *Calpe* slipped back into the safety provided by the smoke.

Arthur Fraser of Les Fusiliers Mont-Royal, recalled the moment a destroyer came out of the smoke, only to turn around and disappear again. Could this have been HMS *Calpe*? According to Arthur, the troops on the beach had been observed by this particular ship's company, so it was most likely one of the other destroyers.

> The raid was finished, the destroyer came forward, they brought down the flag half-mast and everybody on the boat saluted to us on the beach and they raised the flag and all the cannons on that destroyer shot into Dieppe and they went away. A lot of

our boys tried to reach that destroyer but they could not, they didn't have a chance to be picked up. So they came back to the ground and of course, they had no clothes on. They only had their underwear. And they were of course caught as prisoners of war, like we were.

Jacques Cinq-Mars, also of Les Fusiliers Mont-Royal, goes so far as to mention the *Calpe,* although again, the ship he refers too could have been any of the destroyers.

In the Dieppe raid, we had twenty-six men on our ship and twenty-four of them died. Then I was taken prisoner. On the beaches at Dieppe, we didn't do much; we were pinned to the beach and were stuck there. There was a sixty-five-foot cliff and the Germans were above, shooting at us below. It didn't go well. We were like Daniel in the lions' den. At one point I tried to get away; I swam for three miles. I made it to a destroyer called the *Calpe.* It was three miles away from the shore and had come to pick up those who were able to get away. I was about fifty feet away from the destroyer, and I could see the Canadians who had already climbed aboard. Then three German Stukas arrived. They bombed the destroyer; there was fire and explosions and all of that. My friends who were in the destroyer were jumping into the water. I said to myself there's no point in going there, I'll just have to turn around.

On returning to the beach Jacques Cinq-Mars gave aid to a fellow soldier in distress and finally helped him on to a landing craft. Unfortunately, his charity was little appreciated and because of it he was taken prisoner. You can tell that he felt understandably bitter about it:

I said to him: "What are you doing there?" He said to me: "I can't tread water, my back is injured." So I took him on my back and I hauled him to the beach, at least a few hundred feet away, to a small boat, an assault landing craft. I put him on the boat and I grabbed the chain to pull myself up. Then five or six guys came running from the beach; they banged my head and pushed me underwater and then the boat started to back up and I was left there. I got a bullet in the leg because of him and I wasn't able to take the boat since they pushed me down. He wasn't injured. If only he had helped me a bit to get on the boat. He was decorated for bravery and he received a big shiny medal. I never got any medal. Of the prisoners of war, only two got medals. One died and the other is Colonel (John Weir) Foote, the padre. He won the medal of merit – what do you call it, the VC (Victoria Cross). He could have escaped, but he wanted to stay with his men. That was admirable.

Having retreated back through the smoke screen on HMS *Calpe*, Captain Hughes-Hallett decided that in view of the large number of soldiers that were still unaccounted for, he would explore other options for getting them out. He decided to signal the commander of HMS *Locust*, which had a shallower draft and so could get closer to the shore than he had been able to do in the command ship. However, it was while he was engaged in signalling his instructions to HMS *Locust* that Major General Roberts received a signal from the shore. It came from Brigadier Southam's headquarters, saying he was compelled to surrender. The time was 13:08.

As late as 13:45, the Royal Air Force continued to attack the two headlands and other known German defences, even though the battle was effectively now over. In doing this they were responsible for killing a number of Canadian soldiers who were now prisoners of war.

Heading for England now were some 200 vessels in close convoy, with some inevitable stragglers behind. With a renewed effort, the Luftwaffe tried to inflict more casualties. For the RAF fighter pilots flying their third, fourth or even fifth sorties of the day, this was the last challenge. In addition to the general air cover provided, eighty-six additional patrols were put up to intercept specific attacks. It was this devotion to duty, combined with the high degree of skill shown, which caused Major General Roberts to signal from aboard HMS *Calpe* to his Royal Air Force colleague, Air Vice Marshal Trafford Leigh-Mallory at RAF Uxbridge: 'Air co-operation faultless'.

Only one incident was to mar what was otherwise a near-perfect example of fighter cover. At the tail end of the convoy a free-for-all was developing over the last ships getting into station. At 13:08 a section of three Dornier Do 217s, though harried unmercifully by Spitfires, pressed home their attack. Just after 13:14, one bomb exploded under the destroyer HMS *Berkeley*, breaking her back. Her crew were evacuated and she was sunk by a fellow destroyer. The sinking of the *Berkeley* was effectively an accident. The bomb which caused the initial problem had not been targeted at the ship but was jettisoned by the German crew. By ill luck, the *Berkeley* happened to be underneath when the bombs fell and her bridge was destroyed.

Among those on the bridge at the time were Wing Commander Stanley Hewitt Skinner, who was killed, and Lieutenant Colonel Loren Boyd Hillsinger of the US Army Air Corps, who was wounded. They were both acting as observers on the ship and were from the staff of Combined Operations headquarters. Lieutenant Colonel Hillsinger was wearing a pair of smart new shoes. When he came to, after the explosion of the bomb, he saw his left foot floating past with one of them on it. This enraged him, and he took off his other shoe and threw it after his foot in disgust. He was taken aboard an MGB and refusing to go below. He lay on deck directing the AA fire of the ship. He was awarded the US Distinguished Service Cross and the Order of the Purple Heart.

By 15:45, the Luftwaffe, realising the futility of further mass attacks, sent single bombers to harass the convoy, using the gathering overcast for protection. By 20:00 the convoy was nearly home and the RAF had the sky to itself. The expedition returned to the ports from which it sailed, some of the ships not berthing until past midnight.

13

PRISONERS OF WAR

Before we finally analyse the Dieppe Raid to attempt to discover whether or not it did indeed actually achieve anything, a chapter should be reserved solely for one of its major consequences, the fact that the Germans took nearly 2,000 Allied prisoners of war out of the 6,000 men who landed on the beaches. It was, in fact, a total of 1,965 men made up of 1,874 Canadians, eighty-seven British, and four soldiers from the US. This was a catastrophic number, particularly of course for the Canadians and a situation which established a new dimension of interaction for the Allied nations in their wartime diplomacy with Germany.

Although Brigadier William Wallace Southam, the commanding officer of the 6th Canadian Infantry Brigade, was under strict instructions not to take a copy of the official plan for the raid ashore with him, which was classified as a secret document, for some reason known only to himself, he did. This caused him a problem when he was forced to give the order for the final Canadian surrender on Red and White Beaches as he knew he must do all he could to not allow it to fall into enemy hands.

He made the odd choice of trying to bury it under the chert but was spotted in his attempt and the plan was subsequently retrieved by the enemy.

The Germans were thereafter given all the time they liked to mull over it and apparently found it needlessly complex. One disturbing entry in the plan would have ongoing ramifications, which was the order contained therein to shackle German prisoners. One of the objectives of the plan was of course to capture German personnel and return them to England for interrogation and it seems the plan gave the go ahead for what was largely looked upon by The Geneva Convention and other agreements as a breach of human rights when dealing with prisoners of war.

It later transpired that following the Allied withdrawal, the bodies of a number of captured German soldiers were washed up on the shore. It was discovered that their hands had been tied. They had probably been taken aboard an Allied landing craft which had been sunk in the process of leaving the area and having been shackled were unable to swim and save their own lives. When Adolf Hitler was acquainted with this information he was said to have been outraged and ordered the shackling of Canadian prisoners. When they were informed of this, the British and Canadian authorities issued a reciprocating order that German prisoners being held in Canada in the prisoner of war camps there should also be tied.

The Canadians themselves were worried that implementing such an order would put their own personnel then in German hands in grave danger, but they reluctantly agreed to carry it out to maintain unity with the British. The Canadians were right to be concerned as in October 1942 the shackling of Germans led to trouble and brought about an uprising at a Canadian prisoner of war camp, which became known as the Battle of Bowmanville.

The residents of Camp 30 at Bowmanville in Ontario were mostly Germans captured by the British in France and sent to Canada for internment. They were guarded by the Veterans Guard of Canada. The violence began after 126 prisoners were sent to another camp to be shackled as a reprisal for the chaining of Canadian soldiers captured at Dieppe. After a period of hand-to-hand fighting, during which one Canadian guard had his skull fractured, 400 prisoners barricaded themselves in a hall. They remained there for over a day while the guards awaited reinforcements. A group of students at a nearby commando course in Kingston, Ontario, arrived on Canadian Thanksgiving Day, subduing the barricaded prisoners with fire hoses and tear gas.

The Canadians fired three shots during the revolt, two of which wounded a German PoW called Volkmar Koenig. This came about when a soldier in a tower fired on the prisoners after they had grabbed a Canadian officer. Another prisoner was stabbed with a bayonet but survived. There were also a number of minor injuries both to the prisoners and the guards before the situation was got under control.

The Canadians were never whole-heartedly behind the shackling order and in time the whole thing ran out of momentum, with all sides eventually losing interest. Then, both the Germans and the Allies gave up the practice entirely after the intervention of the International Red Cross. But it is true to say that the supposed Anglo-Canadian atrocities committed against Germans captured at Dieppe was one of the reasons Hitler used for issuing his Commando Order in October 1942, which stated that any Allied Commandos captured by German forces should be executed.

We have already read the transcripts of several Dieppe veterans who gave their accounts of the battle to the *Memory Project* of Historica Canada. Most of these soldiers were also taken prisoner after the surrender of Allied personnel and go on to give their accounts of being PoWs. Their accounts are remarkably varied but give a very good idea of what happened to these men after the raid was over. The shackling of prisoners is a recurring theme through all of their accounts.

One of the men in question was Arthur Fraser, who served with Les Fusiliers Mont-Royal. He was taken to Stalag VIII-B which was in Silesia, Poland. It originally housed Polish prisoners from the German September 1939 offensive. Later, approximately 100,000 prisoners – from Australia, Belgium, British India, British Palestine, Canada, France, Greece, Italy, the Netherlands, New Zealand, Poland, South Africa, the Soviet Union, the UK, the Isle of Man, the US and Yugoslavia – passed through the camp. In 1941, a separate camp named Stalag VIII-F was established nearby to accommodate Soviet prisoners only. Later, when the shoe was on the other foot, the Russians interned German prisoners there.

The next day, we took a rail boxcar. It was marked on the side of the car, forty men or eight horses. It took us three days to camp. We were at the camp Stalag VIII-B in Lamsdorf. It was a small village. It was a big camp, I think there was about 10,000 prisoners of war there. Because there was a working party, some of them were working outside the camp and the others inside.

We went into a building, five by five, and they tied our two hands, cross-wise and at the front, with a piece of string. That was twenty-four hours a day. This tying job lasted fifty-five days and then the International Red Cross came and visited us and our hands were all blistered and the officer said to the Germans, they have to think of something else and take these strings away. Oh yes, to go to the bathroom, we had to get ten together and then they would send a first-aid man with us to go to the bathroom, to pull up our trousers. After fifty-five days, they came out with these chains and we were chained up for fourteen months. The chain was better because when winter came, it was very cold but with the chain, we could put our hands in our pockets, which we did.

Roland Gravel also served in Les Fusiliers Mont-Royal, the same regiment as Arthur Fraser. He remembered being shackled and gives further insight into the Dieppe plan and its instructions for the treatment of prisoners. However, other aspects of his story are different to Arthur's, as Roland was an officer and Arthur was an enlisted man, so they went to different camps. Roland Gravel ended up in a camp in Bavaria reserved for officers alone.

We were declared prisoners and we surrendered our weapons. Then we crossed the town of Dieppe by foot, surrounded by guards, until we reached the hospital, the town hospital, where they separated us from our men; the officers on one side and the men – the soldiers – on the other. The first night the officers – I can't speak for the men since I don't know what happened – took us to a church in Envermeu to spend the night, which was about three or four kilometres outside of Dieppe. We spent the night in the church and then after that, a train took us to Verneuil, which was a small town outside of Paris, to a former French army camp which was no longer being used. They took us there and we were there for ten days. The Germans, you could tell, weren't feeding us very much since we were young, well-trained and in good health. They wanted to discourage us from escaping by being too weak. After the ten days, with very little to eat, they put us on trains that transported animals. They were marked twenty horses, forty men and things like that. It took us two days to get to a little town in the south, in Bavaria, in the south of Germany, to a little town called Eichstätt, to a prisoner of war camp for Commonwealth officers.

During raids, we had orders to bind our prisoners. Not bind their feet or hands, but just bind their two thumbs with a cord and then put their hands behind their backs and loop the cord around the neck. This was described in all of our daily orders that were issued at the time. The Germans, in collecting all kinds of things, found a copy of our orders, they saw them. They read the orders and they said that we, not us but our superior officers, acted against the rules of the international court of Geneva. So they handcuffed us – the Canadians only, no other Commonwealth officers – with special handcuffs from 8:00 in the morning until 8:00 at night. That lasted for four months. Then they put us in chains, which was a bit more comfortable since we could put our hands in our pockets, even though there were big metal bracelets. The chains lasted for nine months, from 8:00 in the morning until 8:00 at night. All of that ended the next year, I would say around Christmas time. The hardest thing, funnily enough, was when we saw the mail arrive because of course the mail didn't come every day. Receiving mail from our families was the best for our morale. So if an officer who was particularly difficult knew that we had seen the mail truck arrive, he wouldn't give it to us. He would wait one day, two days, a week before he gave it to us. That was hard, very hard. The liberation happened like this: the Germans, through the intermediary of Red Cross representatives, created a delegation of British and Americans to go meet the American army which was nearby, to request that they allow them a chance to move the camp. The Americans simply said, "Do you want to move or stay here?" They said, "Some have been here for five years and there are others that have spent three years as prisoners." It wasn't just soldiers, but also airmen and sailors. They said, "We're staying; attack, we don't want to move anymore." So they said, "Tell the Germans that we'll attack tomorrow morning at 05:00." So the next day exactly at 05:00 they attacked; but they made sure to overshoot the camp, from one side to the other. It started at 05:00 and towards 11:00, we saw the American tanks roll into the camp. For us, the war was ending.

Jacques Cinq-Mars recalls some of the work that he did while a prisoner of war. Being an enlisted man, having also served with Les Fusiliers Mont-Royal at Dieppe, his liberation would not be the same as the one which Roland Gravel experienced at the officer's camp. He was one of thousands of men forced by the Germans to march huge distances to avoid the Russians. The Germans wanted to hand their prisoners over to the Americans in the west, but more importantly for them, they wished to be taken prisoner themselves by the Americans and not the Soviets, who they feared would mistreat or probably even murder them.

The concentration camp was terrible. They wanted men for work and I did that. I worked in a sugar factory. I worked in the woods. I worked on all kinds of things. I didn't want to sit idle in a concentration camp. I went to different camps. I ran away and I got caught. They sent me to another camp. It wasn't fun. We didn't eat a lot. We were working in the woods. We had to gather a cord and a half of wood per man, per day. Otherwise, we couldn't go back. There was no point in escaping, dammit, because you couldn't. You didn't have any connections, you didn't know anybody. The airmen had people to take care of them, to take them back to England. There weren't very many people who took care of us in the infantry.

I worked on the borders of Russia and Poland. On January 20, 1945, the Germans arrived and said, "We are leaving." We left at around 09:00 in the morning. We were on a hillock and at the bottom of the hill we could see the Russians dressed in white coming towards us with their tanks. The Germans made us walk. The first day we walked almost eighty kilometres. We hadn't walked a lot in three years. Our legs were stiff at night. We would sleep on the side of the road or in barns, depending. The Germans couldn't give us anything to eat, since they didn't have anything for themselves. We walked for 1,800 miles. We would escape at night to go steal things. When I got out of there, I weighed 128 pounds.

The women liked us. They spoke to us in German. We were wondering what was going on there. They all wanted us to go stay overnight with them. I stayed overnight in one house where there were twelve women. During the war, the Germans put out terrible propaganda. They said that the Americans kept black people in cages, and that when they liberated Germany they would set free the black men and the women would be raped and killed. So that's why the women wanted us to stay with them in their houses. We gained life experience that no one else has. I did my part.

Paul Henry DeLorme of the South Saskatchewan Regiment gives an account of his capture at Dieppe and subsequent imprisonment at Stalag IX-C, which was in Thuringia in Germany, situated where many of the prisoners could work in local potassium mines. He was wounded quite badly and at first spent quite some time being treated in hospital. When he got the chance, similar to many prisoners of war, he attempted to escape but as with most, his breakout would fail.

A lot of our boys were killed here and there, and got captured before 16:00 in the afternoon. So I became a prisoner of war and so too did a good many others of the regiment, including the Colonel (Lieutenant Colonel Charles Merritt), who would be decorated with the Victoria Cross for his actions at Dieppe. By midnight, we all got loaded into freight boxcars, horse boxcars, you could smell all the horses; and a few boys died on the way going to Rouen (France). So we were in Rouen overnight, then the next morning the Colonel was going around checking to see how many men he had, and who he could talk to and things like that.

And by the afternoon, we were all loaded onto a Red Cross train heading for Germany.

I was wounded with the second grenade and I couldn't lift my arm or move a finger, or anything. I had shrapnel on the whole side of my body. But I landed in the hospital in Germany and I got unloaded off the train and then we had to get on trucks to go to the hospital. I was in this hospital for eleven months.

I was sent to Stalag IX-C. Immediately I got there, I got chained; they put chains on both arms, about a two-foot chain hanging between your arms. I wasn't there very long with these chains (shackles) because they were shipping guys out to go to work. I was in the salt (potassium) mine for about six months, I guess, something that way. I made friends with an Englishman and we decided we would both run away from that camp together. They had two shifts: day shift; night shift. So when the night shift came along, instead of going in for a shower, we just stood back. It was dark and by this time, the Germans were a little bit slack on their job and not watching. They trusted us and didn't expect anybody to run away. But we did.

So I was on the go for three weeks, but my partner gave up on the way. We got spotted by a single man, a German, in the afternoon while we were walking through the heavy bush in Germany. I noticed he picked up a stick and he himself was scared as hell; and I wasn't scared because I could see that all he had is a stick, so I figured we could knock him out and carry on. But nevertheless, I just said to my friend, George was his name, "George," I said, "let's not stop for this one man with the stick. We could handle him pretty good." So we didn't, at least I didn't; and I started to run. I said, "You run behind me as fast as you can." So I kept running and not looking back for maybe five minutes or so. And finally, I come to a big tree; and I went and swung my arm around the tree, just to see where he is. I didn't see him. I thought, well, I'm going to carry on, so I carried on; and I figured he might catch up with me, and I'd wait for him. After I got myself to a distance, I lay down and covered myself with leaves and things like that. I stayed there and he never showed up; and I've never seen the man since.

On and on until I come to one place and I was seen getting into a little bush. So then that's how I got captured. And pretty soon, while I was in this little bush, I had covered myself, but when I woke up there was a couple of guards on horseback, but they were civilians. They just told me to *raus* out of here, so they took me to a house and I know there was no chance there because they had guns and everything. They didn't know who I was, they thought I was a Russian because they kept asking me and I wouldn't say nothing. They took me to a house. And pretty soon, they called for the army to come and pick me up.

Jack Clifford McFarland of the Hamilton Light Infantry was also wounded at Dieppe, which meant that before entering the world of the PoW camp proper, he spent a good deal of time in a German hospital.

We were first taken to a field dressing station and I think the ladies that were there were German air force medics. Nobody introduced them, naturally, but they gave us a tetanus shot. I thought they were doing bayonet practice as they put a long needle right through our clothing into our stomach and gave us a shot... I hadn't been bandaged or anything yet. I didn't get that until I got to Rouen. I was a month in Rouen and then, believe it or not, by a hospital train, to Lamsdorf. I was then taken to the Lazarett, which is the hospital in the prison camp and I was there for several weeks. They treated me there. I had no complaints. A British doctor once told me, he said, you must have had a darned good German doctor, he said, I would have taken that arm off the minute I saw it.

Like Arthur Fraser, Jacques Nadeau, who served alongside him in
Les Fusiliers Mont-Royal, remembers being taken to Stalag VIII-B
in the first instance. After making several escape attempts, he was
finally liberated by the Russians.

The first September we arrived in Poland in Stalag number
VIII-B. We spent a lot of time there. I tried to escape three
times ... the last was in January 1945. The Russians came by
the place where we were being kept. We had changed stalags: we
were in Pomerania, at first I was in Upper Silesia, Poland, but
then we were transferred to Germany, to Pomerania. Today, it's
Polish territory again. We hid, and when the Russians arrived, we
got out of there.

I returned to England on April 1 after crossing Poland, then
Germany and also Russia, to the Black Sea. A Canadian Pacific
steam liner came to get us. We arrived in England via the Black
Sea, the Aegean Sea and in Malta, we changed ships. That ship
stopped in Algiers and then went from Algiers to Gibraltar and
then we waited a couple of days in Gibraltar for the convoy to
come together since the war wasn't over yet and there were still a
few submarines. Eventually, I arrived in England. From there, we
eventually made our way back to Canada aboard the *Britannia*,
which was a liner that was built just before the war. I arrived in
Halifax on May 23 and the next day I arrived in Montreal, where
my family was waiting for me!

Lamsdorf and Stalag VIII-B was also where Maurice Snook of the
Essex Scottish Regiment ended up after the surrender. He talks
about some of the ways the prisoners had a little fun, at the same
time keeping the German guards thinking.

We got on a train, we got into a place called Lamsdorf in the
dark and then we marched from there into the campsite and we

were billeted to certain buildings, 132 to a building. The next day, we had one inch of bread, that's what we got – we were fed each week four potatoes with skins on, small ones, one-inch in diameter and then we had a bowl of turnip soup. I don't eat turnips to this day.

There were three guys to a bunk. One blanket. One paillasse. Do you know what a paillasse is? A straw mattress, like just straw, horse straw. That was it. You cover it and that's what you had. You had coal once a week, you had a bucket of coal, that's the heat we had. So we were treated very badly at the time but we had a lot of fun.

Actually, what we tried to do is to keep the Germans on their toes. We always found something to do that would get them mad at us. One time was really good. We sat in a bunkhouse, playing cards, no coat on or anything else. But we had chains on… We could always open the lock with a flat nail. But if you complained about it being too tight on your wrist, then they'd put another type of chain on with padlocks that we had. But you couldn't get out of those, but you got out of these all the time. And by the time they yelled get outside with the chains, we walked outside with coats on! To this day, they don't know how we got the coats back on but I was able to unlock those chains with a nail. And then slip them on.

We dug a tunnel in the barracks and there was a guard out in a hut up on the roof – he had a machine gun. So we started a game going. One fellow had a sock and he'd run with a can of stones and they got one guy with it and then he'd try and hit the guy. And the German up there would be laughing so much, and while he was laughing, we had thirty-some-odd people go in the tunnel. They caught them all but at least we got them out. They had a job to do and we had a job to do. They were trying to work for Hitler and we were working the enemy. So nine times out of ten, we got along fine with them.

Jacques Cinq-Mars described how, towards the end of the war, the prisoners at Stalag VIII-B were forced on a long march ahead of the advancing Russian army. Armand Emond, who had served with the 14th Army Tank Regiment at Dieppe, also recalls this experience. This was known as the Lamsdorf Death March and was one of several that occurred at the time.

During the Lamsdorf Death March around 30,000 Allied PoWs were force-marched westward across Poland, Czechoslovakia and Germany in appalling winter conditions. It lasted for about four months, from January to April 1945 – among the coldest winter months of the twentieth century. Most of the PoWs were ill-prepared for the evacuation, having suffered years of poor rations and wearing inadequate clothing. Groups of 250-300 men would march twenty to forty kilometres a day, resting in factories, churches, barns and even in the open. Soon, long columns of PoWs were wandering over the northern part of Germany and neighbouring countries with little or nothing in the way of food, clothing, shelter or medical care. Many did not survive. It is estimated that a large number of PoWs had marched over 500 miles by the time they were liberated, and some had walked nearly 1,000 miles.

So we spent thirty-two months in Poland and fourteen months in handcuffs! We worked from 08:00 in the morning until 18:00 at night. We worked in the woods and then in the summer during the harvest, we would start working at 06:00 in the morning and work until 18:00 at night. The soldiers told us: "Any prisoners who refuse to work will be shot!" So we worked twelve hours per day and then the autumn grain and potato harvest began (in the fields), and we began working a bit later. We worked six days a week. Between us, as prisoners, the relationships were very solid. We were like brothers. Nobody wanted to kill anybody else; everything was going pretty well. Before being liberated, we did the "death march". We walked from Poland all the way to Germany during seven weeks. Sometimes we would get to eat a little something, since we would see a field of carrots or something and we would go dig up the carrots and eat them. They called it the "death march". Some people died along the way. The journey lasted seven weeks and then we met up with the Americans. The Germans didn't want the prisoners to be taken by the Russians, so they took us to Germany. Meanwhile, the Russians were approaching on the other side… The Germans – the soldiers – didn't want to be captured by the Russians, so they went to the Americans' side. It was General Patton's army. It was them who circled us in some place and we were in the middle of it all. We were surrounded by the American army. That's what saved us! Ah, that was such a wonderful day for us. When they saw us, when we arrived face to face with the American tanks, they saw that we were Canadian and British because of the khakis we were wearing, so they let us through. The German guards who were with us threw down their rifles and shouted in German, "Der Krieg ist fertig," which means, "the war is over" in English since they didn't want to be taken prisoners by the Russian army… The greatest day of my life was April 13th; liberation day. Ah, for me, that was the best birthday present. Three days before, I was with René Cardinal and since I knew we were in Germany, I said to him, "For my birthday, I hope that the war will be over." That made him laugh. I remember that I wasn't wrong; we were liberated on the 13th. Oh my goodness, what a relief! I didn't want to be at war anymore. You see, during war, people fight and then they get up the next day and are ready to do it all over again. But if people joined hands, there wouldn't be any war. That is what I hope for: harmony between all people!

David Mann, who served with the Royal Regiment of Canada recalls the surrender, the death march and his final liberation:

When it was finished, they took us off the beach to a small town at a school yard and then some of our own fighter planes strafed, it was one of their targets and it strafed us while we were in there. We had a few casualties there from our own.

They walked us that day, I don't know how far we walked, straggled along, wounded, the whole gang of us. There was a wedding going on in a big French church, people were just coming out on the front steps when we went by. We were dragging a lot of wounded people with missing clothes because they'd been in the water: they'll remember that wedding day.

At one time they put chains on us and that sounds funny, but it wasn't. Actually, before they brought the chains, they tied the boys up. We missed that because we were in hospital and weren't tied. But they tied them up right straight together and tied them tight and if they could find a little slack between their wrists, they'd really crank it, like a binder twine. We wounded that were in hospital missed that but by the time we got out, they brought the damn chains and there was a big cuff on each wrist and about, oh, twelve feet of heavy chain in between the cuffs. They put them on in the morning and took them off at night. And they weren't pleasant.

So they moved us up to another camp and they sent us out to work and there were twenty-four of us. We went out to a big farm. Then we worked there for a year I guess. We did farm work, we planted potatoes, we hoed potatoes, we dug potatoes. And that's the only good thing about that, we could eat all the potatoes we wanted. But anything else, just wasn't there. The work was hard, the hours were long but at least, I think back on it, it kept us from going crazy. You know, if you're just sitting around, with nothing to do, it's pretty hard on the mind.

The spring of 1945, I guess, they started us on the road marching. The prisoners that were in eastern section, we were then getting ready to move into the north-east. They had us moving west. Prisoners in the western section, they had them moving east, so there were prisoners all over the country walking.

That was also damn hard, awfully hard. Just on the road every day. Every night, they'd stop at a farm. All the farms had manure piles and whatnot out in the middle of the yard and that's where we stayed, or in the barn. I was liberated on my 25th birthday, 3 May 1945. That was the best birthday present I've ever had.

14

ANALYSIS

On 8 September 1942, Winston Churchill spoke about the Dieppe raid in the House of Commons:

> The Dieppe Raid must be considered a reconnaissance in force. It was a hard, savage clash, such as is likely to become increasingly numerous as the war deepens. We had to get all the information necessary before launching operations on a much larger scale. This raid, apart from its reconnaissance value, brought about an extremely satisfactory air battle in the west, which Fighter Command wish they could repeat every week. I, personally, regarded the Dieppe assault, to which I gave my sanction, as an indispensable preliminary to full-scale operations.

It would seem from this public statement that Churchill was content with the outcome of the raid: perhaps it suited his own purposes and dialogue with both the Soviet Union and the US. Privately, it would appear that Churchill did have his concerns with regards to the operation. In a minute to Major General Hastings Ismay on 21 December 1942, Churchill's chief military assistant and staff officer and the Prime Minister's principal link to the chiefs of staff committee, he wrote: 'At first sight it would appear to a layman very much out of accord with the accepted principles of war to attack the strongly fortified town front without first securing the cliffs on either side, and to use our tanks in a frontal assault off the beaches.'

That's all well and good, but you have to remember that the plan Churchill sanctioned was exactly that, a frontal attack by infantry and tanks following the capture of the headlands to the east and west of Dieppe. So in some ways he was as culpable as everyone else and should take some of the blame. But did he know the full details of the plan, or had he relied on the chiefs of staff to mull it over and give it the all-clear to proceed with his authority? Did he assume that the attack would not go ahead if the headlands remained in enemy hands? If that was the case, the decision on the day to carry on with the frontal assault, even though the headlands had not been secured, seems to have been made by the military force commander Major General Roberts alone.

Churchill's message to the House of Commons also talks of the perceived necessity of the operation and the benefits of its results. Whereas most people consider that very little was achieved by the raid, even if it had succeeded. So just what were the results to which the Prime Minister eludes?

There seem to be three aspects to his message. Firstly, he states that they needed to get all the information necessary before launching operations on a much larger scale, by which of course he is referring to the second front, when the Allies would return to Europe in the future, before which, of course, an amphibious landing in North Africa was being planned. This is where the reconnaissance in force is justified.

You could argue that reconnaissance can be done by other means, as indeed it was, through photography, by sending agents to get the lay of the land, and through code breaking and intercepting communiques. But again arguably, you can only get a true perspective of what the enemy situation is by seeing it in full operation and testing it in the flesh. Through the battle much was learned about the enemy's defences that other forms of reconnaissance did not pick up. In this instance, notably the guns that were hidden in the cave system to the east of Dieppe, which were totally undetected. I am sure that this rude awakening would have been a high priority in future planning on a larger scale.

Churchill's next point was that he considered it to be an indispensable preliminary to full-scale operations. I suppose here he is talking about all aspects of a real invasion and how men and equipment would perform under such extreme conditions. Did they have the right equipment and was it fit for purpose? Could they attack and capture enemy ports on the day of the invasion? How would tanks deal with the landing conditions? What would be the enemy's reaction and how quickly could they call in reinforcements? These and many other questions could only be answered by launching real attacks, rather than just performing exercises on the training ground and in classrooms.

The third point is of course that it brought about an extremely satisfactory air battle in the west. This was a situation that Fighter Command, as we have already discussed, seemed eager to pursue. They needed to prove that they could gain air supremacy over the battle area for the raid to succeed and in due course, do the same when the real second front was launched. There was also a political desire to draw some of the Luftwaffe's aircraft away from the eastern front to alleviate some of the pressure faced by Russia. In all of this, the RAF did largely succeed.

Yes, Dieppe was a reconnaissance in force, but as we stated at the very beginning, it was also the culminating event in a series of raids which had very much been Churchill's own brainchild. They had varied objectives but collectively all helped to prepare the way for the second front. In the case of Dieppe itself, although having none of its objectives met apart from the capture of the Hess battery, it was suggested by official sources that the results it achieved became visible later when combined operations on larger scales were successfully launched.

At Dieppe, those results were purchased at a very high cost in casualties sustained. We have already noted the number of soldiers taken prisoner during the raid but just as startling perhaps was the number of those who died. Immediately following the operation, it was announced in Canada that of the nearly 5,000-strong Canadian contingent engaged (4,963) a total of 3,350 were killed, wounded or missing. Subsequent announcements raised the total to 3,372. This included 593 officers and other ranks killed or died of wounds, 1,901 who were taken prisoners of war, and 287 missing. Another 591 returned to England wounded.

Today, from all sources the real figure is believed to have been 3,367 casualties for the Canadians, including 916 dead with 1,874 taken prisoner. By taking each unit individually you can break down that number further to give a more comprehensive list of fatalities:

Headquarters and Miscellaneous Detachments = five; 14th Army Tank Regiment (The Calgary Regiment) = thirteen; Royal Canadian Artillery = thirteen; Corps of Royal Canadian Engineers = twenty-seven; Royal Canadian Corps of Signals = nine; The Black Watch (Royal Highland Regiment) of Canada = four; The Royal Regiment of Canada = 227; The Royal Hamilton Light Infantry (Wentworth Regiment) = 197; Les Fusiliers Mont-Royal = 119; The Essex Scottish Regiment = 121; The South Saskatchewan Regiment = eighty-four; The Queen's Own Cameron Highlanders of Canada = seventy-six; The Calgary Highlanders = nil; The Toronto Scottish Regiment (MG) = one; Royal Canadian

Army Service Corps = one; Royal Canadian Army Medical Corps =
four; Royal Canadian Ordnance Corps = two; Canadian Provost
Corps = one; Canadian Intelligence Corps = three.

That makes a total of 907 fatalities among the ground forces,
but the Royal Canadian Navy also lost four men and the Royal
Canadian Air Force five, which brought Canadian fatalities to 916.

The British committed 1,075 ground forces, mainly
Commandos and Royal Marines, which sustained fifty-two
fatalities and eighty-seven taken as PoWs. Many more of course
returned to England with severe wounds that ended their wartime
service. The Royal Navy lost one destroyer (HMS *Berkeley*) and
thirty-three landing craft, suffering seventy-five who were killed
or later died of their wounds and 269 listed as missing or taken
as PoWs.

The RAF lost 106 aircraft to the forty-eight lost by
the Luftwaffe and suffered sixty-two fatalities, having flown
around 2,500 sorties in support of the operation. Among the RAF
losses, six aircraft had been shot down by gunners on their own
side, either Royal Navy or Army batteries. One Typhoon was
shot down by a Spitfire and two others were lost when their tails
broke off, which seems to have been a structural issue with early
Typhoons. Two Spitfires collided during the withdrawal across the
Channel. RAF Air Sea Rescue Services picked up around twenty
pilots who had been brought down in the Channel but lost five of
their high-speed launches in the process.

Although the RAF lost more aircraft than the enemy at
Dieppe it can be argued that they actually won the battle for
air superiority and prevented the Luftwaffe from significantly
interfering with the ships and assault forces. The Allies continued
to lose more aircraft than the Germans over France for the rest
of 1942, but the fact was they could afford to. The German
aircraft industry could not compete or keep up with the

combined productivity of the aircraft industries of the US, Great Britain and Canada. The Allies also had much better training programmes for their pilots and aircrew than the Luftwaffe. So inevitably, Germany slowly lost the war of attrition in the skies above France. The battle for air superiority over the whole of the invasion theatre would therefore be won on several fronts and by continuous effort. Undoubtedly, 19 August 1942 was the start of that achievement.

In other aspects of the battle the RAF had, however, been found grievously wanting. They had not properly assessed the information gathered during aerial photographic reconnaissance missions, so accordingly the results had not been used to proper effect by the ground intelligence. Tactical reconnaissance had not been completely satisfactory either; and in the fields of bombardment and close-support, the RAF had fallen well short. This was not the fault of the aircrew involved as they did everything that was asked of them. It was the fault of the mission planners who didn't seem to know how to use aerial bombardment to maximum effect. The runs were always too short and not sufficient to do any real damage. It was almost as though they were using this as a training exercise, rather than trying to actually quell the enemy's resistance. The same thing applies to the smoke-screens. Fortunately, lessons were learnt from these inadequacies and improved methods in all these spheres would be developed and utilised during subsequent operations.

As for the participation of the United States in the raid, of the fifty US Army Rangers serving with different Commando and Canadian units only fifteen actually went ashore, of which three were killed, five wounded, and four captured. Twenty men from No. 10 (Inter Allied) Commando were also lost.

After the raid the Germans buried the Allied dead in a mass grave, but their bodies were subsequently disinterred and reburied at Vertus Wood, a little to the south of Dieppe. The cemetery contains Canadian and British soldiers killed during the raid. Some 765 identified Allied service personnel are interred in the cemetery, of which 582 are Canadian; another 187 are unidentified. Further casualties from the raid are buried in Rouen, where the Germans took most of the captured soldiers, some of whom later died of their wounds.

Unusually, the headstones in the cemetery are placed back-to-back in double rows, which was the norm for a German war cemetery, but unusual for Commonwealth War Graves Commission sites. When the Allies liberated Dieppe as part of Operation *Fusilade* in 1944, the grave markers were replaced but the layout was left unchanged to avoid disturbing the remains. There are also several monuments and memorials erected in remembrance to those who served and fell at Dieppe, in France, Great Britain and Canada.

As well as losing forty-eight aircraft, the Germans suffered 591 casualties, which included 322 dead. They also lost the patrol boat, The *Franz*. However, although the Luftwaffe admitted to the loss of forty-eight aircraft, that might not have been the true figure. Leigh-Mallory himself insisted the figure, which was based on claims made by the pilots of the raiding force, would have been closer to ninety-one.

The figures for those who died, were wounded or taken prisoner at Dieppe differ greatly in published accounts, which makes it very hard to know exactly what was the truth. For the figures quoted here I have relied upon most of the official accounts and taken the most commonly reported numbers. But I appreciate that these figures might not be 100 per cent accurate. But even if they are close to the truth, they illustrate only too well how brutal the battle was.

As for the Germans, if people here were confused about the raid and its purpose, it must have been an even bigger enigma to them. It was obvious that the Germans knew that the Allies were about to attempt something on a grander scale, as all the signs pointed to it. But the Germans had no way of knowing whether or not this was just another raid, or indeed the start of the invasion. By its scale, in terms of the number of ships used, the vast aircraft cover, and the deployment of assault troops and tanks, their initial reaction would have to be to assume it was the start of an invasion attempt. It was so much bigger than any previous raids on the Atlantic Wall, so their immediate reaction would have been to assume it was something else. Accordingly, the Luftwaffe and the Kriegsmarine spent much of the day patrolling other parts of the Channel on the lookout for other incursions. After all, if it was the opening of the second front, surely other Allied ships would soon be on their way as reinforcements. However, it soon became apparent that there were no further invasion forces steaming towards France, so it was therefore realised this was just another raid.

It has often been stated that because of the scale of *Jubilee's* failure, the Germans must surely have known about the operation in advance. We have noted several times, of course, that they knew an operation of some sort was going to happen in the not too distant future because all the signs pointed to it, not least of which was the discovery of the initial task force for Operation *Rutter*. It would not have taken much to realise that this force was heading for somewhere on the Continent. And there were other clues that the French coast was expecting some sort of attack, for instance, since June 1942 the BBC had been broadcasting warnings to French civilians of a 'likely' action, urging them to evacuate the Atlantic coastal districts of occupied France. In fact, they even made such an announcement on the day of the raid itself.

Many veterans of the raid, especially the Canadians, were convinced that the German defences were prepared for them because of the accuracy and ferocity of their fire. The volume and tone of these accounts meant that a Canadian government report at the end of 1942 concluded that 'They seem to have had ample warning of the raid and to have made thorough preparations for dealing with it.' Lieutenant Colonel Labatt, the officer in command of the Royal Hamilton Light Infantry, testified to seeing markers on the beach which would have been used for mortar practice. He insisted that they appeared to have been recently placed there.

The accounts given by captured German soldiers didn't exactly dispel these beliefs either. For instance, during the interrogation of one German soldier it was discovered that four machine gun battalions had been specially brought in ahead of an anticipated raid. There are numerous accounts of interrogated German prisoners and even French citizens who were of the opinion that the Germans had been making preparations to meet an Allied assault for weeks. However, all of these accounts talk about a potential attack on the Atlantic Wall, but none actually confirm that Dieppe was known as the target, or the date and time when an assault was expected. The argument that they were expecting an attack on Dieppe itself begins to falls apart when you consider that some of the forces, such as those that landed on Green Beach, met with very little resistance. Similarly, No. 4 Commando's troops also reported that they achieved complete surprise.

An intriguing caveat to all of this was the entry of the word 'Dieppe' as an answer to a question in a crossword puzzle published in the *Daily Telegraph* on 17 August 1942, which had been compiled by one Leonard Dawe. The War Office immediately suspected that enemy agents at Whitehall and within the press were using the crossword as a way of passing information to the enemy. Lord Tweedsmuir, who at the time was a senior intelligence officer attached to the Canadian Army, was tasked with investigating the situation. Tweedsmuir later commented: 'We noticed that the crossword contained the word "Dieppe", and there was an immediate and exhaustive inquiry which also involved MI5. But in the end it was concluded that it was just a remarkable coincidence – a complete fluke.' (Dawe would later come under suspicion for including the words Utah, Omaha, Mulberry, Neptune – and Overlord – in May 1944 versions of the *Telegraph* crossword. The coincidence of the insertion of these D-Day code-names beggars belief. Dawe convinced MI5 of his innocence. One intriguing suggestion is that the schoolmaster Dawe was in the habit of asking his sixth-formers to suggest words for the crossword, which he much later confirmed. The school had been evacuated from London to Surrey and at the time the surrounding area was full of US forces. Did the sixth-formers pick up these words from them?)

The enemy's confusion about the Dieppe raid is reflected in the constantly changing and contradictory reports that German wireless stations broadcast throughout the day, again suggesting that they had not known in advance about the exact operation. At first, they claimed that the invasion had begun and their brave troops had thwarted it on the beaches. Their military and political leaders must have revelled in this propaganda. Then when it was realised that it was only a raid, they began to make claims that it was based upon poor and hasty planning, after Winston Churchill had returned from meeting Stalin in Moscow and promised to step up the war effort in the west. This was almost immediately contradicted as the story changed to the raid being the result of ten months of extensive planning and preparations between the Chief of Combined Operations and the military chiefs of the US. Contradictions in reporting continued for some time, as the Nazis attempted to understand for themselves just what had taken place at Dieppe – and how to maximise its propaganda value. That value was certainly enhanced by the fact that the British were slow to publish any official information. This meant that Allied media sources were forced to carry announcements gleaned from German sources.

The capture by the Germans of Brigadier Southam's copy of the Dieppe plan gave the enemy a chance to carry out a thorough analysis of the operation. Having done so, the Germans were not overly impressed. General Haase considered it 'incomprehensible' that a single division was expected to attack and defeat an entrenched German regiment supported by significant artillery. He was also reported to have expressed the opinion that the strength of the Allied naval and air forces was entirely insufficient to suppress the defenders during the landings in question. General Kuntzen believed it 'inconceivable' that tanks had not been used to support the landings at Pourville-sur-Mer.

At Dieppe the Germans also captured numerous Churchill tanks, Britain's latest elite weapon, and again, were not very impressed with either its armour or weaponry. One report decided, 'In its present form the Churchill is easy to fight.' Its gun was described as 'poor and obsolete', and the armour was compared unfavourably with that of German and Soviet tanks.

The main concern for the Germans after the dust had settled was the realisation of the scale of resources that the Allies had at their disposal. If this was indeed just a raid to test the enemy's defences both on the ground and in the air, they had been able to gamble with and lose huge amounts of men and equipment for what was, effectively, only a practice run. If that was the case, the Nazi regime must have been shaken by the prospect of what would be launched against them when the actual invasion began. Any reasonable military commander must have been quaking in his boots at the firestorm that was undoubtedly heading their way at some point and would have known that they would not be able to stop it when it came, in spite of the rantings of Hitler and their disillusioned political leaders.

One thing the Germans certainly appreciated after the raid was that the Allies could only learn from the mistakes they made during the operation. Field Marshal Gerd von Rundstedt, German commander in chief in the west observed that, 'Just as we are going to evaluate these experiences for the future so is the assaulting force ... perhaps even more so as it has gained the experience dearly. He will not do it like this a second time!'

One thing was for sure; since the very beginning of the war, the Germans had been on the offensive, but after Dieppe the Germans now had to look towards a defensive strategy for the first time. Their fears were well founded as on 8 November 1942, the Allies launched Operation *Torch*, the invasion of French North Africa, when they carried out a large-scale and successful amphibious assault. Everything the Allies had leant at Dieppe was used to good effect and the war had turned for the first time in their favour.

As for France itself, how was the raid taken there? Marshal Philippe Pétain, the head of state of the Vichy government collaborating with the Nazis, wrote a public letter to Adolf Hitler in which he congratulated him on the Wehrmacht's recent victory at Dieppe in repulsing what he termed 'this latest act of British aggression against France'. Pétain took the opportunity to suggest that in the future French troops should also be permitted to help defend their country against an invasion from the western Allies. He expressed his deep regret that Vichy forces had not played a part in stopping these attackers.

French forces had been barred from defending the Atlantic Wall since the signing of the armistice between the French and Nazi administrations in June 1940 and Hitler had no interest in allowing their return any time soon. However, the Nazis did appreciate the propaganda benefits of flaunting Petain's letter in the media, using it to illustrate that the citizens of France were fully behind Germany's efforts to defend them. Pétain's letter would later be used as evidence for the prosecution when he was put on trial for high treason in 1945. He claimed that the letter was a forgery, but this was overwhelmingly rejected.

To show his appreciation to the citizens of Dieppe for not seeming to help the enemy in any way, Hitler made the decision to reward the town both financially and with a more human gesture. He gave the town ten million francs, which was to be used to repair any damage that had been caused by the Allies during the raid, both on public and domestic buildings. The gesture was to free any French PoWs in German camps who either came from Dieppe or had lived there before the war, and subsequently on 12 September 1942 a train carrying an estimated 1,500 French ex-PoWs arrived in the port.

Why had the raid been permitted to go so badly wrong? Initially, the Canadians came under huge criticism as the chosen troops for the operation; they were untested in the field, and the blame was pointed in their direction. Likewise, those who had put them forward, particularly Lieutenant General Bernard Montgomery from whose South Eastern Army they had been selected, and Lieutenant General McNaughton, the commander in chief of Canadian forces in Britain, were criticised for making this choice.

The fact of the matter was that given the circumstances under which they were required to attack the beaches, without the enemy positions having first been, if not silenced then at least weakened, even the most battle-hardened of troops would have found it impossible to have done better under the unacceptable conditions forced on them by their superiors. This was an attempt by the western Allies to attack and capture a German-held port. Bearing in mind this simple fact, planning by the force commanders in preparation for the raid was totally inadequate and almost casual. It was as though the planners assumed everything would go according to their instructions without fail, as if the enemy didn't actually come into the equation.

In terms of its immediate objectives the raid of course failed to complete any of its allotted tasks, except for the destruction of the Hess battery. So in order to find any positives you can only look at it in terms of the bigger picture. Mountbatten later justified the raid by arguing that lessons learned at Dieppe in 1942 were put to good use later in the war. He claimed, 'I have no doubt that the Battle of Normandy was won on the beaches of Dieppe. For every man who died in Dieppe, at least ten more must have been spared in Normandy in 1944.' And in a direct response to the raid, Winston Churchill remarked that, 'My Impression of *Jubilee* is that the results fully justified the heavy cost ... it was a Canadian contribution of the greatest significance to final victory.'

The lessons learned at Dieppe essentially became the textbook of what not to do in future amphibious operations and laid the framework for the Normandy landings two years later. Most notably, Dieppe highlighted the need for preliminary artillery support, including aerial bombardment; the need for a sustained element of surprise; the need for proper intelligence concerning enemy fortifications; the avoidance of a direct frontal attack on a defended port; and the need for proper re-embarkation craft.

As a consequence of the lessons learned at Dieppe, the British developed a whole range of specialist vehicles that allowed their engineers to perform many of their tasks protected by armour. Because the tracks of most of the Churchill tanks were caught up in the shingle beaches of Dieppe, the Allies started a new policy of learning the exact elements of every beach they intended to land upon and devising appropriate vehicles for those beaches. Reconnaissance took on a new dimension.

Perhaps the most significant effect of the raid was that it changed the Allies' previously held belief that seizure of a major port would be essential in the creation of a second front: after all, that was the bottom line, and exactly what the Dieppe raid was all about. Their revised view was that the amount of damage that would be done to a port by the necessary bombardment to take it would almost certainly render it useless as a port afterwards. As a result, the decision was taken to construct prefabricated harbours, codenamed Mulberry, and tow them to lightly defended beaches as part of a large-scale invasion. The driving force behind the creation of the Mulberry harbours was none other than Captain John Hughes-Hallett, who had been the naval force commander at Dieppe. At a meeting following the raid, he declared that if a port could not be captured, then one should be taken across the Channel. Although this was met with derision at the time, the concept of Mulberry harbours began to take shape when Hughes-Hallett became Naval Chief of Staff to the Operation *Overlord* planners. The rest, as they say, is history.

APPENDIX ONE

Commando raids on the Atlantic Wall, June 1940–May 1944

1) Codename: Operation *Collar*
   Date: 24 - 25 June 1940
   Target: Neufchâtel-Hardelot, Stella Plage, Berck, and Le Touquet, France
   Objectives: Reconnaissance and capture prisoners
2) Codename: Operation *Ambassador*
   Date: 14 - 15 July 1940
   Target: Guernsey, Channel Islands
   Objectives: Capture prisoners, attack airfield
3) Codename: Operation *Claymore*
   Date: 4 March 1941
   Target: Lofoten Islands, Norway
   Objectives: Attack industrial sites and capture prisoners
4) Codename: Operation *Chess*
   Date: 27 - 28 July 1941
   Target: Ambleteuse, France
   Objectives: Reconnaissance and capture prisoners
5) Codename: Operation *Gauntlet*
   Date: 25 August - 3 September 1941
   Target: Spitsbergen, Norway
   Objectives: Deny Germany natural resources, prevent Germans receiving weather reports and repatriate local population, scientists and POWs

6) Codename: Operation *Acid Drop*
   Date: 30 - 31 August 1941
   Target: Neufchâtel-Hardelot and Merlimont, France
   Objectives: Reconnaissance and capture prisoners

7) Codename: Operation *Chopper*
   Date: 27 - 28 September 1941
   Target: Saint-Aubin-d'Arquenay, France
   Objectives: Reconnaissance and capture prisoners

8) Codename: Operation *Deep Cut*
   Date: 27 - 28 September 1941
   Target: Saint- Vaast-la-Hougue, France
   Objectives: Reconnaissance and capture prisoners

9) Codename: Operation *Astrakan*
   Date: 12 - 13 November 1941
   Target: Houlgate and Les Hemmes, France
   Objectives: Beach reconnaissance

10) Codename: Operation *Sunstar*
    Date: 22 - 23 November 1941
    Target: Houlgate, France
    Objectives: Destroy gun battery and capture prisoners

11) Codename: Operation *Anklet*
    Date: 26 - 27 December 1941
    Target: Lofoten Islands, Norway
    Objectives: Capture prisoners and destroy radio transmitters

12) Codename: Operation *Archery*
    Date: 27 December 1941
    Target: Vågsøy, Norway
    Objectives: Destruction of industrial sites and military
    installations

13) Codename: Operation *Curlew*
    Date: 11 - 12 January 1942
    Target: Saint-Laurent-sur-Mer, France
    Objectives: Reconnaissance of beach defences

14) Codename: Operation *Biting*
    Date: 27 - 28 February 1942
    Target: Bruneval, France
    Objectives: Capture of radar equipment

15) Codename: Operation *Chariot*
    Date: 28 March 1942
    Target: Saint-Nazaire, France
    Objectives: Destruction of harbour installations

16) Codename: Operation *Myrmidon*
    Date: 5 April 1942
    Target: Adour Estuary, France
    Objectives: Disrupt road and rail transport between France and Spain

17) Codename: Operation *J V*
    Date: 11 - 12 April 1942
    Target: Boulogne-sur-Mer, France
    Objectives: Attack German shipping

18) Codename: Operation *Abercrombie*
    Date: 21 - 22 April 1942
    Target: Neufchâtel-Hardelot, France
    Objectives: Beach reconnaissance, capture prisoners and destroy installations including a searchlight battery

19) Codename: Operation *Bristle*
    Date: 3 - 4 June 1942
    Target: Plage-Ste-Cecile, France
    Objectives: Attack on German radar installation

20) Codename: Operation *Barricade*
    Date: 14 - 15 August 1942
    Target: Pointe de Saire, France
    Objectives: Attack radar and anti-aircraft gun installations

21) Codename: Operation *Jubilee*
    Date: 19 August 1942
    Target: Dieppe, France
    Objectives: Seize and hold port, reconnaissance in force, capture prisoners, destroy coastal defences and other installations

22) Codename: Operation *Dryad*
    Date: 2 - 3 September 1942
    Target: Les Casquets, Channel Islands
    Objectives: Reconnaissance and capture prisoners

23) Codename: Operation *Branford*
    Date: 7 - 8 September 1942
    Target: Burhou, Channel Islands
    Objectives: Reconnaissance

24) Codename: Operation *Aquatint*
    Date: 12 - 13 September 1942
    Target: Sainte-Honorine-des-Pertes, France
    Objectives: Reconnaissance and capture prisoners

25) Codename: Operation *Musketoon*
    Date: 11 - 21 September 1942
    Target: Glomfjord, Norway
    Objectives: Attack industrial site
26) Codename: Operation *Basalt*
    Date: 3 - 4 October 1942
    Target: Sark, Channel Islands
    Objectives: Reconnaissance and capture prisoners
27) Codename: Operation *Fahrenheit*
    Date: 11 - 12 November 1942
    Target: Pointe de Plouézec, France
    Objectives: Reconnaissance and capture prisoners
28) Codename: Operation *Batman*
    Date: 15 - 16 November 1942
    Target: Omonville, France
    Objectives: Objective not known
29) Codename: Operation *Freshman*
    Date: 19 November 1942
    Target: Telemark, Norway
    Objectives: Destroy German heavy water production
30) Codename: Unknown
    Date: 22 - 29 November 1942
    Target: Bergen, Norway
    Objectives: Reconnaissance and capture prisoners
31) Codename: Operation *Frankton*
    Date: 7 - 12 December 1942
    Target: Bordeaux, France
    Objectives: Attack shipping
32) Codename: Operation *Cartoon*
    Date: 23 - 24 January 1943
    Target: Stord Island, Norway
    Objectives: Attack industrial site
33) Codename: Operation *Crackers*
    Date: 23 February - 3 March 1943
    Target: Sognefjord, Norway
    Objectives: Reconnaissance
34) Codename: Operation *Huckaback*
    Date: 27 - 28 February 1943
    Target: Herm, Channel Islands
    Objectives: Capture prisoners and gain information about
               the situation in the occupied islands

35) Codename: Operation *Brandy*
    Date: 14 February 1943
    Target: Florø, Norway
    Objectives: Attack German shipping
36) Codename: Operation *Roundabout*
    Date: 23 March 1943
    Target: Stad, Norway
    Objectives: Destroy a bridge over fjord
37) Codename: Operation *Pussyfoot*
    Date: 3 - 4 April 1943
    Target: Herm, Channel Islands
    Objectives: Reconnaissance and capture prisoners
38) Codename: Operation *Checkmate*
    Date: 28 April - 15 May 1943
    Target: Haugesund, Norway
    Objectives: Attack shipping
39) Codename: Operation *Forfar Easy*
    Date: 3 - 4 July 1943
    Target: Onival, France
    Objectives: Reconnaissance and capture prisoners
40) Codename: Operation *Forfar Dog*
    Date: 5 - 6 July 1943
    Target: Biville, France
    Objectives: Reconnaissance and capture prisoners
41) Codename: Operation *Forfar Beer*
    Date: 3 - 5 August and 1 - 2 September 1943
    Target: Eletot, France
    Objectives: Reconnaissance and capture prisoners
42) Codename: Operation *Forfar Love*
    Date: 3 - 4 August 1943
    Target: Dunkirk, France
    Objectives: Reconnaissance of pier and capture prisoners
43) Codename: Operation *Forfar Item*
    Date: 2 - 3 September 1943
    Target: Saint-Valery-en-Caux, France
    Objectives: Reconnaissance of searchlight battery and
               capture prisoners
44) Codename: Operation *Pound*
    Date: 3 - 4 September 1943
    Target: Ushant, France
    Objectives: Reconnaissance and capture prisoners

45) Codename: Operation *Hardtack* 1 1
    Date: 24 - 25 December 1943
    Target: Gravelines, France
    Objectives: Reconnaissance of beaches and sand dunes
46) Codename: Operation *Hardtack* 1 3
    Date: 26 - 27 December 1943
    Target: Bénouville-Etretat, France
    Objectives: Reconnaissance and capture prisoners
47) Codename: Operation *Hardtack* 2 8
    Date: 25 - 26 December 1943
    Target: Jersey, Channel Islands
    Objectives: Reconnaissance and capture prisoners
48) Codename: Operation *Hardtack* 4
    Date: 26 - 27 December 1943
    Target: Criel-sur-Mer, France
    Objectives: Reconnaissance and capture prisoners
49) Codename: Operation *Hardtack* 5
    Date: 26 - 27 December 1943
    Target: Onival, France
    Objectives: Reconnaissance and capture prisoners
50) Codename: Operation *Hardtack* 7
    Date: 25 - 26 and 27 - 28 December 1943
    Target: Sark, Channel Islands
    Objectives: Reconnaissance and capture
               prisoners
51) Codename: Operation *Hardtack* 2 1
    Date: 26 - 27 December 1943
    Target: Quineville, France
    Objectives: Reconnaissance and capture prisoners
52) Codename: Operation *Hardtack* 2 3
    Date: 27 - 28 December 1943
    Target: Ostend, Belgium
    Objectives: Reconnaissance and capture prisoners
53) Codename: Operation *Hardtack* 3 6
    Date: 24 - 25 December 1943
    Target: Wassenaar, Holland
    Objectives: Reconnaissance and capture prisoners
54) Codename: Operation *Tarbrush* 5
    Date: 15 - 16 May 1944
    Target: Dunkirk, France
    Objectives: Beach reconnaissance

55) Codename: Operation *Tarbrush 8*
    Date: 15 - 16 May 1944
    Target: Quend, France
    Objectives: Beach reconnaissance
56) Codename: Operation *Tarbrush 3*
    Date: 16 - 17 May 1944
    Target: Bray-Dunes, France
    Objectives: Beach reconnaissance
57) Codename: Operation *Tarbrush 10*
    Date: 17 - 18 May 1944
    Target: Onival, France
    Objectives: Beach reconnaissance

APPENDIX TWO

Allied Order of Battle (Ground Forces)

2nd Canadian Infantry Division – Major General John Roberts

4th Canadian Infantry Brigade – Brigadier Sherwood Lett

The Essex Scottish Regiment – Lieutenant Colonel Frederick K. Jasperson

The Royal Hamilton Light Infantry – Lieutenant Colonel Robert Ridley Labatt

The Royal Regiment of Canada – Lieutenant Colonel Douglas Cato

5th Canadian Infantry Brigade

C Company of The Black Watch (Royal Highland Regiment) of Canada

Mortar Platoon of The Calgary Highlanders

6th Canadian Infantry Brigade – Brigadier William Southam

Les Fusiliers Mont-Royal (Floating reserve) – Lieutenant Colonel Dollard Menard

The Queen's Own Cameron Highlanders of Canada – Lieutenant Colonel Alfred Gosling

The South Saskatchewan Regiment - Lieutenant Colonel Charles Merritt

No. 6 Defence Platoon (Lorne Scots)

14th Canadian Tank Regiment (Calgary Regiment) Lieutenant Colonel John Andrews

Detachment of 3rd Light Anti-Aircraft Regiment, Royal Canadian Artillery (RCA)

Detachment of 4th Field Regiment, RCA

The Toronto Scottish Regiment (Machine Gun)

No. 3 Commando (British Army) – Lieutenant Colonel John Durnford-Slater

No. 4 Commando (British Army) – Lieutenant Colonel Simon Fraser, 15th Lord Lovat

No. 10 Inter-Allied Commando (French speakers attached to other units as interpreters)

No. 40 Commando Royal Marines – Lieutenant Colonel Joseph Picton-Phillips

No. 30 Commando (intelligence gathering)

In addition a detachment of fifty men of the 1st US Ranger Battalion was assigned to various units to act as observers

Free French troops (number uncertain)

APPENDIX THREE

Allied Order of Battle (Naval Forces)
The naval forces were under the command of Captain John Hughes-Hallett RN

Destroyers:
   HMS *Calpe* - Headquarters ship
   HMS *Fernie* - reserve HQ ship
   HMS *Albrighton*
   HMS *Berkeley*
   HMS *Bleasdale*
   HMS *Brocklesby*
   HMS *Garth*
   ORP *Slazak* (Polish Navy)
Landing Ships, Infantry:
   HMS *Duke of Wellington* LSI (hoisting)
   HMS *Glenqyle* LSI (large)
   HMS *Invicta* LSI (small)
   HMS *Prince Charles* LSI (small)
   HMS *Prince Leopold* LSI (small)
   HMS *Princess Beatrix* LSI (medium)
   HMS *Princess Astrid* LSI (small)
   HMS *Prins Albert* LSI (small)
   HMS *Queen Emma* LSI (medium)
Landing Craft, Tanks (LCT): x 24

Landing Craft, Flak (LCF 1) (LCF 2)
9th Minesweeping Flotilla (MSF):
    HMS *Bangor* (J00)
    HMS *Bridlington* (J65)
    HMS *Sidmouth* (J47)
    HMS *Tenby* (J34)
    HMS *Bridport* (J50)
    HMS *Blackpool* (J27)
    HMS *Rhyl* (J36)
13th Minesweeping Flotilla (MSF):
    HMS *Eastbourne* (J127)
    HMS *Ilfracombe* (J95)
    HMS *Blyth* (J15)
    HMS *Stornoway* (J31)
    HMS *Clacton* (J151)
    HMS *Felixstowe* (J126)
    HMS *Polruan* (J97)
Motor Gun Boats (MGB):
    Nos. 50, 51, 52, 57, 312, 315, 316, 317, 320, 321, 323 and 326
Steam Gun Boats of the 1st SGB Flotilla:
    Nos. 5, 6, 8 and 9
Motor Launches (ML):
    Nos. 114, 120, 123, 171, 187, 189, 190, 191, 193, 194, 208, 214, 230, 246, 291, 292, 309, 343, 344 and 346
Gunboat: HMS *Locust*
Sloop: HMS *Alresford*
Free French Chasseurs:
    Nos. 5, 10, 13, 14, 41, 42 and 43

APPENDIX FOUR

Allied Order of Battle (Air Forces)
Commander in chief: Air Vice Marshal Trafford Leigh-Mallory

No. 11 Group RAF Fighter Command
(Supermarine Spitfire squadrons)
    No. 19 Squadron RAF
    No. 41 Squadron RAF
    No. 43 Squadron RAF
    No. 64 Squadron RAF
    No. 66 Squadron RAF
    No. 71 (Eagle) Squadron RAF
    No. 81 Squadron RAF
    No. 87 Squadron RAF
    No. 91 Squadron RAF
    No. 111 Squadron RAF
    No. 121 (Eagle) Squadron RAF
    No. 122 Squadron RAF
    No. 124 Squadron RAF
    No. 129 Squadron RAF
    No. 130 Squadron RAF
    No. 131 Squadron RAF
    No. 133 (Eagle) Squadron RAF
    No. 134 Squadron RAF
    No. 154 Squadron RAF

No. 165 Squadron RAF
No. 222 Squadron RAF
No. 232 Squadron RAF
No. 242 Squadron RAF
No. 302 City of Poznan (Polish) Fighter Squadron
No. 303 Kosciuszko (Polish) Fighter Squadron
No. 306 City of Torun (Polish) Fighter Squadron
No. 308 City of Krakow (Polish) Fighter Squadron
No. 310 (Czechoslovak) Squadron
No. 312 (Czechoslovak) Squadron
No. 317 City of Wilno (Polish) Fighter Squadron
No. 331 (Norwegian) Squadron
No. 332 (Norwegian) Squadron
No. 340 GC/IV/2 Ile de France (French) Squadron
No. 350 (Belgian) Squadron
No. 401 Squadron RCAF
No. 403 Squadron RCAF
No. 411 Squadron RCAF
No. 412 Squadron RCAF
No. 416 Squadron RCAF
No. 501 Squadron RAF
No. 602 Squadron RAF
No. 610 Squadron RAF
No. 611 Squadron RAF
No. 616 Squadron RAF
(Hawker Hurricane squadrons)
No. 3 Squadron RAF
No. 32 Squadron RAF
No. 43 Squadron RAF
No. 87 Squadron RAF
No. 174 Squadron RAF
No. 175 Squadron RAF
No. 245 Squadron RAF
No. 253 Squadron RAF
(Hawker Typhoon squadrons)
No. 56 Squadron RAF
No. 266 Squadron RAF
No. 609 Squadron RAF
(Douglas Boston squadron)
No. 418 (City of Edmonton) Squadron RCAF

RAF Army Cooperation Command
(North American P-51 Mustang squadrons)
(No. 35 Wing)
  No. 26 Squadron RAF
  No. 239 Squadron RAF
  No. 400 Squadron RCAF
  No. 414 Squadron RCAF
(Bristol Blenheim squadrons)
  (No. 36 Wing)
  No. 13 Squadron RAF
  (No. 32 Wing)
  No. 614 Squadron RAF

No. 2 Group RAF Bomber Command
(Douglas Boston squadrons)
  No. 88 Squadron RAF
  No. 107 Squadron RAF
  No. 226 Squadron RAF

USAAF Eighth Air Force
No. 97 Bombardment Group
(Boeing B-17 Flying Fortress squadrons)
  No. 340 Bombardment Squadron
  No. 341 Bombardment Squadron
  No. 342 Bombardment Squadron
  No. 414 Bombardment Squadron

No. 31 Fighter Group
(Supermarine Spitfire squadrons)
  No. 307 Fighter Squadron
  No. 308 Fighter Squadron
  No. 309 Fighter Squadron

The RAF Air Sea Rescue Service also operated some aircraft

APPENDIX FIVE

German Order of Battle (Ground Forces)
302nd Static Infantry Division – *Generalleutnant* Konrad Haase
    570th Infantry Regiment
    571st Infantry Regiment
    572nd Infantry Regiment
    302nd Artillery Regiment
    302nd Anti-tank Battalion
    302nd Reconnaissance Battalion
    302nd Engineer Battalion
    302nd Signal Battalion
    302nd Supply Battalion
    302nd Divisional Supply detachment

Batteries
    (2/770) Berneval Battery (Goebbels)
    3 x 170 mm guns; 4 x 105 mm guns; 20 mm flak gun
    (813) Varengeville-sur-Mer Battery (Hess)
    6 x 155mm guns; 7 x 20 mm flak guns
    (B/302) Puys Battery (Rommel)
    4 x 155 mm guns; 3 x 88 mm guns
    Pourville Battery (Hindenburg)
    French captured 75 mm guns and light artillery
    Calnon Battery (Hitler)
    4 x 150 mm guns; 3 x 88 mm guns

APPENDIX SIX

German Order of Battle (Air Forces)
Jagdeschwader 2 (JG 2) 'Richthofen' (Fighter Wing) –
Oberstleutnant Walter Oesau
    I Gruppe – Hauptmann Erich Leie
    II Gruppe – Hauptmann Helmut-Felix Bolz
    III Gruppe – Hauptmann Hans 'Assi' Hahn
    Aircraft: Focke-Wulf Fw 190
    (1 staffel flying high-altitude Messerschmitt Bf 109G-1)

Jagdeschwader 26 (JG 26) 'Schlageter' (Fighter Wing) – Major
Gerhard Schöpfel
    I Gruppe – Major Johannes Seifert
    II Gruppe – Hauptmann Conny Meyer
    III Gruppe – Hauptmann Josef Priller
    Aircraft: Focke-Wulf Fw 190

Kampfgeschwader 2 (KG 2) 'Holzhammer' (Bomber Wing) –
Oberstleutnant Hans von Koppelow
    I Gruppe – Major Karl Kessel
    II Gruppe – Major Walter Bradel
    III Gruppe – Major Kurt Leythaeuser
    IV Gruppe – Hauptmann Helmut Powolny
    Aircraft: Dornier Do 217

MAPS

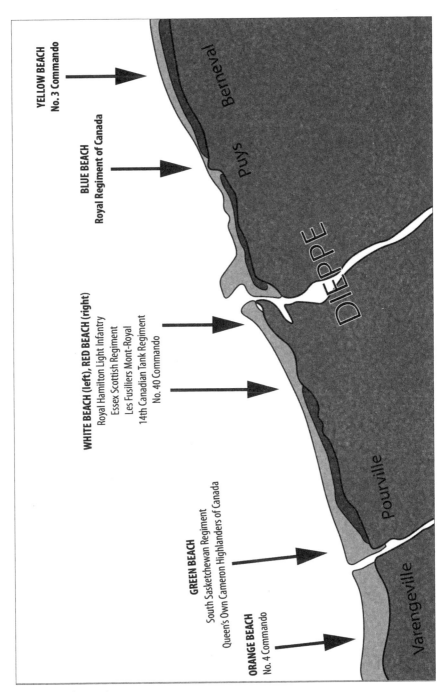

YELLOW BEACH
No. 3 Commando

BLUE BEACH
Royal Regiment of Canada

WHITE BEACH (left), RED BEACH (right)
Royal Hamilton Light Infantry
Essex Scottish Regiment
Les Fusiliers Mont-Royal
14th Canadian Tank Regiment
No. 40 Commando

GREEN BEACH
South Saskatchewan Regiment
Queen's Own Cameron Highlanders of Canada

ORANGE BEACH
No. 4 Commando

Berneval

Puys

DIEPPE

Pourville

Varengeville

The beaches of Dieppe.

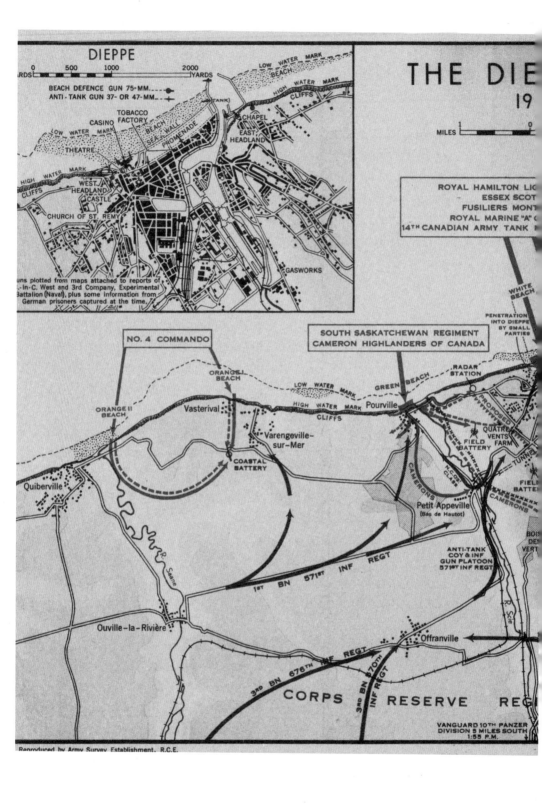

DIEPPE

0	500	1000	2000
RDS | | | YARDS

BEACH DEFENCE GUN 75-MM......●
ANTI-TANK GUN 37- OR 47-MM...+

LOW WATER MARK
BEACH
HIGH WATER MARK
EAST
CLIFFS

TOBACCO FACTORY
CASINO
THEATRE
BEACH
SEA WALL
PROMENADE

CHAPEL
EAST,
HEADLAND

LOW WATER MARK

HIGH WATER MARK
WEST.
HEADLAND
CLIFFS
CASTLE

CHURCH OF ST. REMY

GASWORKS

uns plotted from maps attached to reports of
.-in-C. West and 3rd Company, Experimental
Battalion (Naval), plus some information from
German prisoners captured at the time.

THE DIE

19

MILES

ROYAL HAMILTON LIC
ESSEX SCOT
FUSILIERS MONT
ROYAL MARINE "A"
14TH CANADIAN ARMY TANK

WHITE
BEACH

PENETRATION
INTO DIEPPE
BY SMALL
PARTIES

NO. 4 COMMANDO

SOUTH SASKATCHEWAN REGIMENT
CAMERON HIGHLANDERS OF CANADA

ORANGE I
BEACH

RADAR
STATION

LOW WATER MARK
GREEN BEACH

ORANGE II
BEACH

Vasterival

HIGH WATER MARK
CLIFFS
Pourville

PROPOSED

Varengeville-
sur-Mer

QUATRE
VENTS
FARM
FIELD
BATTERY

COASTAL
BATTERY

RC-02
CLASS

TUNN

Quiberville

CAMERONS

FIELD
BATTE

CAMERONS

Petit Appeville
(Bas de Hautot)

BOIS
DES
VERT

ANTI-TANK
COY & INF
GUN PLATOON
571ST INF REGT

R. Saane

1ST BN 571ST INF REGT

R. Scie

Ouville-la-Rivière

Offranville

3RD BN 570TH INF REGT

3RD BN 676TH INF REGT

CORPS
RESERVE
REG

VANGUARD 10TH PANZER
DIVISION 5 MILES SOUTH
1:55 P.M.

Reproduced by Army Survey Establishment. R.C.E.

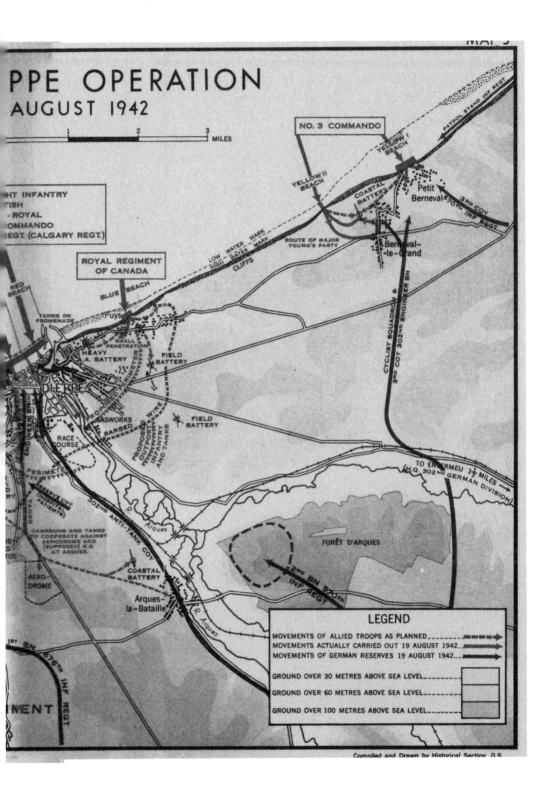

PPE OPERATION
AUGUST 1942

MILES 1 2 3

NO. 3 COMMANDO

HT INFANTRY
TISH
- ROYAL
OMMANDO
EGT (CALGARY REGT.)

ROYAL REGIMENT
OF CANADA

YELLOW II BEACH

YELLOW I BEACH

PATROL 572ND INF REGT

Petit Berneval

3RD COY 570TH INF REGT

COASTAL BATTERY

ROUTE OF MAJOR YOUNG'S PARTY

Berneval-le-Grand

LOW WATER MARK
HIGH WATER MARK
CLIFFS

RED BEACH

BLUE BEACH

Puys

TANKS ON PROMENADE

SMALL PENETRATION

HEAVY A. BATTERY

FIELD BATTERY

DIEPPE

GASWORKS

BARBED WIRE

PROPOSED OUTPOST INFANTRY AND TANKS

FIELD BATTERY

RACE COURSE

PERIMETER

CYCLIST SQUADRON & 3RD COY 302ND ENGINEER BN

TO ENVERMEU 1½ MILES
(H.Q. 302ND GERMAN DIVISION)

RESERVE COY (HOSPITAL PATIENTS)

TANKS

302ND ANTI-TANK COY

R. Arques

CAMERONS AND TANKS TO COOPERATE AGAINST AERODROME AND (SUPPOSED) H.D. AT ARQUES.

FORÊT D'ARQUES

AERO-DROME

COASTAL BATTERY

Arques-la-Bataille

R. Arques

2ND BN 570TH INF REGT

1ST BN 570TH INF REGT

MENT

LEGEND

MOVEMENTS OF ALLIED TROOPS AS PLANNED
MOVEMENTS ACTUALLY CARRIED OUT 19 AUGUST 1942
MOVEMENTS OF GERMAN RESERVES 19 AUGUST 1942

GROUND OVER 30 METRES ABOVE SEA LEVEL
GROUND OVER 60 METRES ABOVE SEA LEVEL
GROUND OVER 100 METRES ABOVE SEA LEVEL

Compiled and Drawn by Historical Section G.S.

ACKNOWLEDGEMENTS

My main sources of reference in telling the story of the Dieppe Raid are the books *Combined Operations 1940-1942* published by His Majesty's Stationery Office and prepared for The Combined Operations Command by The Ministry of Information. Crown copyright 1943: and *Combined Operations the official story of the Commandos* by Louis Mountbatten published by His Britannic Majesty's Stationery Office. Crown copyright 1943.

https://www.historicacanada.ca

I would also like to thank Historica Canada for their permission to use the transcripts of interviews made with the following Dieppe veterans for The Memory Project. I have included the URLs to these interviews for your interest, so you can read their complete interviews as I have edited them for clarity.

Don Wolfe: http://www.thememoryproject.com/stories/2147:don-wolfe.
Arthur Fraser: http://www.thememoryproject.com/stories/184:arthur-philip-fraser.
Roland Gravel: http://www.thememoryproject.com/stories/596:roland-rolly-gravel.
Jacques Cinq-Mars: http://www.thememoryproject.com/stories/949:jacques-cinq-mars.
Paul DeLorme: http://www.thememoryproject.com/stories/1958:paul-henry-delorme.

Acknowledgements

John Barron: http://www.thememoryproject.com/stories/
2161:john-joseph-reid-johnny-barron.

Jacques Nadeau: http://www.thememoryproject.com/stories/
467:jacques-nadeau.

Maurice Snook: http://www.thememoryproject.com/stories/
828:maurice-ypres-junior-snook.

George Marchant: http://www.thememoryproject.com/stories/
862:george-edmund-jim-marchant.

Paul Dumaine: http://www.thememoryproject.com/stories/
950:paul-dumaine.

Louis Pantaleo: http://www.thememoryproject.com/stories/
3418:louis-pantaleo.

Armand Emond: http://www.thememoryproject.com/stories/
221:armand-emond.

Albert Kirby: http://www.thememoryproject.com/stories/
327:albert-kirby.

Amos Wilkins: http://www.thememoryproject.com/stories/
1134:amos-wilkie-wilkins.

Jack McFarland: http://www.thememoryproject.com/stories/
333:jack-clifford-mcfarland.

Theodore Bennett: http://www.thememoryproject.com/stories/
449:theodore-j.-bennett.

Wilson Large: http://www.thememoryproject.com/stories/
741:wilson-howard-howard-large.

David Mann: http://www.thememoryproject.com/stories/
2466:david-mann.

I have also found the following websites useful for further information:

https://www.normandywarguide.com/articles/operation-barricade
www.historyofwar.org
www.flamesofwar.com
http://www.warfaremagazine.co.uk/articles/Dieppe-Operation-Jubilee/61
http://gallery.commandoveterans.org/cdoGallery/v/WW2/sbs/goulding
https://www.blighty-at-war.net/dieppe-raid.html
https://www.veterans.gc.ca/eng/remembrance/history/second-world-
war/1942-dieppe-raid

The following publication was also useful for reference: *The South African Military History Society Military History Journal* Vol 1 No 5 – December 1969, 'Air Umbrella – Dieppe' by Michael Schoeman

INDEX

Also available from Amberley Publishing

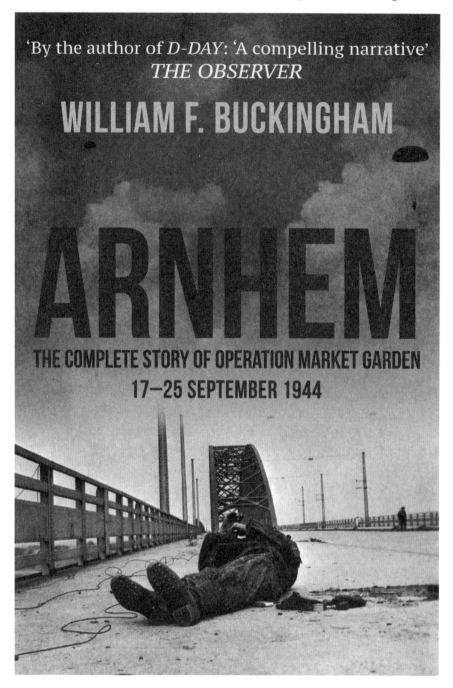

'By the author of *D-DAY*: 'A compelling narrative'
THE OBSERVER

WILLIAM F. BUCKINGHAM

ARNHEM

THE COMPLETE STORY OF OPERATION MARKET GARDEN
17–25 SEPTEMBER 1944

Available from all good bookshops or to order direct
Please call **01453-847-800**
www.amberley-books.com